International Pressures for Accounting Change

Edited by

Anthony G. Hopwood

*Arthur Young Professor of International Accounting and
Financial Management, London School of Economics*

Prentice Hall
In association with

D1388976

The Institute of Chartered Accountants in England and Wales

First published 1989 by
Prentice Hall International (UK) Ltd
66 Wood Lane End, Hemel Hempstead
Hertfordshire, HP2 4RG
A division of
Simon & Schuster International Group

This book consists of a research study undertaken on behalf of The Institute of
Chartered Accountants in England and Wales. In publishing this book the
Institute considers that it is a worthwhile contribution to discussion but neither the
Institute nor the Research Board necessarily shares the views expressed, which are
those of the authors alone.

No responsibility for loss occasioned to any person acting or refraining from action
as a result of any material in this publication can be accepted by the authors or
publisher.

Printed and bound in Great Britain by
BPCC Wheatons Ltd, Exeter.

British Library Cataloguing in Publication Data

International pressures for accounting
change.
1. Accounting standards
I. Hopwood, Tony, *1944*- II. Series
657'. 0218
ISBN 0-13-470873-3

12345   93 92 91 90 89

Contents

Foreword

This is the first volume in the Research Studies in Accounting Series to contain a collection of conference papers on different aspects of a single research topic. The conference, which addressed the topic of international pressures for accounting change, was held at the London Business School in September 1986 and was attended by a distinguished group of practising and academic accountants. The conference was sponsored jointly by the Research Board of the Institute of Chartered Accountants in England and Wales and by Deloitte Haskins and Sells. The sponsorship of conferences such as this which bring together practitioners and academics to discuss problems of topical interest, is an important part of the activities of the Research Board.

Professor Hopwood assembled for the conference a list of topics and contributors which covered a wide variety of perspectives on international aspects of accounting. That rich variety is reflected in the papers in this volume. The study of international accounting is often thought of in purely comparative terms. This book breaks away from that rather limited view. It includes comparative analysis and some individual country studies but also contains major contributions on professional and business perspectives (the chapters by Cook, Hanson, Mitchell, Scheid and Standish, and Takatera and Daigo); regulatory aspects (the chapters by Rutteman and Elsafty); particular problems and issues in transnational accounting (the chapters by Archer and McLeay and by Gray and Roberts); and overviews of the nature of international accounting and its development (the chapters by Hopwood, Parker, Peasnell and Shaw).

Accountants in the United Kingdom are sometimes accused of having a parochial view of their subject. This book, and the conference from which it derives, could not be so accused. The collected papers present a stimulating view of a variety of international accounting problems and of the international pressures of change in accounting.

John Arnold
Director of Research
ICAEW

Acknowledgements

The papers included in this volume were prepared for and presented at the Accounting Research Symposium which was held in London in September 1986. Co-sponsored by Deloitte Haskins and Sells and the Institute of Chartered Accountants in England and Wales, the Symposium was one of a series designed to provide an opportunity for academics and senior practitioners to discuss the state of the art of research in key accounting areas.

I would like to acknowledge the generous support of Deloitte Haskins and Sells and the Research Board of the Institute of Chartered Accountants in England and Wales which enabled the Symposium to take place.

Kim McCarthy served as the efficient administrator for the Symposium and all who attended appreciated her help. I also would like to thank Ann Cratchley for her help in dealing with the seemingly endless correspondence associated with both the organisation of the Symposium and its editing. Marion Crouch and Anne Gleeson for so efficiently typing the final manuscript, and Stuart Turley for his editorial assistance.

Anthony G. Hopwood

Contributors

Simon Archer is Senior Lecturer in Accounting and Finance at the University of Lancaster. He qualified as a Chartered Accountant with Arthur Andersen & Co., and then joined the Paris office of Price Waterhouse where he became partner in charge of management advisory services. His previous academic appointments have been at The City University, London, and the London Business School. He is the co-author of *The Implementation of SSAP16 Current Cost Accounting by UK Listed Companies*, and is currently engaged in research into corporate reporting by European multinationals.

Allan Cook is Head of Accounting Research at Shell International Petroleum Company Limited. He has spent most of his career working for two Anglo-Dutch multinationals, Unilever 1966-81, and the Royal Dutch/Shell Group, from 1982. During 1979-81 he served on secondment from Unilever as the Secretary of the International Accounting Standards Committee. He is currently a member of various ICAEW committees concerned with legal or accounting development and led the BIAC (Business and Industry Advisory Committee) Working Group at informal consultations with the OECD's Working Group on Accounting Standards.

Satoshi Daigo is Associate Professor of International Accounting at the University of Kyoto. He was formerly Associate Professor of Financial Accounting at the Nagoya City University (1978-85). He is the author of *A Critical Study of Accounting for Public Enterprises*, and *Studies in the Accounting History of Large Firms* (with S. Takatera), both of which are written in Japanese. His current research interests focus on the economic impact of accounting standards and accounting for business reorganisations (such as business combinations and separations, and privatisations) with a special focus on their distributive fairness.

M. Adel Elsafty is a Minister Plenipotentiary in the Egyptian Ministry of Foreign Affairs where he holds the post of Deputy Director of the International Organisations Department. He has held posts in the Embassies of Egypt in Oslo, Norway, Belgrade, Yugoslavia and the Mission of Egypt to the United Nations in New York. He also has represented his country in many political, economic and technical conferences. He graduated from the Faculty of Commerce, Ein Shams University. While beginning his career as an accountant and internal auditor in Bank Al-Gomhouria of Egypt (previously the Ottoman Bank), he has pursued post-graduate studies in the Egyptian Institute for

Banking and Statistical Studies. He has represented Egypt as an expert diplomat in the work of the United Nations Intergovernmental Working Group of Experts on International Standards of Accounting and Reporting since its inception in 1980. He was elected Vice Chairman of the Group for six consecutive years. His country has presented his name as a candidate for the chairmanship of the 1987 session of the Group.

Sidney J. Gray is a Professor of Accounting and Finance and Director of the Glasgow Business School in the University of Glasgow. Prior to joining Glasgow University in 1978, he held teaching appointments at the University of Sydney and the University of Lancaster where he earned his Ph.D. His business experience includes several years working for international trading and industrial companies in India and Australia. He is a Fellow of the Chartered Association of Certified Accountants. He was formerly Secretary General of the European Accounting Association. He is currently Chairman of the British Accounting Association and Vice President-Europe of the International Association of Accounting Education and Research. He has been a member of the Accounting Standards Committee since 1984. His research interests focus on information disclosure, international accounting, takeovers and mergers, and corporate strategy.

J. Don Hanson is the senior partner and managing partner of Arthur Andersen & Co. in the United Kingdom. He is also a member of the Arthur Andersen Worldwide Board of partners with responsibility for operations in Scandinavia, Turkey, the Middle East, Africa and India. He qualified as a chartered accountant in 1951 after training with a small firm in the North of England. He has worked with Arthur Andersen & Co. since 1958 in their London and, subsequently their Manchester office, which he started in 1966. He was elected managing partner of the UK practice in 1982 and since that time has concentrated on the strategic management of the UK practice and its integration and co-ordination with the rest of the worldwide firm. He is a member of the Council of the Confederation of British Industries and of the Council of Business in the Community and is a member of the Court of Manchester University.

Anthony G. Hopwood is the Arthur Young Professor of International Accounting and Financial Management at the London School of Economics and Political Science. He also holds visiting professorships at the European Institute for Advanced Studies in Management, Brussels, and Pennsylvania State University. Prior to joining the LSE in 1985, he held the ICAEW Chair at the London Business School and had served on the faculties of the Manchester Business School and the Oxford Centre for Management Studies. President of the European Accounting Association in 1977-9 and 1987-8, in 1981 Anthony Hopwood was the American Accounting Association's Distinguished International Visiting Lecturer. His research and publishing interests focus on the organisational, social and comparative aspects of accounting and management information systems. He is Editor-in-Chief of the international research journal *Accounting, Organisations and Society*.

Stuart McLeay is a Lecturer in Accounting and Finance at the University of Lancaster and a Fellow of the International Centre for Research in Accounting. He is also a Fellow of the Institute of Chartered Accountants in England and Wales and has worked with major accounting firms in Italy, France and Germany and as a financial analyst and loan co-ordinator with the European Investment Bank. A former contributor to the *Financial Times World Survey of Annual Accounts*, his current research interests are in the areas of international financial reporting and the statistical modelling of large-scale accounting data sets. At present, he is organiser of the Statistical Modelling of Corporate Financial Indicators project funded by the ESRC.

Geoffrey B. Mitchell is Technical Director of the Institute of Chartered Accountants in England and Wales where he is responsible for the co-ordination and direction of technical activities undertaken in the ICAEW's Technical Directorate. He was previously Secretary-General of the International Accounting Standards Committee and previously held appointments at the Flinders University of South Australia and University of Adelaide. He is co-author of *Principles of Accounting* and his publications have appeared in *Journal of Accounting Research, The Accounting Review, Australian Economic Papers, The Chartered Accountant in Australia,* and *The Australian Accountant.*

Robert H. Parker is Professor of Accountancy at the University of Exeter. Previously he held a similar position at the University of Dundee. he has also held appointments at the University of Adelaide, the University of Western Australia, the Manchester Business School, INSEAD and LSE. A graduate of University College, London, and a member of the Institute of Chartered Accountants in England and Wales, he is joint editor of numerous books and papers on accounting, especially in the fields of accounting history, international and comparative accounting, and income measurement. His recent publications include *Papers on Accounting History* (1984), *Macmillan Dictionary of Accounting* (1984), the second edition of *Comparative International Accounting* (with C.W. Nobes, 1985), and the second edition of *Readings in the Concept and Measurement of Income* (with G.C. Harcourt and G. C. Whittington, 1986).

Kenneth V. Peasnell is the Wolfson Professor of Accounting and Finance at the University of Lancaster. He is a Fellow of the Institute of Chartered Accountants in England and Wales and was educated at the Universities of Sheffield, London and Lancaster. His publications have appeared in various accounting journals, including *The Accounting Review*, the *Journal of Accounting Research, Accounting and Business Research, Abacus* and the *Journal of Business Finance and Accounting*. He is the co-author of *British Financial Markets and Institutions*. His current research interests are in the areas of pricing in financial markets and corporate financial reporting.

Clare B. Roberts is a Lecturer in Accounting and Finance in the University of Glasgow. She earned her B.Sc. and M.Sc. degrees from the University of Southampton. Prior to taking up her current post she was lecturer at Portsmouth Polytechnic and a Research Assistant on an ESRC funded project at Glasgow University. Her research interests focus on information disclosure, segmental reporting, and international accounting.

Paul Rutteman is a partner in Arthur Young in London. Previously the firm's senior technical partner, he is currently in charge of its Financial Services Group. He was President of the Groupe d'Etudes des Experts Comptables de la CEE until December 1986, when the organisation became part of the Federation of European Accountants. He is a member of the Council of the Institute of Chartered Accountants in England and Wales and Chairman of its Parliamentary and Law Committee. He has worked for Arthur Young in continental Europe and the United States and has a particular interest in international accounting.

Jean-Claude Scheid is a graduate of the University of Paris (Sorbonne), where he obtained his doctorate in management science. He qualified as an *expert comptable* in 1964. He has taught at the University of Grenoble, the Ecole Normale Supérieure de L'Enseignement Technique, Cachan, and currently holds the chair of management science at the University of Limoges. Since 1985 he has been the technical and research director of the French Institute, l'Ordre des Experts Comptables et Comptables Agréés in Paris. He has written many articles in the fields of information science, organisation theory, cost and financial accounting. He is also the author of several books. He has wide consulting experience with French companies and with French national organisations. He is the technical adviser of the French delegates at the IAS Board.

Jack Shaw is Executive Director of Scottish Financial Enterprise. He was until recently the senior partner in the Edinburgh office of Deloitte Haskins & Sells. He was President of The Institute of Chartered Accountants of Scotland in 1983-4, and held the part-time post of Johnstone Smith Professor of Accountancy at the University of Glasgow between 1977 and 1982. He has served on the Council of the Chartered Institute of Management Accountants, and is on the Executive of the Scottish Council for Development and Industry.

Peter Standish is Professor of Accounting at the University of Tasmania. He was formerly Institute of Chartered Accountants Professor of Accounting and Financial Reporting at the London Business School. His principal interests are in the field of financial reporting by business enterprises, especially from a comparative international viewpoint. He has contributed the chapter on Britain and Australia in both editions of C.W. Nobes and R.H. Parker (eds), *Comparative International Accounting*, and published widely elsewhere. More recently, he spent seven months in 1987 in France based at the Ordre des Experts Comptables for the purpose of carrying out a detailed study of the French national accounting code, the *Plan comptable général,* and is currently writing a book offering a critical explanation of French experience with the code.

Sadeo Takatera is Professor of the Principles of Accounting at the University of Kyoto. He served as Dean of the Faculty of Economics of the University of Kyoto from 1979 to 1980. His main books on professional subjects are *General Theory of Bookkeeping, Developing Accounting Policy and Bookkeeping, Studies in Depreciation Accounting of the Meiji Era, Studies in the Accounting History of Large Firms* (with S. Daigo), *Accounting à la carte,* and *Paradoxes in Accounting,* all of which are written in Japanese. He has contributed more than 130 articles in the professional journals and co-authored books. His current research interests include the application of economic and organisational theories to accounting phenomena, the development of accounting systems for the public interest, and comparative accounting history. He also serves on the editorial boards of *Accounting, Organisations and Society, Accounting Historians Journal, Kyoto University Economic Review, Japan Business History Review,* and the *Year Book of the (Japanese) Accounting History Association.*

1

International Pressures for Accounting Change: An Introduction

Anthony G. Hopwood

Accounting has never been a purely national phenomenon. As an influential means of economic calculation, both its techniques and the significances that are in part created by them have a history of penetrating national boundaries, moving along the pathways established by commerce and patterns of political influence. As Parker illustrates so well in his subsequent chapter, early forms of multinational commerce and finance provided one of the means by which the technique of double-entry bookkeeping was diffused throughout Europe and the reproduction of the institutions of a professionalised accountancy reflected both the spread of imperial power and the close trading and commercial ties established on the basis of a shared language.

More recently, however, more explicit consideration has been given to the international aspects of accounting, not least in respect of the variety of different national embodiments of the craft and a resultant interest in both the rationales and possibility for some form of standardisation or harmonisation. The origins of such an awareness are numerous, but include the internationalisation of business, the rapid development of financial markets which are increasingly autonomous of national states, the concerns of supra-national institutions which in their desire to equalise the conditions for trade and competition within their domains have focussed, amongst other things, on national differences in forms of economic calculation and the availability of public information on business enterprises, and the emergence of a research and teaching interest in the area (e.g. Nobes and Parker, 1985). Both singly and together these factors have resulted in a growing appreciation of accounting diversity and the problems that this can sometimes create for the efficient conduct of both business and regulatory endeavours.

As Hanson makes clear later in this volume, such pressures have not only had a significance for accounting itself. Accounting firms, as practitioners of the craft, also have had to be conscious of the growing internationalisation of the accounting environment. With their clients increasingly operating in multinational contexts, financing their operations in a variety of different national capital markets and subject to an ever increasing range of both national and supra-national regulatory authorities, there has been a major increase in the interest attached to questions of corporate standardisation amidst national diversity and the problems associated with managing, financing and reporting in a diversity of accounting formats. As we are all well aware by now, such pressures have had a rapid and significant influence on the size, structure and internal patterns of control of audit firms. What until quite recently were national entities or often quite loose affiliations across national boundaries, have now become multinational organisations themselves, increasingly mirroring the structure of their clients and facing many of the same problems of management, internal coherence and a uniformity of standards.

However, although there is now an awareness of the significance of the international pressures operating on accounting, the practice of accounting still has an equivocal relationship to them. As Archer and McLeay illustrate in their detailed and intriguing study of financial reporting by European Companies listed on more than one capital market, which is included in this collection, disclosures remain diverse even amongst this, the most multinational set of enterprises, not least with respect to the listing requirements themselves, issues of both textual and currency translation, and the forms of audit pronouncements. On the latter point, noting the increasingly multinational nature of audit firms, Archer and McLeay nevertheless note the absence of standardisation even in areas where the firms might conceivably have been able to influence matters themselves.

Equally, Gray and Roberts illustrate the diversity of response of British multinational companies in the extent to which they voluntarily modify their reporting formats to provide greater insight into the impact that multinational trading has on their operations and financial performance. Rather than revealing any strategies of enlightenment directly responsive to the changing nature of their domain of operations, the study not surprisingly suggests a more cautious, interested and calculative response, seemingly moderated by an awareness of market and political contingencies.

Accounting seemingly is an area where a rhetoric of internationalisation advances more rapidly than practical achievements. Whilst pointing to the 'fundamental ... differences in accounting practice ... between different countries', Rutteman's contribution to this volume nevertheless points to the 'incredibly slow progress towards harmonisation even in the context of the European Community'. Impatiently commenting that 'it is time for all [national] standard setting bodies to recognise that they should not be producing standards in isolation', he emphasises the constraining influence of the factors that maintain accounting practice within a nexus of national, institutional and practical influence, something that is also made manifestly clear by the subsequent

discussions of particular national patterns of response to international
pressures for standardisation.

In an analysis of the standardisation initiatives of the British
Accounting Standards Committee, Mitchell simply notes that 'there has
been little external influence on the Accounting Standards Committee's
(ASC) agenda or even on the methods finally adopted by the ASC'.
Although the enactment of the European Fourth Directive into British law
provided a potential for a wider range of influences to infuse the practice
and regulation of accounting, that potential remains to be realised. Indeed
as Rutteman notes, commenting on actual practice as distinct from
Mitchell's concerns with its standardisation, 'a survey of published
accounts today shows less conformity with the Fourth Directive
accounting principles and rules than there was before it was even
introduced into the United Kingdom'.

Although Scheid and Standish point to increasing international
influences on French accounting, both in terms of practice and its
regulation, the origins of this are seen as diverse. International and
European standardisation and harmonisation initiatives were amongst
these, although Scheid and Standish are at pains to note that the
'soothing overtones of reasoning' suggested by the vocabulary of
harmonisation often contrast with a realpolitik that requires 'non-English-
speaking countries to give up whatever indigenous accounting practices
they may have developed in favour of Anglo-American accounting
standards'. A growing similarity of practices can occur outside of such
attempts to harmonise, however. In the case of France, indigenous
interests in capital market regulation started in the 1960s and have
subsequently developed in the context of shifting macro-economic policy
concerns which have attributed a greater significance to the efficient
functioning of capital markets and their information requirements.
Although such influences have worked alongside rather than in any way
replacing or even substantially modifying the existing regulatory
apparatus of French accounting, they nevertheless have provided a
different set of institutional contexts, issue arenas and discursive
frameworks (see, for instance, Colasse and Boussard, forthcoming) within
which accounting practices have been examined and reformed. Such
pragmatic realignments might provide a basis whereby different
functionalities are attributed to the accounting craft, thereby enabling a
concern with the informative to complement the regulatory. To the extent
that such transformations have been at work, they might provide a means
through which differences are reduced, albeit slowly, by an emerging
similarity rather than a more radical harmonisation.

Japan also provides a case where it is difficult to disentangle
international and indigenous influences. As Takatera and Daigo note in
a wider context: 'while new management methods and systems have been
introduced into Japanese enterprises, the traditional management

philosophy has been maintained unchanged as the core organisational culture'. Although pressures for accounting change have resulted from the very significant internationalisation of Japanese business and its increasing involvement in international capital markets and the international regulatory community, national circumstances and interests have played an important role in filtering those pressures and determining which come to bear on the practice and regulations of domestic accounting. In the blunt terms of Takatera and Diego: 'the truth of the matter is that Japanese accounting policy makers, who were and still are honest spokesmen for powerful large corporations, accepted international pressures only when they resulted in insignificant adverse effects on those corporations ... or when they might even produce favourable effects ...'.

All too clearly international pressures cannot be analysed in isolation of national ones. Nor can international standardisation be seen as a smooth process of harmonisation or even a gradual process of encroachment. More active forces are at work whereby national influences permeate and often, in the process, considerably modify, if not change, the international pressures and influences, however real the latter may be. Interests in new and different accountings, internationally orientated or otherwise, have to confront the nexus of national institutions, regulations and practices, and problem agendas that give a particular significance to accounting and embed it in a quite specific institutional setting such that it functions in quite particular ways.

Seen in such terms, it is not surprising that Parker's analysis of the transference of the British concept of 'true and fair' to Continental Europe leads him to conclude that 'it is clear that what they have really imported is a form of words which they are translating and applying so as not to disturb unduly what already exists'. Nor is it surprising that countries of the Third World, usually subject to internationalisation rather than agents of it, find it difficult to have any influence whatsoever on the process of accounting change in the industrialised nations. In his discussion contained in this volume, Elsafty is therefore right to identify the problem, from the perspective of the Third World, as being one of power. However uncertain the prospects of reform may be in the foreseeable future, the other analyses of the processes of accounting change nevertheless imply that it is correct to perceive the problem in institutional terms involving questions of representation, the influencing of agendas and the possibilities for exercising authority.

Some of these points, and others, are elaborated upon in Shaw's insightful and critical concluding analysis for this volume. Drawing on his experience in practice, he emphasises both the limited national horizons of accounting discussions and the conflicts of interests and concerns that increasingly infuse accounting practice and policy formulation. He sees limitations in the visions that mobilise practice, the institutional forums that shape its development and the concerns articulated by both practitioners and members of the academic community.

However much needed, accounting change is seemingly both difficult to achieve and little understood (Burchell et al., 1985; Hopwood, 1987). Although the problem of practical action might initially be the concern of the practitioner, the regulator and the politician, the problem of understanding is also the concern of the academic, as researcher. And in areas as complex as this, new understandings can sometimes play important roles in mobilising action.

As Peasnell points out, the task of gaining such an understanding is both challenging and complex. For at present we even have relatively few insights into the processes by which specific national accountings start to become what they are not. Whilst there is no shortage of chronologies of accounting developments, insights into both the forces which result in them and their consequences for wider economic and social action are far fewer. In the research community, although quite obviously not in the world at large (if not of accounting practice), accounting has tended to be seen as just accounting, and so far that very characterisation has constrained our ability to probe into what are now increasingly seen to be significant preconditions of accounting change that reside outside of the realm of accounting itself but can nevertheless become interconnected with it. But if our understanding of national processes of change is minimal, that of the factors implicated in national diversity, its consequences and the preconditions for its reduction is even less. Although there are classifications of different national forms of accounting, the resultant insights are relatively static, often infused by a concern with technical differentiation rather than a probing into questions of preconditions, contextual embodiment and the attribution of functionalities and significance. Yet it is the latter understandings that are needed to confront, appreciate and explain both the subsequent national and institutional analyses of accounting change and, as Peasnell points out in his concluding review of research implications, the processes which activate changing concerns and modes of operation in those institutions which mediate and can create wider international pressures for continued change.

The task of understanding, like that of action itself, therefore remains a large one. The following analyses by both practitioners and researchers hopefully will contribute to this end, both by the rich and varied insights which they contain and the stimulus they provide for further questioning and exploration.

References

Burchell, S., Clubb, C., and Hopwood, A.G., Accounting in its Social Context: Towards a History of Value Added in the United Kingdom,

Accounting, Organizations and Society (1985).

Colasse, B., and Boussard, D., From Funds Flow Statements to Cash Flow Accounting: Research in Progress in the French Context, in A.G. Hopwood and H. Schreuder, eds., *Accounting Research and Accounting Practice: European Perspectives* (ICAEW and Prentice-Hall, forthcoming).

Hopwood, A.G., The Archaeology of Accounting Systems, *Accounting, Organizations and Society* (1987).

Nobes, C.W., and Parker, R.H., *Comparative International Accounting*, (2nd edn) Philip Allan/St Martin's Press, 1985).

2
Importing and Exporting Accounting: The British Experience[1]

Robert H. Parker

Accounting techniques, institutions and concepts are all capable of being imported and exported from one country to another. The following discussion considers, by way of three case studies, the British experience of such imports and exports and in particular the way in which the British have imported double entry bookkeeping (a technique) and have exported professional accountancy (an institution) and a 'true and fair view' (a concept).

The analysis focusses on the British experience for two reasons. First, it is the one with which the writer is most familiar. Secondly, and more importantly, British accounting history is not just of parochial interest. From being, in the sixteenth century, distinctly underdeveloped in mercantile accounting, Britain became in the nineteenth the pioneer of modern professional accountancy. In the twentieth century, however, the United States has become the pace-setter in many aspects of accounting.

The scope of the discussion has been limited as follows. First, there is no consideration of which accounting techniques, institutions or concepts *ought* to be transferred from one country to another and how this can best be done (Seidler, 1969; Needles, 1976). There is no assumption that one set of techniques, institutions or concepts is inherently better than another.

Secondly, countries are taken as a whole, with no attempt to distinguish between early and late adopters of an import. This means that the emphasis is placed on economic rather than sociological variables (cf. Griliches, 1960 in Rosenberg, 1971, page 266). Thirdly, the analysis is not concerned with imports which may be regarded as choices among accounting policies and analysed as part of a contracting process between

---

[1] Earlier drafts of this chapter were presented in 1985 at an EIASM workshop on 'Accounting and Culture' at the Free University of Amsterdam, at a number of Australian universities and at the national University of Singapore. I have benefited greatly from comments received.

managers and owners. (The literature in this area is summarized in Watts and Zimmerman, 1986).

The discussion is concerned with the international transfer of accounting technology (AT) in its widest sense. AT differs from physical productive technology in that it is non-proprietary (Taylor and Turley, 1985, page 3) and more specific to particular countries (Seidler, 1969, pages 36-7).

Each case study is built around the following questions:

1. What was available for import?
2. Who were the importers and exporters? Were they active or passive?
3. How did the importers find out about the potential import?
4. How did importers and exporters assess the costs and benefits?
5. How, if at all, were imports adapted, i.e. made appropriate to an environment different from that of the exporter?
6. How were problems of terminology dealt with?

Double entry bookkeeping

Double entry bookkeeping is a technique of recording economic events which was evolved by merchants in the Italian city states from the end of the thirteenth century onwards. It is not the only such technique and until about the year 1500 it was not used outside Italy except by Italian merchants who had established branches of their firms in other countries, including England (de Roover, 1956).

In principle, techniques are easier to import than institutions or concepts since there are presumably no cultural, social or political costs or benefits attached to them, but British merchants, the potential importers, did not start to adopt double entry until the sixteenth century.

To adopt a technique one must first find out about it. This was relatively easy since Italian merchants made no attempt to keep double entry a trade secret. On the other hand they were not active exporters. Italian cultural influence was strong throughout Europe, including England, during this period (as the settings of many of Shakespeare's plays attest) but both England and Scotland were influenced more by France and the Low Countries. The main commercial link with continental Europe was Antwerp, the port through which most English exports passed in the sixteenth and seventeenth centuries (Davis, 1973).

The ways in which British merchants could obtain a knowledge of double entry can be listed as follows:

1. Reading a manuscript or book
   (a)   in a language other than English
   (b)   in English

2. Learning from a native teacher in Britain
3. Learning from a foreign merchant or teacher resident in Britain
4. Learning abroad from a foreign merchant or teacher.

There is evidence that all these sources were used. Textbooks on double entry were published in Italy from 1494 (Pacioli's *Summa*) and in the Netherlands, France and Britain from 1543 onwards. A book which illustrates the way in which knowledge of doubt entry spread from country to country is Jan Ympyn's *Nieuwe Instructie ...* published in Antwerp in Flemish (Dutch) and French (as the *Nouvelle Instruction ...*) in 1543 and in London in 1547 (as *A Notable and Very Excellente Woorke ...*). In his Prologue the author states that his book is based on a translation of a work in Italian by one Juan Paulo di Bianchi. No published work by an author of this name is known and there has been much speculation about the existence of a manuscript which may have been used not only by Ympyn but also by Pacioli (Yamey, 1967). Appended to Ympyn's work, unlike Pacioli's or Oldcastle's, is an illustrative set of books which, it has been plausibly suggested, may have been based on Ympyn's own business. The long title of the English version states that the book has been:

> Translated with great diligence out of the Italian toung into Dutche, and out of Dutche, into French, and now out of French into Englishe.

It is clear from this (and other similar evidence) that knowledge of double entry was made available throughout sixteenth century Europe through both books and manuscripts; that these were translated into various languages; and that they often contained illustrative sets of books (the first to do so was an Italian work by Tagliente published in 1525).

For merchants and their apprentices who needed oral as well as written instruction, teachers were available, many of whom were also textbook writers. Sixteenth century English examples (with the dates of their books in brackets) include Hugh Oldcastle (1543), James Peele (1553, 1569) and John Mellis (1588).

It is also possible that some British merchants learned double entry from foreign merchants or teachers resident in Britain. The earliest double entry or near double entry record written up in England which has survived is an account book (1305-8) of the London branch of the Gallerani company of Siena. There is no evidence, however, that the Gallerani had any influence on indigenous English accounting records (Nobes, 1982). More interesting in the history of *English* accounting are the four ledgers (1436-9) bound together in one volume of the London branch of the Borromei, a firm of merchant bankers with its main office in Milan. According to Kats (1926) the textbooks of James Peele have a number of features to be found in the Borromei ledgers but not in Pacioli.

Kojima (1980, page 63) has suggested that Oldcastle, a citizen and shearman (i.e. draper) acquainted with wool merchants, might have worked in an Italian firm or might have learnt the Italian language or Italian bookkeeping from contacts with Italian merchants. This, while plausible, is, of course, no more than conjecture.

It is possible that many British accountants learned more accounting from practical experience than they learned from books and teachers. The double entry or near double entry records of the sixteenth century which have survived suggest that English merchants may have gained such experience overseas (Ramsey, 1956). These account books include the ledger of Thomas Howell, a member of the Drapers' Company resident and trading in Spain; the ledger of John Smythe, a leading merchant of Bristol; the journal of Sir Thomas Gresham; the ledger of John Johnson, a merchant of the Staple at Calais (a French port which was an English possession from 1347 to 1558); and ledgers and a journal of Thomas Laurence, a Merchant Adventurer. Howell's ledger was written up in Spain; Smythe also had strong Spanish connections (Vanes, 1974). Gresham spent much of his career in the Netherlands. Johnson's business was in Calais; Laurence traded overseas.

One of the earliest English language texts, John Weddington's *A Breffe Instruction ...* (1567) was even published in Antwerp rather than London. Weddington was an English merchant resident in Antwerp and at one time an agent of Gresham. His book differs in many ways from others of the time and it 'is highly probable that Weddington encountered the particular arrangement of the records, as taught by him in his book, in some business firm or firms in Antwerp' (Yamey, 1958, page 124).

There is no record of the use of double entry in Scotland before the seventeenth century, the first text of double entry, Colinson's *Idea Rationaria*, being published as late as 1683. The books (1696-1707) of the ill-fated Darien Scheme ('The company of Scotland trading to Africa and the Indies') were, it has been said, kept 'in exact concordance with the methods ... in the schoolmasters' lesson-books' by a 'clerk who might have been Pacioli himself' (Row Fogo in Brown, 1905, page 157). In Scotland, textbooks were, of course readily available from England, but Dutch influence was also important. Colinson had lived and traded in the Netherlands, includes a Dutch quotation in his book, and dedicates it to the 'Lord Conservator of the Privileges of the Scots Nation in the 17 Provinces of the Netherlands ...' (Parker, 1974).

It is clear from the above that British merchants in the sixteenth and seventeenth centuries had every opportunity to adopt double entry if they wished to do so. In fact it appears that double entry made slow headway and was not in widespread use until the nineteenth century (Yamey, 1977, page 17). It was only in that century that it ceased to be generally known as the 'Italian method' of bookkeeping: an indication perhaps that the import had been completed.

Such a slow adoption presumably reflects British merchants' assessment of the costs and benefits. It can be argued that Britain's stage of commercial development when double entry was first available for import was such that double entry was not an 'appropriate technique'. At the beginning of the sixteenth century, and for some time afterwards, England and Wales was 'a small poor country with a single-crop economy [wool]' (Kenyon, 1978, page 15). Scotland was even smaller and poorer. Nearly two centuries later, however, (about 1780) London had become the commercial centre of Europe.

There is little direct evidence of how British merchants perceived the benefits of double entry. The textbook writers who, in order to sell their books were more likely to overestimate than to underestimate – saw double entry as creating order from chaos by providing complete, integrated and interlocking records within a self-correcting system; better knowledge of, and hence control of, amounts owed and owing and of merchandise; and better profit calculations on individual ventures. They placed little emphasis on profit calculations and measures of wealth related to the whole enterprise (Winjum, 1972, pages 239-40). Yamey (1977, page 17) finds little evidence in pre-nineteenth century British accounting practice of systematic income measurement and asset valuation. Balancing was highly irregular and merchants more usually prepared inventories of their fortunes at irregular intervals. The profit and loss account was used as a place to which detailed but unwanted information could be removed. Winjum (1972, Chapter 11) concludes that double entry was valued more for its ability to provide systematic and comprehensive recording than for its ability to provide accurate income determination.

It would appear that most British merchants did not, until the nineteenth century, require much of what double entry had to offer. Orderliness and control were of course worth having but could often be achieved without double entry. Interlocking and self-correcting records were not always regarded as worth the effort. Annual profit calculation and asset valuation were of little use in the absence of sophisticated capital markets and income tax collectors, neither of which, so far as most business enterprises were concerned, were present until the late nineteenth century. It was only then that the benefits of double entry were generally perceived to exceed the costs.

One problem that any importers of a technique, institution or concept must face is that of terminology, especially when importer and exporter do not share a common language. The importer has a number of options (Parker, 1984, page 119). He can: treat the foreign words as native words; change them into native words; invent new words in his native language; or use already existing native words. English writers on double entry mainly chose the second option, taking and adapting from Italian such words as journal, folio, capital (replacing stock), cash (replacing money) and bank. It is also possible that the word bookkeeping is an adaptation of the equivalent Dutch word (Parker, 1984, pages 114-16).

What can we conclude about the import of double entry into Britain? Double entry was a technique which reached British merchants without any active exporting on the part of its Italian inventors. It was adopted because of its merits but only to the extent that it was thought to be an appropriate technology and it thus spread only slowly. Although it was close trading ties with the Netherlands that first made British merchants aware of the technique, its Italian origins have left a lasting mark on English accounting terminology.

Professional accountancy

We turn next to professional accountancy. We may note first of all that this is a more difficult import or export than double entry because it is an institution rather than a technique. Acceptance of the existence of self-regulating professional organisations, especially when they act as qualifying associations independent of any government control, implies acceptance of a particular form of economic and social structure.

There was little need for professional accountancy in Britain before the nineteenth century. Previously, accounting was regarded simply as one of the necessary skills of a merchant. In the nineteenth century, however, the growth of large-scale organisations and in particular of the railways, the development of the limited liability company, the high rate of insolvencies, and the introduction of income taxation produced demands for insolvency, auditing, costing and tax services. These demands led to the emergence of specialist experts who came together to discuss common problems, to distinguish competent and honourable practitioners from incompetent and dishonourable ones, to raise their status and to protect their material interests. They endeavoured to achieve these aims by formal association (Parker, 1986).

The way in which this took place (the 'British model' of professional accountancy) can be deduced from Table 2.1 which lists the numerous professional accountancy bodies established during the period 1853 to 1919. Three characteristics of these bodies may be discerned:

1. Many were formed on a regional basis and there are indeed still three separate Institutes of Chartered Accountants in the British Isles: of Scotland, in England and Wales, and in Ireland (covering both the Republic of Ireland and Northern Ireland).
2. If, in the absence of government regulation, the founders of an association are allowed to decide who is to be allowed to join and who is not, those who are excluded are likely to consider themselves harshly treated and to go out and form their own association (which explains the present existence of a Chartered Association of Certified

Table 2.1 Accountancy bodies formed in the British Isles:1853-1919

1853	Society of Accountants in Edinburgh (Royal charter 1854)[1]
1853	Institute of Accountants and Actuaries in Glasgow (royal charter 1855)
1867	Society of Accountants in Aberdeen[1]
1870	Incorporated Society of Liverpool Accountants[2]
1870	Institute of Accountants in London[2]
1871	Manchester Institute of Accountants[2]
1872	Society of Accountants in England[2]
1877	Sheffield Institute of Accountants[2]
1880	Institute of Chartered Accountants in England and Wales
1880	Scottish Institute of Accountants[3]
1885	Society of Accountants and Auditors[4]
1885	Corporate Treasurers' and Accountants' Institute[5]
1888	Institute of Chartered Accountants in Ireland
1891	Corporation of Accountants in Scotland[6]
1903	Institute of Certified Public Accountants[7]
1904	London Association of Accountants[6]
1905	Central Association of Accountants[8]
1919	Institute of Cost and Works Accountants[9]

Notes to Table 2.1
[1] *Merged to form Institute of Chartered Accountants of Scotland, 1951*
[2] *Merged to form Institute of Chartered Accountants in England and Wales, 1880*
[3] *Absorbed by the Society of Accountants and Auditors, 1899*
[4] *Name changed to Society of Incorporated Accountants and Auditors, 1908; to Society of Incorporated Accountants, 1954; integrated into the English, Scottish and Irish Chartered Institutes, 1957.*
[5] *Name changed to Institute of Municipal Treasurers and Accountants, 1901; to Chartered Institute of Public Finance and Accountancy, 1973.*
[6] *Amalgamated in 1939 to form the Association of Certified and Corporate Accountants.*
[7] *Amalgamated in 1941 with the Association of Certified and Corporate Accountants (from 1971 the Association of Certified Accountants and from 1984 the Chartered Association of Certified Accountants).*
[8] *Absorbed by the Institute of Certified Public Accountants, 1933.*
[9] *Name changed to Institute of Cost and Management Accountants, 1972; to Chartered Institute of Management Accountants, 1986.*

Accountants).
3. Since accountants practise not one technique but a related set of techniques, specialized associations may be formed, as happened with local government accountants in 1885 and cost accountants in 1919.

Professional accountancy can be imported and exported in a variety of ways, which may be listed as follows:

1. The *idea* of professional accountancy is exported, i.e. local accountants form their own association on:
   (a) the British model, or
   (b) some other model.
2. British accounting *qualifications* are exported, i.e. local accountants either:
   (a) form a local branch of a British body, or
   (b) become full members of a British body, by
       (i) qualifying in Britain, or

(ii) qualifying in their own country

The combination of British political and economic dominance and technological advances meant that knowledge of professional accountancy developments in Britain could spread rapidly. By the end of the nineteenth century, the British Empire covered Canada, the Australian continent and New Zealand, much of southern, central, east and west Africa, India, Ceylon, parts of South East Asia, and numerous islands in the Mediterranean, Caribbean, Atlantic, Indian and Pacific Oceans. Moreover, Britain's 'informal empire' (Gallagher and Robinson, 1953) of overseas trade and investment spread well beyond these, notably to the United States, Argentina and Brazil. Many 'local accountants' were in fact British accountants (not necessarily members of a formal association) who had emigrated overseas. Steamships and the telegraph gave even remote Australia reliable and fast links with Britain and helped to defeat the 'tyranny of distance' (Blainey, 1966, Chapter 9).

The formation of associations on the British model, but independent of British bodies, was most common in Canada, Australia, New Zealand and South Africa, as is demonstrated in Table 2.2. The merits of such associations were expressed by a pioneer accountant in Melbourne, Thomas Brentnall, as follows:

> It was gradually borne in upon a few of us that if those who were holding themselves out as public practitioners were to gain the confidence and support of the public, there must be a standard fixed which would connote the possession of the necessary qualifications for this special work. To that end a meeting was held [in Melbourne] on April 12, 1886, at which thirty practising accountants met to consider the propriety of establishing an 'Association of those having kindred interests in their common calling, and a desire to place their profession on a higher plane that it had previously occupied in public esteem'. We knew the position attained by the Institute of Chartered Accountants in England and Wales, which had been incorporated by Royal Charter in 1880, by the Society of Accountants and Auditors in 1885, as well as the three Scottish Institutes which had come into existence some years previously. With these examples before us, we had no difficulty in arriving at the conclusion that our object could best be attained by following in their footsteps (Brentnall, 1938, page 64).

As we shall see later, the accountants of Melbourne consciously rejected the alternative of constituting themselves a branch of a British body.

Table 2.2 clearly shows the inheritance of both regionalism (e.g. by 1904 there was a separate professional body in every Australian state) and duplication (e.g. the larger Australian states had more than one body).

Table 2.2 Accountancy bodies formed in Canada, Australia, New Zealand and South Africa:1880-1904

1880	The Association of Accountants in Montreal
1883	The Institute of Chartered Accountants of Ontario
1885	The Adelaide Society of Accountants (renamed The Institute of Accountants in South Australia, 1889)
1886	The Chartered Accountants' Association of Manitoba
1887	The Incorporated Institute of Accountants of Victoria (renamed Commonwealth Institute of Accountants, 1921)
1891	The Queensland Institute of Accountants
1894	The Sydney Institute of Public Accountants
1894	The Incorporated Institute of Accountants of New Zealand
1894	The Federal Institute of Accountants and Auditors in the South African Republic (became Transvaal branch of the [British] Society of Accountants and Auditors, 1902)
1895	The Institute of Accountants in Natal
1897	The Tasmanian Institute of Accountants
1898	The New Zealand Accountants' and Auditors' Association
1899	The Corporation of Accountants of Australia (Sydney)
1900	The Institute of Accountants and Auditors of Western Australia
1900	The Society of Accountants and Auditors of Victoria
1900	The Institute of Chartered Accountants of Nova Scotia
1902	The Dominion Association of Chartered Accountants (Canada)
1903	The Institute of Chartered Accountants in South Africa
1904	The Institute of Accountants of British Columbia
1904	The Transvaal Society of Accountants

Later (and thus not shown in the table), specialised bodies were also formed.

American accountants also formed their own associations but they adapted the British model to their own needs. The right to practise public accountancy came to depend upon a licensing authority (normally one of the States) with not all public accountants so certified considering it necessary to join a professional body. Unlike Britain, Canada and Australia, the United States managed to avoid a multiplicity of competing professional bodies. In the first comprehensive survey of accountancy bodies round the world, made on the occasion of the fiftieth anniversary of the Edinburgh Society of Accountants, Brown (1905, page 274) compared the advantages of the two models:

> The American plan prevents more effectively the misuse of the title adopted, while the British insures the benefits of association. There is greater freedom and elasticity under the British system, which is, however, accompanied by some liability to abuse.

Brown could also have pointed out that the British model lends itself more easily to the export of professional qualifications, since the barrier of a home-based licensing authority does not exist (Seidler 1969, page 44). British accountants have in fact been active exporters of professional accountancy qualifications. By the 1900s there were about 400 members of British accountancy bodies around the British Empire, forming 6 per cent of a total membership of about 7,000. In round terms 200 of the 400 were in Africa (mainly South Africa) and 100 in Australasia. Of the 400 over 70 per cent were incorporated accountants (Johnson and Caygill, 1971).

The attitudes of the various British bodies to accountancy overseas differed in interesting ways. The English Institute insisted that English chartered accountants could only be trained in England and Wales; the Scottish bodies, with their small home base, allowed training in England and Wales as well as in Scotland. The smaller home base also meant a greater migration of Scots CAs not only to England and Wales but also to the Empire and Commonwealth. In the 1960s, 4 per cent of them were located there; in the 1920s, 1940s and 1960s, 11 per cent (Johnson and Caygill, 1971, Table 1 page 158); in the 1970s and 1980s 7 per cent. Unlike certified accountants (see below) they were and are mainly to be found in the 'old' Commonwealth.

The Society of Incorporated Accountants and Auditors, however, kept in second place by the chartered bodies in the United Kingdom, made, under the indefatigable leadership of James Martin, determined efforts to expand through the British Empire. The historian of the Society (Garrett, 1961, page 14) reports that 'At an early stage the Society claimed for itself a "British Empire" policy'. The success of this varied from country to country.

In Australia it was unsuccessful. A commissioner for Australia (a Mr Charles A. Cooper) appointed in 1886 established a Committee in Victoria but was not able to make the Society the nucleus of a nascent profession in Australia. The first annual report of The Incorporated Institute of Accountants of Victoria (the body of which Brentnall was a founding member) records that 'Mr Cooper's proposals were, after careful consideration, set aside in favour of a local independent body'. Martin was, however, appointed in 1888 as a corresponding member of the Institute in London (Commonwealth Institute of Accountants, 1936, pages 8, 17). Nevertheless Martin complained at the First International Congress of Accountants in St Louis that Australia was 'dominated very largely by the working classes, and the working classes of Australia have nothing in common with professional men, and they brought our efforts to naught' (Official Record, 1904, page 105). Local practitioners in each colony formed their own accountancy bodies which after many vicissitudes were merged into the Institute of Chartered Accountants in Australia (1928) and the Australian Society of Accountants (1958).

What it failed to do in Australia, the Society was successful in achieving in South Africa (Garrett, 1961, pages 14, 55-9) – perhaps because Martin was able to go to South Africa personally (yet another example of the 'tyranny of distance' so important in Australian history); perhaps because South African governments were not dominated by the working classes; but also perhaps because accountants in Johannesburg 'having regard to the wide ramifications and finance of the mining industry … preferred to become part of a British Society with world-wide connexions, rather than remaining members of a body with local limitations' (Garrett, 1961, page 57). A mining industry also existed in Australia but its links with Britain were rather less. The South African arrangement lasted until the late 1950s.

Apart from Australia and South Africa, the Society established branches in Canada (Montreal, 1905), India (Bombay, 1931; Bengal, 1933) and Central Africa (Salisbury, 1954). A president of the Society, Harry L. Price, has even been claimed as the 'unlikely father' of the present organisational form of chartered accountancy in Canada. It was under Price's chairmanship during the 1908 conference in Atlantic City, New Jersey, of the American Association of Public Accountants, that the Dominion Association of Chartered Accountants and the Institute of Chartered Accountants of Ontario were reconciled. The event has a symbolic significance and according to the historian of the Ontario Institute is 'so beautifully and typically Canadian it is hard to imagine how it could be improved' (Creighton, 1984, page 63).

As the Society became stronger in the United Kingdom, its overseas activities became less important, and it underwent a 'loss of enthusiasm for Empire glory once it had fully established its position at home' (Johnson and Caygill, 1971, page 159).

By 1957, when the Society merged with the Chartered Institutes, the Association was already playing the leading role in this area which it has retained ever since. Between 1913 and 1967 the Association established branches in South Africa, India, Malaya, Jamaica, Trinidad, Hong Kong, Central Africa, Cyprus, British Guiana, Nigeria, the Bahamas, Canada and Tanzania (Johnson and Caygill, 1971). The Chartered Association, as it has now become, remains the world's largest exporter of accountancy qualifications. Six per cent of the Association's members were in the Commonwealth in the 1920s, rising to 11 per cent in the 1960s and 33 per cent in the 1980s. As already noted, overseas certified accountants, unlike overseas Scots CAs, are to be found in the 'new' Commonwealth rather than the 'old'. The Institute of Cost and Management Accountants has also built up a significant overseas membership in the last two decades (Banyard, 1985, pages 56, 79, 89).

As was the case with incorporated accountants in South Africa, many of the overseas members of the Association are also members of their own local accountancy bodies. It is a measure of the prestige value attaching to a word that most of these are 'chartered' rather than 'certified'. The historian of the English Institute (Howitt, 1966, pages 194-5) noted that 'chartered' bodies had been formed outside the United Kingdom as follows: Canada (1902, earlier in some provinces), Australia (1928, the only one based on a royal charter), Rhodesia (now Zimbabwe) (1928), South Africa (1946, earlier in some provinces), India (1949), Ceylon (now Sri Lanka) (1959), Pakistan (1961), Ghana (1963), Jamaica (1965) and Nigeria (1965). Since that date may be added the Bahamas, Bangladesh, Barbados, and Trinidad and Tobago.

What can we conclude about the British experience as an exporter of the institution of professional accountancy? Professional accountancy was both actively exported and actively imported. On the exporting side, some British bodies have been much more active than others, the difference being explainable in terms of their relative strengths in the *home* market. On the importing side, the United States actively imported the idea of professional accountancy (but not on the British model); Canada, Australia and New Zealand actively imported the British model but preferred to form their own local bodies rather than import British accounting qualifications; the countries of the 'new' Commonwealth have been twentieth century importers of British qualifications and have formed local bodies only recently; South African accountants until the 1950s were willing to hold both local and British qualifications.

How can these differences be explained? The active *nineteenth century* importers were in general located in those temperate regions of recent settlement which were recipients of British overseas investment; which had experienced British colonial rule but attained independence or a considerable measure of self-government; and where British cultural influence was strong and the English language dominant.

It is important to note the complex pattern of influences. Professional accountancy on the British model did not simply follow the direction of British investment which appears to have been a necessary but not a sufficient condition. Thus, the British model was *not* adopted in those areas (the United States and South America) to which British investment was directed most (see Table 2.3). Nor was it adopted first in those areas where British political power was the strongest but, on the contrary, succeeded best in those parts of the Empire which had achieved most self-government. In the *twentieth century* professional accountancy bodies have developed most rapidly *after* the achievement of independence. Under colonial rule development was sometimes slowed down by, for example, restricting public company audits to members of British bodies (Johnson and Caygill, 1971, page 170; Kapadia, 1973). On the other hand professional accountancy made little headway in areas such as South America where Britain had considerable investments but no political power.

For local professional bodies to develop on the British model, the further factor of strong British cultural influence (as in Australia, New

Table 2.3 Direction of new British portfolio investment 1865-1914

		%
By continent	North America	34
	South America	17
	Asia	14
	Europe	13
	Australasia	11
	Africa	11
		100
By political status	Independent	59
	British Empire	40
	Foreign Dependencies	1
		100
By climatic-ethnic category:	Temperate Regions of recent European settlement	68
	Tropics	27
	Non-tropical Asia	5
		100

Source: Simon (1967)

Zealand, Canada, and to a lesser extent South Africa) was needed. British investment alone was not sufficient. 'In neither [the United States nor Argentina]', a distinguished economic historian has concluded, 'did the British create the social structure they encountered. Their [economic] activity aided and abetted the tendencies that were already there ...' (Jenks, 1951, page 388). These conclusions can be extended to professional accountancy.

True and fair view

We turn finally to a discussion of an accounting concept, that of a true and fair view. In principle, just as an institution should be more difficult to export or import than a technique, a concept should be more difficult than an institution, since what is being transferred is part of a culture and a culture cannot easily be transferred piecemeal. On the other hand, concepts are expressed as forms of words rather than as actions or physical things, so apparent exports or imports may be easier.

The concept of a true and fair view received its first legal formulation in the British Companies Act 1947 but its origins can be traced back to the mid-nineteenth century (Chastney, 1975). It represents an amalgam of the previous Acts (see Table 2.4). The provisions of the 1947 Act (re-enacted in the 1948 Act) followed the recommendations of the Cohen Committee on Company Law Amendment (1945) which in turn followed the memorandum submitted to it by the Institute of Chartered Accountants in England and Wales.

It is much less easy than in the previous sections of this chapter to state what was available for import, for British accountants have never defined very clearly what a true and fair view is or how to make it operational. An authoritative view of one of the accountant members of the Cohen Committee (Kettle, 1950, page 117) was that:

> A true and fair view implies that all statutory and other essential information is not only available but is presented in a form in which it can be properly and readily appreciated.

Asked for an explanation by continental Europeans when the Fourth Directive was under discussion in the 1970s, British accountants referred to 'fairness of presentation (i.e. unbiased as between the different users of financial information) and frank[ness] in the recognition of economic substance rather than mere legal form'. (Rutteman, 1984, page 8). One British commentator has concluded that 'True and fair is what you make it' (Chastney, 1975, page 92).

The potential importers of the concept in the 1950s were those countries which were accustomed, when amending their company legislation, to give great weight to British law, i.e. most of the member countries of the British Commonwealth. Australia may be taken as an example.

The legislation of the Australian States echoed the requirements of United Kingdom legislation fairly closely until the 1970s (NCSC, 1984, pages 8-9). There were originally good reasons for this which were expressed by parliamentarians and lawyers as follows:

> Investors at Home [i.e. in the United Kingdom] were shy about investing in a State whose company law they did not understand (Manifold, quoted Gibson, 1971, page 48).

> ... uniformity would give to Victoria the guidance of English decisions and English textbooks on the Act would continuously furnish precedents and illustrations. Divergence would mean uncertainty ... access to a wide range of experience is vital, and ... this the narrow limits of a small community cannot furnish (Moore, 1934, page 182).

Table 2.4 Extracts from British Companies Acts

1844 ... the Directors ... shall cause ... a full and fair Balance Sheet to be made up ... (s.35)

1862 The Auditors shall make a Report to the Members upon the Balance Sheet and Accounts, and in every such Report they shall state whether, in their Opinion, the Balance Sheet is a full and fair Balance Sheet, containing the Particulars required by these Regulations, and properly drawn up so as to exhibit a true and correct View of the State of the Company's Affairs ... (para.94, Table A).

1879 (Banking Companies) The auditor or auditors ... shall state whether, in his or their opinion, the balance sheet ... is a full and fair balance sheet properly drawn up so as to exhibit a true and correct view of the state of the company's affairs, as shown by the books of the company ... (s.7)

1900 ... the auditors ... shall state whether, in their opinion, the balance sheet ... is properly drawn up so as to exhibit a true and correct view of the state of the company's affairs as shown by the books of the company ... (s.23)

1948 (1) Every balance sheet of a company shall give a true and fair view of the state of affairs of the company as at the end of its financial year, and every profit and loss account of a company shall give a true and fair view of the profit or loss for the financial year.
(3) ... the [detailed] requirements of [the 8th Schedule] shall be without prejudice either to the general requirements of subsection (1) of this section or to any other requirements of this Act (s.149, re-enacting s.13, Companies Act 1947).

1985 (2) The balance sheet shall give a true and fair view of the state of affairs of the company as at the end of the financial year; and the profit and loss account shall give a true and fair view of the profit or loss of the company for the financial year.
(3) Subsection (2) overrides—
(a) the requirements of Schedule 4, and
(b) all other requirements of this Act as to the matters to be included in a company's accounts or in notes to those accounts:
and accordingly the following two subsections have effect.
(4) If the balance sheet or profit and loss account drawn up in accordance with those requirements would not provide sufficient information to comply with subsection (2), any necessary additional information must be provided in that balance sheet or profit and loss account, or in a note to the accounts.
(5) If, owing to special circumstances, in the case of any company, compliance with any such requirement in relation to the balance sheet or profit and loss account would prevent compliance with subsection (2) (even if additional information were provided in accordance with subsection (4)), the directors shall depart from that requirement in preparing the balance sheet or profit and loss account (so far as necessary in order to comply with subsection (2)).
(6) If the directors depart from any such requirement, particulars of the departure, the reasons for it and its effect shall be given in a note to the accounts (s.228 = re-enactment of s.149 of 1948 Act as amended by 1981 Act; s.230 provides similarly for group accounts).

These views prevailed into the 1950s and 1960s and the Victorian Act of 1955 and the Uniform Companies Acts based on it all included the phrase 'true and fair view'. The requirement remains in the present Australian Companies Act and Codes.

By the 1960s, however, the United States was replacing Britain as Australia's main trading partner and source of investment, and knowledge of American accounting was spreading. Australian accountants began to define a true and fair view in an American as well as a British way.

Recommendation on Accounting Principles No.1 (1963) of the Australian Institute, for example, stated that a true and fair view 'implies appropriate classification and grouping of the items … [and] also implies the consistent application of generally accepted principles'. In 1984 the Auditing Standards Board (AuSB) of the Australian Accounting Research Foundation (AARF) issued Statement of Auditing Practice AUP3, 'The Auditor's Report on Financial Statements' (Pound, 1984), which sought to introduce a reporting format in which the auditor's opinion was formed and expressed in the context of whether financial statements 'present fairly the financial position and results in accordance with Australian Accounting Standards'.

However, a consultative document of the Australian National Companies and Securities Commission (written by Professor R.G. Walker of the University of New South Wales) rejected suggestions that a true and fair view should be stated to be in accord with generally accepted accounting principles or approved accounting standards and proposed the following addition to the Australian Act:

> Without affecting the generality of the meaning of the term, '*true and fair view,*' a 'true and fair view' in relation to accounts or group accounts means a representation which affords those who might reasonably be expected to refer to those accounts (including holders or prospective purchasers of shares, debentures, notes or other interests, and creditors or prospective creditors) information which is relevant to the decisions which may be made by those persons in relation to the purchase, sale or other action in connection with their securities or interests (NCSC, 1984, page 3).

The Auditing Standards Board reacted strongly against this recommendation which it regarded as placing 'an impossible responsibility on accountants, auditors and directors' and recommended instead the phrase 'present fairly … in accordance with approved accounting standards and comply with the Companies Code' (Edwards, 1985).

Whilst Australian accountants have begun to doubt the wisdom of their import, continental Europeans have been persuaded to write the concept of a true and fair view into their legislation. Table 2.5 shows how the wording of the relevant clause, which at first closely followed German law, was changed during the discussions of the various drafts. The changes were made at the suggestion of the United Kingdom negotiators but at the same time a minute of the Council of Ministers was recorded to the effect that in general following the provisions of the directive would be sufficient to achieve a true and fair view of a company's economic situation (Rutteman, 1984, page 8).

British accountants were keener to export the concept of a true and fair view than accountants of other EEC member states such as France and Germany were to import it. Whilst British accountants genuinely believe in the importance of the concept and its general applicability, the export took place in order to protect its role in British accounting rather than in the expectation of other countries making radical changes in their own accounting styles. It may be doubted whether a concept developed in a country where the main users of financial statements are investors is appropriate to countries where the main users are government (as tax collectors), creditors and trade unions. This may not matter, however, if the concept is interpreted in such a way as to fit its new environment.

This is quite likely to happen. In France, for example, there was, before the Fourth Directive, already a requirement for financial statements to be *régulier* (in accordance with the letter of the regulations) and *sincère* (in accordance with the spirit of the regulations). French law now requires that the statements be not only *régulier et sincère* but also show a true and fair view (*une image fidèle*). What this means has led to considerable debate (Pham, 1984) but the most probable result is that the concept will have no effect on the balance sheet and profit and loss account but will lead to additional disclosures in the notes to the accounts (which have assumed a new importance in France as a result of the Directive). It is not expected that German financial statements will change their nature unless the underlying economic and social structures do so first (Busse Von Colbe, 1984). The general idea of a true and fair view existed in Dutch law before the Fourth Directive, although not in so many words. The law (as now stated in the Civil Code, article 362) has not been substantially changed in this respect and there is, for instance, no explicit reference to a true and fair view in Moret and Limperg's (1984) commentary on the new Dutch legislation on annual reports.

The phrase 'true and fair view' is Britain's contribution to twentieth century accounting terminology. Those importers for whom English is a native language have not had to translate it. Continental European importers on the other hand have had the task of translating the phrase into their own language (Rutherford, 1983). In French a true and fair view becomes *une image fidèle*, in Italian *un quadro fedele*, in Dutch *een getrouw beeld*. German speakers have had difficulty in finding the right translation. The more or less literal *ein den tatsachlichen Verhaltnissen entsprechendes Bild* may be translated as 'a picture corresponding to actual conditions'.

It is interesting to note that all four languages prefer a 'picture' to a

Table 2.5 'True and Fair' in the Fourth Directive

1971 Draft	1. The annual accounts shall comprise the balance sheet, the profit and loss account and the notes on the accounts. These documents shall constitute a composite whole.
	2. The annual accounts shall conform to the principles of regular and proper accounting.
	3. They shall be drawn up clearly and, in the context of the provisions regarding the valuation of assets and liabilities and the lay-out of accounts, shall reflect as accurately as possible the company's assets, liabilities, financial position and results.
1974 Draft (Art 2)	1. (as 1971 Draft)
	2. The annual accounts shall give a true and fair view of the company's assets, liabilities, financial position and results.
	3. They shall be drawn up clearly and in accordance with the provisions of this Directive.
1978 Final	1. (as 1971 Draft)
	2. They shall be drawn up clearly and in accordance with the provisions of this Directive.
	3. The annual accounts shall give a true and fair view of the company's assets, liabilities, financial position and profit or loss.
	4. Where the application of the provisions of this Directive would not be sufficient to give a true and fair view within the meaning of paragraph 3 additional information must be given.
	5. Where in exceptional cases the application of a provision of this Directive is incompatible with the obligation laid down in paragraph 3, that provision must be departed from in order to give a true and fair view within the meaning of paragraph 3. Any such departure must be disclosed in the notes on the accounts together with an explanation of the reasons for it and a statement of its effect on the assets, liabilities, financial position and profit or loss. The Member States may define the exceptional cases in question and lay down the relevant special rules.

Source: Nobes and Parker, 1984, page 84

'view' and (except the 1978 German) express 'true and fair' by one word whose most literal translation is 'faithful'. This at least avoids the British and Australasian discussions about financial statements which are true but not fair. An American accountant unaware of the original English might translate the continental phrases as 'representational faithfulness' or 'faithful representation'. Whilst it is at first sight surprising that the Continental European countries have accepted such a concept it is clear that what they have really imported is a form of words which they are translating and applying so as not to disturb unduly what already exists. Perhaps this is the fate of all indefinable concepts.

Some conclusions

An analysis of the case studies presented in the preceding sections suggests two sets of conclusions. First, both exporters and importers must be considered and there is an important distinction between active exporters and importers on the one hand and passive exporters and importers on the other. Secondly, in assessing costs and benefits the position of exporters in their home markets is important, whilst it makes a difference to the importer whether it is a technique, an institution or a concept that is being imported.

The relationship between exporters and importers can be set out as follows:

A Active exporter	Active importer
B Active exporter	Passive importer
C Passive exporter	Active importer
D Passive exporter	Passive importer

Clearly, an import and export is likely to take place most quickly and effectively when an active exporter is faced with an active importer (situation A) and is least likely to be quick and effective when a passive exporter is faced with a passive importer (situation D).

Active exporters and importers are those who have made an assessment of the costs and benefits of importing or exporting a technique, institution or concept, have decided that the benefits outweigh the costs and are eager to go ahead. Examples of active exporters in this chapter are British accountancy bodies interested in expanding overseas and the United Kingdom negotiators keen to get the EEC to accept the concept of a true and fair view.

Success has for such exporters depended in part upon what importers were willing to accept. British accountancy bodies have regarded the British Empire and Commonwealth as a legitimate market and have used appropriate economic, political and cultural influence. The more advanced countries politically and economically have, however, preferred, and been able, to set up their own bodies rather than accept membership of British bodies. Continental Europeans have been willing to accept the concept of a true and fair view in the knowledge that they could adapt it to their own needs and also because they could successfully export standardized formats and valuation rules to Britain.

Examples of active importers are the Australian and Canadian accountants of the nineteenth century who formed accountancy bodies on the British model. They were also for a time active importers of British company accounting (including, in the case of Australia, the concept of a true and fair view).

Passive exporters and importers are those who have either not made an assessment of costs and benefits (perhaps through lack of knowledge) or have made the assessment and decided that the costs outweigh the benefits. An example of a passive exporter in this chapter is the early Italian practitioner of double entry. An example of a passive importer is a continental European negotiator who accepted the British concept of a true and fair view.

The three cases studied in this discussion can thus be entered in a matrix shown in Table 2.6.

Table 2.6 Importing and Exporting Options

EXPORTER	IMPORTER	
	Active	Passive
Active	Professional Accountancy	True and Fair View
Passive	-	Double Entry

The position of the exporter in the home market has been seen to be important both in the spread of professional accountancy throughout the British Empire and Commonwealth and in the export of the true and fair view to continental Europe. The former would probably have happened anyway, given the existence of active importers, but the latter would not have taken place if British practitioners had not been concerned to make sure that the concept survived in *British* law and practice.

It is easier to import a technique than an institution or a concept. Double entry has spread from Italy not just to Britain but to the whole world. Professional accountancy has spread more selectively. We have already noted Brown's (1905) findings for the United States and for Canada, Australia, South Africa and New Zealand. In other British colonies Brown found accountants but not, at that date, professional bodies. In continental Europe he noted the existence of bodies in Italy, Holland (from 1895) and Sweden (from 1899) but found none in any other European country. Where professional accountancy developed late in Europe it did so with more government intervention than in Britain or the United States and the bodies so created are less influential. They have not been created on either the British or American model and can hardly be regarded as imports from the United Kingdom or the United States.

Until recently, the concept of a true and fair view had spread even more selectively than professional accountancy, being confined to the United Kingdom and members of the British Commonwealth such as Australia, New Zealand, Nigeria and Singapore. It was not found in Canada or the USA. How real its export to continental Europe will be remains to be seen.

References

Banyard, C.W., *The Institute of Cost and Management Accountants – A History* (London: The Institute of Cost and Management Accountants, 1985).

Blainey, G., *The Tyranny of Distance* (Melbourne: Sun Books, 1966).

Brentnall, T., *My Memories* (Melbourne: Robertson and Mullins, 1938).

Brown, R., *A History of Accounting and Accountants* (Edinburgh: Jack, 1905).

Busse von Colbe, W., A True and Fair View: A German Perspective, in S.S.J. Gray and A.G. Coenenberg (eds), *EEC Accounting Harmonisation: Implementation and Impact of the Fourth Directive* (Amsterdam: North-Holland, 1984)

Chastney, J.G., *True and Fair View – History, Meaning and the Impact of the Fourth Directive* (London: Institute of Chartered Accountants in England and Wales, 1975).

Commonwealth Institute of Accountants, Historical Survey 1886-1936,in *Commonwealth Accountants' Year Book 1936* (Melbourne Commonwealth Institute of Accountants, 1936).

Creighton, P., *Sum of Yesterdays* (Toronto: The Institute of Chartered Accountants of Ontario, 1984).

Davis, R., *English Overseas Trade 1500-1700* (London: MacMillan, 1973)

de Roover. R., The Development of Accounting Prior to Luca Pacioli According to the Account-Books of Medieval Merchants, in A.C. Littleton and B.S. Yamey, *Studies in the History of Accounting* (London: Sweet & Maxwell, 1956).

Edwards, B., 'True and Fair'– Not Just An Academic Debate, *Chartered Accountant in Australia*, March 1985.

Gallagher, J, and Robinson, R., The Imperialism of Free Trade, *Economic History Review*, 2nd ser., vol. VI, 1953, reprinted in W.R. Louis (ed.), *Imperialism* (New York: New Viewpoints, 1976).

Garrett, A.A., *History of the Society of Incorporated Accountants 1885-1957* (Oxford: The University Press, 1961).

Gibson, R.W., *Disclosure by Australian Companies* (Melbourne: Melbourne University Press, 1971).

Griliches, Z., Hybrid Corn and the Economics of Innovation, *Science*, 29 July 1960, reprinted in N. Rosenberg (ed.), *The Economics of Technological Change* (Harmondsworth: Penguin Books, 1971).

Howitt, (Sir) H.G., *The History of The Institute of Chartered Accountants in*

England and Wales 1880-1965 and of its Founder Accountancy Bodies 1870-1880 (London: Heinemann, 1966).

Jenks, L.H., Britain and American Railway Development, *Journal of Economic History*, Fall 1951.

Johnson, T.J. and Caygill, M., The Development of Accountancy Links in the Commonwealth, *Accounting and Business Research*, Spring 1971.

Kapadia, G.P., *History of the Accountancy Profession in India* (New Delhi: The Institute of Chartered Accountants of India, 1973).

Kats, P., Double Entry Book-keeping in England before Hugh Oldcastle, *Accountant*, V.74, 1926.

Kenyon, J.P., *Stuart England* (Harmondsworth: Penguin Books, 1978).

Kettle, R., Balance Sheets and Accounts under the Companies Act, 1948, in W.T. Baxter, *Studies in Accounting* (London: Sweet & Maxwell, 1950).

Kojima, O., James Peele and his Works, essay appended to 1980 reproduction of *The Pathe waye to perfectnes in th' accomptes of Debtour and Creditour* by James Peele 1569.

Harrison Moore, W., A Century of Victorian Law, *Journal of Comparative Legislation and International Law*, 3rd ser., vol.16, 1934.

Moret and Limperg, *New Dutch Legislation on Annual Reports* (Rotterdam, 1984).

National Companies and Securities Commission, *'A True and Fair View' and the Reporting Obligations of Directors and Auditors* (Canberra: Australian Government Publishing Service, 1984).

Needles, B.E., Implementing a Framework for the International Transfer of Accounting Technology, *International Journal of Accounting*, Fall 1976.

Nobes, C.W., The Gallerani Account Book of 1305-1308, *Accounting Review*, April 1982.

Nobes, C.W. and Parker, R.H., The Fourth Directive and the United Kingdom, in S.J. Gray and A.G. Coenenberg, *EEC Accounting Harmonisation: Implementation and Impact of the Fourth Directive* (Amsterdam: North-Holland, 1984).

Official Record of the Proceedings of the Congress of Accountants ... 1904 (New York: Arno Press, 1978).

Parker, R.H., The First Scottish Book on Accounting: Robert Colinson's *Idea Rationaria* (1683), *Accountants Magazine*, September 1974.

Parker, R.H., Reckoning, Merchants' Accounts, Bookkeeping, Accounting or Accountancy? The Evidence of the Long Titles of Books on Accounting in English, in B. Carsberg and S. Dev, *External Financial Reporting* (London: Prentice Hall International, 1984).

Parker, R.H., *The Development of the Accountancy Profession in Britain to the Early Twentieth Century* (The Academy of Accounting Historians, Monograph Five, 1986).

Pham, D., A True and Fair View: A French Perspective, in S.J. Gray and A.G. Coenenberg (eds), *EEC Accounting Harmonisation:*

Implementation and Impact of the Fourth Directive (Amsterdam: North-Holland, 1984).

Pound, G., New Statement of Auditing Practice – AUP 3, *Chartered Accountant in Australia*, May 1984.

Ramsey, P., Some Tudor Merchants' Accounts, in A.C. Littleton and B.S. Yamey, *Studies in the History of Accounting* (London: Sweet & Maxwell, 1956).

Rutherford, B.A., Spoilt Beauty: The True and Fair Doctrine in Translation, *AUTA Review*, Spring 1983.

Rutteman, P., *The EEC Accounting Directives and their Effects* (Cardiff: University College Cardiff Press, 1984).

Seidler, L.J., Nationalism and the International Transfer of Accounting Skills, *International Journal of Accounting*, Fall 1969.

Simon, N., The Pattern of New British Portfolio Foreign Investment, 1865-1914, in J.H. Adler, *Capital Movements and Economic Development* (London: Macmillan, 1967).

Taylor, P. and Turley, S., The International Transfer of Accounting Technology, University of Manchester Working Paper Series No. 8502, 1985.

Vanes, J (ed.), *The Ledger of John Smythe* 1538-1550 (Bristol Record Society's Publications, vol. 28, 1974).

Watts, R.L. and Zimmerman, J.L., *Positive Accounting Theory* (Englewood Cliffs, N.J.: Prentice-Hall, 1986).

Winjum, J.O., *The Role of Accounting in the Economic Development of England: 1500-1750* (Centre for International Education and Research in Accounting, University of Illinois, 1972).

Yamey, B.S., John Weddington's *A Breffe Instruction*, 1567, *Accounting Research*, April 1958.

Yamey, B.S., Fifteenth and Sixteenth Century Manuscripts on the Art of Bookkeeping, *Journal of Accounting Research*, Spring 1967.

Yamey, B.S., Some Topics in the History of Financial Accounting in England 1500-1900, in W.T. Baxter and S. Davidson (eds), *Studies in Accounting* (London: Institute of Chartered Accountants in England and Wales 1977).

Accounting and International Pressures for Change

3
International Business: A Channel for Change in United Kingdom Accounting

Allan Cook[1]

Before examining the particular role of international business as a channel for change, it is useful to consider briefly the nature of accounting changes and the extent to which in the United Kingdom they may be expected to reflect their environment.

Pressure for accounting change may have a number of different causes – often in combination. A new business practice may emerge calling for new concepts or more precise calculations; examples might be lease accounting and accounting for deep discount bonds. Similarly and perhaps more fundamentally, general economic and financial conditions may so change that previous assumptions can no longer be maintained; the most obvious examples in our own time have been the move to floating exchange rates and the onset in major economies of sustained moderate to high inflation. In contrast to these causes, changes in accounting and reporting practices may reflect primarily new levels of accountability either voluntarily adopted or imposed by a regulatory authority; changes of this kind generally focus on disclosure: examples might be segment reporting and related party disclosures.

Another way of classifying changes in accounting and reporting requirements is to enquire how far the change is responding to what one might call a 'real world' problem for the enterprise or country concerned and how far it merely represents standardisation for its own sake. The first two causes of change mentioned above – responses to new business practices and to changed economic and financial conditions – appear to be rooted firmly in the real world. Even here, however, a particular change may be difficult to justify in relation to an individual enterprise.

Moreover, the intensive debates over the appropriate accounting responses to changing exchange rates and to changing prices are evidence of the divisions of opinion regarding what the Americans would call the 'representational faithfulness' of the solutions proposed. Resistance,

---

[1]The views expressed here are the author's personal ones and do not necessarily represent those of his company.

especially in continental European countries, to the adoption of so-called 'Anglo-Saxon' accounting methods also reflects a belief that the treatments in question are inappropriate in their environments. Although the Accounting Standards Committee's constitution refers to the intention of the governing bodies to 'narrow the areas of difference and variety in accounting practice', the Explanatory Foreword to Statements of Standard Accounting Practice makes it clear that 'accounting standards are not intended to be a comprehensive code of rigid rules' ... catering for 'all business situations and circumstances and every exceptional or marginal case'. Compliance with the spirit of accounting standards is stressed as well as the overriding requirement to give a true and fair view. At least in intention, therefore, the Accounting Standards Committee sets out to apply appropriate rules rather than rules for rules' sake.

The existence of the Accounting Standards Committee and the participation of its governing bodies in the International Accounting Standards Committee (IASC) create a screening process that evaluates accounting changes adopted or proposed in other countries to ensure that they are appropriate in a United Kingdom context before they are adopted in this country. A similar process is at work in the development and implementation of EEC directives, though in this case participation in the development is all important, since the scope for adapting the terms of a directive, once adopted, to the special circumstances of a particular country is severely limited. The United Kingdom has established a good reputation for the effectiveness of its public consultation during the preparatory stages of the company law and stock exchange directives. Nevertheless, it was inevitable that compromises were necessary and many believe that in consequence a number of misfits have now found their way into United Kingdom legislation.

International business

'International business' is sometimes taken to refer in a general sense to all aspects of international trade. For the purposes of this discussion it is interpreted in a narrower sense as the activities of multinational enterprises, though at a number of points reference will be made to practices or influences that are not unique to multinationals.

Accounting change was categorised above as stemming from three causes: new business practices, changes in the financial and economic environment, and new levels of accountability. The experience and needs of international business will now be examined in relation to each of these categories.

New business practices

The advent of microcomputers and improved communications has made possible an upsurge in new forms of financial instruments on a scale that would have been unthinkable a few years ago. The first currency swap was arranged between IBM and the World Bank in 1981. By 1985 the value of deals, counting both sides of the transaction, had risen to $23 billion. The scale of the business has itself created an industry within the international banks which may have even more far-reaching effects as the market for the original deals becomes saturated and their inventors turn their attention to new and riskier schemes. The development of the futures markets and the possibilities of arbitrage between them and the stock markets has given a frightening, new significance to the close of the account, as huge portfolios identically matching the components of a futures contract based on a stock market index are triggered for sale or purchase in the last few minutes of trading.

In line with their cautious traditions, the big multinationals have usually steered clear of the more speculative or borderline deals. Nevertheless, the international nature of their business naturally involves them in many aspects of the new opportunities. A recent example of financial innovation undertaken by a multinational was the issue by Standard Oil, the troubled US subsidiary of BP, of a bond, interest on which varied with the oil price. An investment of this kind blurs the textbook distinction between risk capital and debt and creates a new concept for the financial analyst, if not for the accountant. A similar effect is achieved by the perpetual floating rate notes issued in the past two years by a number of the big banks. Under Bank of England rules the finance so raised may be treated as equivalent to equity for the purposes of calculating the liquidity ratios which govern the permitted level of a bank's lending. For the purposes of the balance sheet, the notes are effectively equity; for the purposes of the profit and loss account, the interest seems nevertheless to be a financial charge rather than a preference dividend.

The extent to which a new business practice can be internationalised often depends on the circumstances of its birth. Financial innovation is frequently a response to tax, exchange control and other regulations imposed by a national government. As such, its effects may be limited, at least initially, to the country for which it was designed. A good example, which has created its own accounting problems, is the 'daisy chain' of North Sea oil sales and purchase contracts, under which a cargo of oil for future delivery may change hands thirty or forty times between the producer and the ultimate buyer. The music stops at 5 p.m. on the nomination date, when the destination of the cargo must be notified to the producer. The accounting problem arises when a company that appears more than once in the same chain attempts by agreement with all the intermediate parties to 'book-out' the intervening contracts so that margins are settled, but not the full amounts. On the assumption (itself open to debate) that forward purchase and sale contracts by the same company would normally be recorded gross, the question arises whether the terms of settlement should be allowed to affect the accounting for the transaction itself. The book-out problem does not occur on a large scale outside the North Sea, partly because the daisy chain is a direct result of British Government oil taxation policies, which require evidence of market prices even for intra group deliveries, partly because of the proximity of North Sea oil production to the markets and partly because in the United States, the other major oil trading country, such 'paper' transactions would normally be conducted on a futures market.

As accounting and reporting become regulated, more and more frequent examples recur of financial innovation designed to secure a desired accounting or disclosure treatment. The trend is illustrated by the growing concern expressed in the United States and in this country at the use of 'off balance sheet finance'. The occasions for such finance and the forms that it takes naturally depend on the prevailing regulations but the idea is easily transferable between countries even if the exact schemes are not. One type of scheme, in the United States, whose accounting effects were removed by FAS 68, was to fund a company's research and development activities by means of an associated company, a limited partnership or an independently constituted trust. The company would contract to buy the research and development services over a period of time and would often find it necessary also to guarantee repayment of the finance in the event that the research and development did not produce usable results. Apart from the implications for federal and state income taxes, such arrangements would, until FAS 68, have enabled a company to charge research and development only as it was 'used' instead of as the expense was incurred in accordance with FAS 2. In the United Kingdom, the more flexible accounting requirement of SSAP 13, which allows the carry forward of development expenditure subject to certain conditions, would remove some of the accounting motivation for such arrangements, though the off balance sheet finance advantages would still remain.

It would seem unlikely that multinationals are disproportionately significant to United Kingdom accounting through the introduction of new business practices. New markets and the availability of international financial advice are open to all. Non-banking multinationals with their long term perspectives and high levels of accountability are usually averse to engaging in the type of borderline practices that are often the stimulus for new accounting regulations. Whether or not a new business practice capable of generating an accounting change takes root in this country is likely to depend much more on the legal fiscal and regulatory environment than on its popularity with multinational business.

Changes in the financial and economic environment

By definition, multinational companies operate in not one but a variety of financial and economic environments. From an accounting standpoint this variety has been most significant in relation to the development of SSAP 20, the standard on foreign currency translation.

During the early stages of the preparation of SSAP 20, the responses to ED 21 showed an interesting division of opinion. Business was solidly in favour of the use of the closing rate, whereas accounting firms and academics generally preferred the temporal method on the grounds of its (supposed) conceptual purity, while recognising that it was unlikely to be accepted in practice in this country. The eventual acceptance both in the United Kingdom and in North America of the theory of the 'net investment', which underlies the closing rate method, was largely the result of the testimony of multinational business, which demonstrated from its own experience that the theory and its sometimes novel corollaries fitted the realities of a world of floating exchange rates much more closely than any alternative.

The variety of financial and economic environments of multinationals also influences the attitudes of some of them to accounting for the effects of changing prices. The most direct way in which this happens is of course that the effects of hyper-inflation cannot be ignored. In accordance with SSAP 20, the accounts of subsidiaries operating in highly inflationary economies are normally adjusted for changing price levels before translation and consolidation. Less directly but perhaps more significantly, recognition of the complexities of measuring and communicating the interplay between changing exchange rates and changing price levels has dampened enthusiasm for applying in their case such apparently straightforward techniques as the indexation of current cost profit by the United Kingdom retail price index. An adjustment of this kind presupposes that it is acceptable to translate local profits to sterling before restating them in units of constant purchasing power. Some, however, believe that restatements by local indices followed by translation at the current exchange rate is the more correct procedure, particularly if the objective is to indicate the trend of sustainable growth in the countries of operation. Apart from these complexities, a multinational is more likely than a purely domestic company to have an international spread of shareholders. These may not find it particularly helpful to be presented with trend information adjusted by the United Kingdom retail price index.

Looking to the future, one detects a growing readiness on the part of both users and preparers of multinationals' accounts to attempt to identify the underlying movements of key figures over successive years after eliminating the effects of translation at different sets of exchange rates. For example, both Unilever and BAT regularly present their preliminary group results on both an actual and a constant exchange rates basis. The effect is to reveal more clearly the underlying trends in the countries of their operations. Unfortunately, press comment about stripping away the effects of currencies sometimes refers to adjustments such as these but somtimes to quite different elements which ought not to be excluded.

In one sense the international nature of the operations of multinationals inevitably influences United Kingdom accounting, since it raises a number of problems not found elsewhere. A deeper issue is the extent to which general accounting problems are influenced by international developments.

Accounting developments involving new techniques or insights generally originate as a response to a new business practice or a changed financial and economic environment. Once established and working in one country, however, the new development may transfer to other countries with less difficulty than was met with in the original development, provided always that the circumstances in those countries are sufficiently similar to justify the new accounting approach.

Two areas in which the presence of multinationals may act as a bridge for the transfer of new accounting developments to the United Kingdom are accounting for pensions and the use of LIFO for accounting for stocks.

The Accounting Standards Committee has recently published ED 39, Accounting for Pension Costs. These proposals have been some ten years in gestation and by and large reflect the view that pensions are a long-term cost that is essentially insulated from the immediate effects of volatility in both stock markets and pay levels. Accordingly, the emphasis is more on preserving a level charge for pensions in relation to pensionable pay than on specifying precise rules for reflecting current events in the accounts or on identifying potential balance sheet effects of those events. Over the past five years, however, first in the United States and latterly in the United Kingdom, companies have found ways of recovering substantial sums from their pension funds, thus demonstrating a close link between the condition of the pension scheme and the net income and financial position of the sponsoring employer. In these circumstances it is not surprising that the two US standards, FAS 87 and FAS 88 published in December 1985, also resulting from ten years of work on the subject, should have taken a far more prescriptive line than ED 39 in relation to both accounting and disclosures. United Kingdom multinationals that file their accounts with the US Securities and Exchange Commission will be obliged to familiarise themselves with the US standards in order to provide supplementary information on that basis. It is possible that this experience, together with United Kingdom developments such as the new statutory rules for regulating the over or under-funding of pension schemes, will lead eventually to the adoption of more prescriptive rules for pensions accounting in the United Kingdom.

The LIFO method of accounting for stocks is familiar to a number of multinationals with subsidiaries operating in the United States and other countries where the method is accepted for tax purposes. Because it charges something close to the current cost of goods sold the method might be expected to be acceptable in this country to those who wish accounts to reflect current rather than historical costs. Nevertheless, though permitted by the Companies Act the method is virtually prohibited by SSAP 9. The reason is probably that under LIFO the balance sheet figure for stocks tends to be seriously understated; furthermore, when volumes reduce so that old layers of LIFO are drawn down, very out of date costs are charged to the profit and loss account with potentially highly significant effects on profit for the period. These drawbacks could be eliminated by a proposal currently under discussion in the United States. The suggestion is that LIFO should be used in the income statement but FIFO in the balance sheet, the difference being taken to what we would call a reserve account forming part of shareholders' funds. At the same time LIFO 'drawdown' profits would cease to be recognised in income. The system has obvious similarities with current cost accounting for stocks, since it transforms LIFO into a technique that satisfactorily measures both current performance and current financial position. Multinationals at present operating a variety of stock accounting systems for similar products could find such a reformed LIFO highly attractive to them.

The conclusion of this section is that multinationals have influenced United Kingdom accounting developments by requiring appropriate accounting responses to their own international financial and economic environment and that they at least have the potential to act as a channel for changes developed in other countries whose environments are sufficiently similar to that of the United Kingdom.

New levels of accountability

It is in relation to new levels of accountability that multinationals ultimately may be expected to have the most far reaching influence on United Kingdom accounting developments. This being said, it is necessary to make some distinctions. Multinationals face a bewildering array of demands for information, often at a level of detail that could not be granted without infringing conditions of business confidentiality or disclosing competitive or price sensitive information. Much information is provided under a variety of accounting regulations in the statutory accounts of individual subsidiaries. Additional information may also be supplied to the appropriate authorities or employee representatives in the form of special purpose reports. For the purposes of this paper, however, 'new levels of accountability' are taken to refer not to these levels of information or requests for information but to the legitimate interests of the international investment community in the financial statements of the enterprise as a whole.

The growth of investment analysis over the last two decades has heightened the importance of a clear presentation of a company's performance and financial position. For companies whose shares are quoted only on the United Kingdom stock exchange it has been sufficient for this purpose to provide a true and fair view in the context of the Companies Acts and the Accounting Standards Committee's statements of standard accounting practice. Even in the past, however, a number of multinationals have sought quotations on foreign stock exchanges. The reasons include access to new capital markets, provision of a service to shareholders and reinforcement of the presence in the foreign country of an important operating subsidiary.

The next few years could well witness an explosion in the international trading of equities, even though differences in regulations and market practices will tend to make simultaneous international public offerings of the Reuters and British Telecom variety relatively rare. The new foreign shareholders will probably be more volatile than domestic ones since they are unlikely to be motivated either by traditional loyalties or by the belief that a particular United Kingdom share should be a normal component of their portfolio. In these circumstances, clarity of communication between management and the international investment community will be an essential element of support for the share price.

Clear communication of financial information relies heavily on the use of appropriate and widely recognised accounting principles. To some extent differences between the accounting requirements of countries can be overcome by providing reconciliation for net income and the key balance sheet figures between the amounts reported and their equivalents under US generally accepted accounting principles. There are limits, however, to the effectiveness of such reconciliations. Sometimes the differences of accounting treatment may be so fundamental that they transform every aspect of the accounts. Prior to the adoption of FAS 52 in the United States, the different treatments in use in that country and the United Kingdom for foreign currency translation were a case in point. Other significant differences that persist between these countries are the treatments of tax, goodwill and, most recently, pensions and the fact that revaluations of fixed assets are not permitted in the United States.

Reconciliations may permit compliance with the law and provide the means for the meticulous analyst to obtain the data he requires for the purpose of comparisons against other companies and the market. Reconciliations, however, do not usually hit the headlines – or, if they do, they are liable to gross misinterpretation. Furthermore, the management commentary, to which increasing importance is nowadays being attached, particularly by the SEC, can normally only be framed in terms of one set of accounting standards – those of the home country used in the published accounts. Managements are likely to become increasingly dissatisfied by their inability to communicate in one language to the international users of their companies' accounts.

For reasons such as these, United Kingdom multinationals have for the past ten years been actively fostering the international harmonisation of accounting standards. They have urged the Accounting Standards Committee to attach a high priority to this goal. At the international level they have joined with business colleagues from other countries in participating in regular discussions on accounting topics with government representatives at the OECD and in supplying a representative from business on the Consultative Group of the International Accounting Standards Committee (IASC). They have also monitored developments at the EEC and in the political (rather than technical) forum of the United Nations. Some have also participated in consultations in connection with significant accounting developments in individual foreign countries. At a forum on the International Harmonisation of Accounting Standards organised by the OECD in April 1985, representatives of international business made a strong plea to the members of accounting standard setting bodies present to raise the priority of international harmonisation on their agendas and to educate public opinion in their countries by researching the international background to all major domestic proposals. It was suggested that a starting point could be for all national standard setting bodies to compare their own requirements with those of IASC, identifying the reasons behind any significant differences.

These activities in support of harmonisation and the successes already achieved have been made possible because international business has taken a serious view of the importance of the subject and been prepared to devote a sustained effort to understanding the issues and practicalities involved rather than pressing narrowly for its own advantage. It is not to be expected that the encouragement of international harmonisation in accounting standards will lead to immediate far-reaching results. Nor should it be thought that pressure by multinationals in support of this cause should always be in the direction of advocating change in United Kingdom accounting to accommodate a practice developed elsewhere. As the foreign currency debate showed, it is sometimes the smaller countries, whose businesses are more exposed to the international environment, that are more ready to adopt appropriate accounting changes. What is needed is an attitude to accounting change that is both open and informed. The City of London as an international financial centre and multinationals with international reporting responsibilities are well placed to stimulate such an attitude in this country.

Conclusion

The discussion has drawn attention to ways in which accounting changes can transfer between countries when they respond to real world needs in the recipient country. International business is an agent for change of this kind because its own activities, environment and responsibilities reflect a changing real world.

4
Internationalisation of the Accounting Firm

J. Don Hanson

Let me begin my remarks by clearly identifying the role of the international accounting firm. The accounting profession around the world plays a vital role in society. Without the Good Housekeeping seal of approval on the financial statements of major corporations, capital allocation would be very inefficient and the cost of capital to such corporations much higher. In fulfilling its audit responsibilities the profession assumes a public responsibility transcending any employment relationship with the client.

This is by no means a new situation. As long ago as 1935 Arthur Andersen in the aftermath of the US securities legislation of 1933 and 1934, stated, 'It has long been recognised that the published financial statements of corporations are clothed with the public interest and that the accountant has a responsibility to the public as well as to his client.' Writing in 1972, Robert Trueblood, former chairman of Touche Ross asserted, 'the public is the accountant's only client in the world today. The public is the accountant's consumer.' Thus, while the authorities acknowledge the practice of public accounting as a business, the leaders of our profession also established an important understanding and that was that the success of the business depends on public acceptance of the accountant's unique role as a public watchdog. Such a public service role demands a careful, consistent and dedicated campaign to balance commercial concerns against public responsibility. A recent quotation by Duane R. Kullberg, Managing Partner and Chief Executive Officer of Arthur Andersen summarises our own views, 'The purpose of a business should be to make a profit – and, incidentally, render a service. The difference is subtle, but vital.'

Thus our greatest challenge is how to retain the professionalism that has been the hallmark of our role in world society for many years. This role is under constant and growing threat of commercialism in the profession. By commercialism I mean the assumption of general business standards regarding such matters as growth, profit and market share which, if not carefully balanced, could frustrate our public service role.

Key challenges

Let me now summarise my perception of some of the key challenges facing the international accounting firms. These are: how to respond to changing expectations; how to design a management structure that will last; and how to develop a worldwide ethic.

How to respond to the rapidly changing expectations resulting from the move to a single world capital market is a major challenge to the world profession and its major players. Historically, it was multinational companies that demanded comparable service around the world. They were greatly concerned that the quality of the accounting, auditing and tax services provided in each country in which they operated was comparable to that which they received in their base country. It was this need that was the prime impetus to the international accounting firms to expand around the globe and to organise themselves to provide broadly comparable service throughout their organisations. As United Kingdom capital went around the world, United Kingdom accountants followed. As US capital went around the world, US accountants followed.

Today not only do multinationals expect comparable service around the world but increasingly users of financial statements in various countries are demanding financial statements which conform to either their home standards or some internationally recognised standards. The impetus for this is coming from the regulatory bodies, such as the SEC in the United States, which requires foreign owned companies reporting there to conform with their reporting standards, and the Commission of the EEC, which under the Seventh Directive permits the top holding company in an EEC country to file accounts prepared for use in another country (i.e., EEC or worldwide) provided such accounts are comparable to the requirements in that EEC country. However, the regulatory impetus is only part of the story. Increasingly, sophisticated users in the capital markets of the world are requiring the preparation of financial statements of whatever source under some broad concept of generally accepted accounting principles. This demand will grow rather than subside as securities and financial markets become international in character and break through regional and national barriers.

How to develop a management structure that will stand the test of time is an issue that has vexed the international firms for some decades. These structures must not only meet the administrative goals and needs of the firms but must respond to the paradox of increasing international integration and interdependence at the same time as increased political nationalism and fragmentation.

Historically such nationalism and fragmentation have been exercised largely at the national level by restrictions on the international firms' right to practice. Indeed, such restrictions have generally taken the form of requiring local national practices to be owned and managed nationally and in many cases prohibiting any outsider in the management of the firm. This has generally meant that the international firms have had to develop their worldwide practices while maintaining the integrity of their local national practices. Perhaps the most unique response to such national fragmentation is the one we use in Arthur Andersen in the form of our Swiss Society Cooperative which I will return to later.

More recently, the demands for fragmentation have come in the form of attempts to separate the practices of accounting, audit and consultancy. Such attempts have occurred simultaneously on both sides of the Atlantic. In the United States, in 1978, the SEC promulgated ASR 250 which required listed companies to file an annual return identifying some twenty different categories for non-attest services as a percentage of attest services. This was really an attempt to determine the magnitude of the problem and in 1981 ASR 250 was withdrawn. In the meantime, the SEC had endeavoured in another statement, ASR 264, to sensitize the risk to independence if the proportion of advisory and non-audit services to attest services became too high. Again by 1981 the concern with this issue had subsided and ASR 264 was also withdrawn. More recently several committees are revisiting the subject, namely the Dingell Committee and the Treadway Commission. The Treadway Commission established by the Public Oversight Board is likely to be highly critical of the profession in this area. Thus the issue is unlikely to go away

In Europe there has long been the perception in some countries, notably France, and more recently, Italy, that the services of audit, tax and consultancy, should not be furnished to the same client by the same professional firm. These countries have endeavoured to export this notion to other European countries with the assistance of the Commission of the EEC. Various attempts have been made to incorporate independence requirements based on such fragmentation in both the Eighth Directive (now promulgated) and the Fifth Directive (currently under consideration).

Again, the international firms have had to respond to this challenge through structural arrangements which meet local needs but nevertheless preserve the reality of a worldwide practice.

More recently, fragmentation has shown signs of becoming an issue in the United Kingdom, which has hitherto been regarded as a bastion of the integrated profession. The leader in the Financial Times of 10 July, 1986, states: 'The firms need strong regulation because conflicts of interest are intensifying as they diversify out of their core business of auditing.' It continues, 'one solution would be to extend to the private sector the rules presently in force in the public sector. The Audit Commission ... stipulates that a firm cannot both audit a public sector body and act as its management consultant.' At the ICAEW Cambridge conference, Mr Paul Channon echoed these fears when he asserted that this general area should be carefully thought through as part of our consideration of the Eighth Directive. This will be an issue for some years to come.

The third major challenge concerns the role of the international firm as an inter-face between different accounting regimes. The international firm is faced with a myriad of national positions and practices on such issues as accounting, auditing, ethics (particularly those relating to the scope of practice), accepted business practices, regulatory intervention and many others. One of the critical issues facing an international firm is whether, and if so how, to establish worldwide standards in these areas.

To accept whatever goes in a particular country is of course the easy and to some extent a legitimate response. However, a truly worldwide firm cannot be built on such accommodation. It must articulate what is good and bad, acceptable or unacceptable, preferred or accepted in all facets of its operations. Without such articulation, an international firm is in reality no more than a loose affiliation

In today's environment there is an even more critical aspect of this notion. A truly international firm must ensure that its technology is subject to instant transfer around the world. Historically, such technology transfer could take place more slowly since developments in various countries took place at different paces. Today, time is of the essence because the world capital markets expect and demand that technology be transferred worldwide in a short space of time.

This applies not just to the accounting and audit practice but increasingly to tax and above all to our consultancy practice. The firm that can achieve instant transfer of its technology throughout the world is in a unique position. It has, in the words of Michael Porter, a 'unique competitive advantage'.

Need for worldwide values

Let me now turn to how the worldwide accounting firms endeavour to respond to these and other challenges. I must clearly do this by telling you how Arthur Andersen endeavours to respond. In doing so, I will identify many of the factors that need to be addressed in building a practice that can weather the storms of our complex society.

Let me begin by illustrating the enormity of the problem – a few statistics on the size and geographic dispersion of our practice (in the year to 30 August 1986) may help to dramatise the problems:

1. Worldwide fees will exceed $1.8 billion.
2. Accounting and audit practice   45%.
   Tax   23%.
   Management information consulting   32%.
3. Total of 215 offices located in 49 countries around the world.
4. Fees represent some 30.5 million hours of professional services.

5. Rendered by over 30,000 total personnel.
6. Rendered to over 110,000 clients.

As you will have gathered, by now the truly international accounting firm does not just happen. Its member firms and individuals do not assimilate its ethics by osmosis alone. It needs principles and guidelines which the worldwide organisation undertakes to pursue in preference to their own national aspirations. It means working at them day by day in country after country and continually reconciling and rationalising differences.

Within my firm we have identified the following basic concepts as values that guide our practice.

'One firm' service concept

This concept recognises that independent and autonomous national practice entities serving common clients must adopt compatible policies with respect to the performance of professional practice, accounting principles, personnel policies, and administration and finance. This 'One Firm' service concept requires that the partners and member firms speak with one voice outside the firm on professional matters, while retaining freedom of discussion and exchange of ideas within, subject always to each partner's responsibility to his or her national profession, and it goes without saying, his or her nation's laws.

Professional leadership

Our emphasis on professional leadership requires that all partners work toward the adoption by the profession as a whole of principles adopted within the firm, that no compromises on issues or principles be made, and that no rationalised immunity be sought from public accountability.

Optimum service

Under this concept, Arthur Andersen SC is expected to explore and implement programmes of professional development which will improve the potential of the firm for rendering service in all areas falling within its professional competence. Such programmes will include the following:

1. Expansion of the geographic coverage as rapidly as it is feasible to do so in order to render proper service.
2. Anticipation of the future personnel requirements of present and prospective offices, and investment of the necessary preliminary training to meet these requirements.
3. Maximum development of special and expert competence on an individual industry basis and sponsorship of the research necessary to identify the opportunities for service in all major industries.

4. Maximum development of the ability to perform tax consulting and management information consulting and to perform special work of a distinctive quality and character, and recognition that such development contributes exceptionally to the quality of the personnel, general professional ability and reputation for public service.
5. Continued emphasis on quality audit work.

Merit approach

Another important concept underlying professional development in Arthur Andersen is that additional responsibility is given as the result of clearly demonstrated ability and willingness to assume it. Such a philosophy is inherent in all advancement within the firm and applies to the partner level as well as to personnel. It ensures that salary and promotion are related only to performance. This concept denies any vested interest or other rights as a result of seniority or other factors not directly related to one's contribution to the development of the firm.

The fact that we have a true worldwide partnership makes us unique among public accounting firms. This is referred to as our 'one-firm' concept. We adopted this concept to ensure a uniform level of client service wherever we practice. This consistent level of performance is important to our multi-location clients, especially those who are trans-national. Our clients know what they can expect from us without regard to geography, function or industry.

By comparison, most public accounting firms operate with a looser affiliation and co-ordination of national entities. This may lead to less assurance that responses will be consistent, and less assurance that the level of service will be uniform.

I will return to some of these themes as I turn to the management of an international accounting firm.

Management of an international firm

In candour, this is a topic that is rarely discussed outside the individual firms. This is in part due to the intricacies of partnership agreements, to the intricacies of internal management and also, in part, to the fact that it is very difficult for us to articulate how we manage an accounting firm.

Peter Drucker has maintained that it is nearly impossible to run a multinational public accounting firm in the manner that we do. And in many respects, he is correct. However, when he made this comment our firm was 500 partners and now we are 2,000. Having got the formula (which we will not share even though we describe) we have every confidence that we will continue to do the nearly impossible. In fact as our national practices 'mature' we are more than ever convinced that our formula is impregnable even though we have to work at it continually.

It is individuals – not our structure, not our rules, and not our bureaucracy – that infuse an entrepreneurial spirit in our daily operations. We pay a tremendous amount of attention to this entrepreneurial spirit. It is extremely important to us and one that we continually reinforce. Teamwork is the cement which binds us together in continually striving to improve our service.

Creating and managing this teamwork, making the total of 2,000 entrepreneurial parts greater than the simple addition of those parts, results from attention to principles, concepts, style and culture rather than matrix management or organisational theory.

Legal structure

It is easy to speak of a 'one-firm' concept – most firms claim worldwide co-ordination – and we believe it is harder to accomplish this unless you have the sort of financial and legal ties that we do. For example, in 1977 we established Arthur Andersen & Co. Société Cooperative (SC) as our worldwide coordinating entity. Our SC is physically located in Geneva, Switzerland. Each partner in our worldwide organisation is a member of the SC and a member of another partnership. For example, a partner in France is a member and owner of both the French Arthur Andersen firm doing business in that country and a member of the Arthur Andersen SC. Because the SC does not engage in any accounting or professional service practice, our French partner in this example does not violate any professional requirements in effect in that country.

Because we have a worldwide partnership, we have a worldwide sharing of certain costs such as training, methodology, Research and Development and (topically and unfortunately) professional indemnity insurance.

Democratic process

We do not – as distinct from other public accounting firms – have a number of different classes of partners. We have only one class of partner; anyone who votes on an issue in the firm has one vote. Also there is no distinction in voting power of partners in regard to how long they have been with the firm or their level of responsibility – again, the rule is one partner, one vote. The difference is that some other firms have a system by which the number of votes that a partner has relates to the number of shares of ownership held by a partner. It also differs in that some firms do not allow all partners, depending on their geographic location, to vote on all issues raised before management.

Like the democratic process, however, this decision-making and more open style of management does force you to think through your principles, think through your policies and think through your practices and it makes certain that you need the overwhelming support of your partners before you move ahead. Because of the gestation period, it also means that when you do move ahead, you do so with the full force and consent of the partnership and the entire organisation.

If I can digress to give you an illustration at an international level in our firm, we recently had some new firms join us in the Far East and their association with us required virtually the unanimous support of our partners in the various partnerships we operate around the world. We got this on a virtually unanimous basis, not because it wasn't something that was questioned, it was severely questioned, but rather because by a great deal of information, a great deal of dialogue, documentation and discussion, we thrashed out all the advantages and disadvantages so that every partner in each of our partnerships was absolutely sure of the facts of the circumstances and the benefits that would be derived from the association.

Organisation

While our legal structure is very real and important, it is only rare in our modern and complex society that an entity's management structure can exactly mirror its legal structure. This brings me to what I would describe as our matrix organisational structure. Essentially, we have an organisation that follows three dimensions:

1. Geography – the various offices in different countries, areas or regions
2. Practice – our services in accounting and audit, management information consulting, and tax.
3. Functions – such as finance and administration, personnel, professional education and others.

Overall, our line organisation is geographically oriented. There is, of course, nothing unusual in this, other than to mention that our offices throughout the world tend to be a microcosm of each other, while obviously catering for the local scene.

The really unique feature of our organisation is, however, that our practice organisation (audit, tax and consultancy) and our functional organisation (finance, personnel) cut across the geographic line organisations, creating a matrix structure. While each office comprises three primary divisions each with a division head reporting to an office managing partner, and through him to various regional managing partners, the practices in each division have a dual reporting responsibility to the regional and worldwide practice management. It is through such practice management that our practice philosophies are disseminated, used and reviewed on a worldwide basis. It is through the practice organisation that we seek to achieve the instant transfer of technology.

What this means in practice is that an audit performed in Houston, Paris or Tokyo, or a tax return, or consultancy assignment performed in one of those offices will have been conducted using essentially the same methodology, principles, skills and discipline applied by people of similar background, training and experience. This common approach to practice methodology and practice issues is the hallmark of our international organisation and I believe no other firm has attempted or achieved the same degree of uniformity. To date this has been a desirable and effective approach. As technology revolutionises our methodology, it is an essential approach.

Such uniformity is also mirrored in the functional aspects of our practice. Thus, our approach to finance and administration, our personnel policies, our training and recruiting are all pursued with common philosophies and reviewed on a worldwide basis.

Cutting across this structure is our industry programme. In this area we pay special attention to forty-two industries that represent some 90 per cent of our fees. Examples of these would be banking, insurance, energy, utilities, transportation, health care, manufacturing and others.

National practices

Our offices around the world are unique local practices managed and staffed by host country nationals. This has always been most important to us and we believe it to be an essential hallmark of our international success. Our origins in most countries lie in a small nucleus of local personnel whom we imbued with the same dedication, principles, methodologies and aspirations as are evident in our worldwide practice. We have but rarely merged. While this has meant we have taken longer to establish ourselves, we believe it has resulted in a more unique practice. Our mergers, although unusual, have demonstrated a flexibility which is often lacking in one-firm firms.

Worldwide quality control

While I hope my brief overview of the management of Arthur Andersen and Co. will have been of interest to you, I now turn to what is really the single most important question concerning the internationalisation of an accounting firm. How does it control quality on a worldwide basis? I believe that we are perhaps the only accounting firm that really seeks to manage quality control on a worldwide basis. Let me expand on how we try to achieve this while ensuring that the local practice entities remain the dynamic entities we would want them to be.

To ensure a uniformly high quality of service, our national partnerships around the world are committed to applying the worldwide standards established by our Worldwide Committee on Professional Standards, created about thirty years ago and reconstituted to emphasise our worldwide perspective in 1975.

Worldwide committee on professional standards

The Committee on Professional Standards is responsible for the promulgation of the policies of the SC relating to professional standards in all practice disciplines including accounting and audit, management information consulting, and tax. Specifically, the Committee is charged to (a) provide active leadership in the promulgation of sound standards in the accounting profession and in the business world, (b) initiate or approve all policies and statements of position on accounting, auditing and other practice standards, including ethical standards and scope of practice and (c) engage in long-range policy planning in the area of professional standards

The Committee is of course staffed with many of our most experienced personnel who are used to developing standards intended to be applied on a worldwide basis. This is no mean feat. As the world of accounting, auditing and reporting moves forward in the leading western countries, the decision has to be made as to whether a particular development (e.g., lease accounting or property accounting) should be applied worldwide or only in a particular country. The answer lies in the pervasiveness of the question and how well we like the answers already developed. For instance, in the area of goodwill we have never endorsed the amortisation approach followed in the United States and have instead advocated immediate write-off. In contrast, we believe that the approach to lease accounting developed in the United States whereby leases are classified as either finance or operating leases was sound and we advocated this solution long before such an approach was endorsed by pronouncements around the world.

Worldwide standards

To guide us in this difficult area we have had to develop the notion of worldwide accounting reporting, auditing and ethical principles. For instance, our definition of worldwide (and individual country) GAAP would embrace the following notions:

1. The fairness of the result of applying an accounting practice is our basis for judging the acceptability of the practice, and this applies regardless of the practices that may prevail in any particular country.
2. We do not regard an accounting practice as being 'generally accepted' for this purpose merely because it is in use; judgements in this respect must be made in the light of all the related conditions, including legal requirements and business and economic factors.

3. Laws, business customs, and other conditions affecting financial reporting differ from country to country; therefore, we may regard a practice as acceptable in issuing an unqualified opinion in one country but not in another.
4. However, the main body of generally accepted accounting principles (as we define the term) has universal application, and the differences from country to country in what we consider to be acceptable practice are relatively few.

The policies established worldwide are administered by the line organisation of the national practice entities. While these entities are committed to applying our worldwide policies, their application is achieved not so much through structure, supervision or management. Rather, they are achieved through a recognition by dedicated professionals that the resources devoted to developing our practice methodologies worldwide provides them with the most current, efficient and effective tools with which to serve their clients.

Core literature

The consistent standards are achieved through common internal material which comprises a core practice literature and a worldwide information system whereby our personnel in every country are kept up to date with significant developments in their own country and in all other major countries. Such core literature applicable in each country would comprise:

1. Audit Objectives and Procedures – five volumes that deal with our worldwide policies on how to perform an audit (translated into Spanish, Portuguese, etc. – including chapters on such issues as acting as a statutory auditor).
2. Auditors' Reports – covers our policies on the form and content of virtually every conceivable kind of auditors' report in close to 500 pages (including our policies on auditors' reports on financial statements prepared for use outside the country of origin).
3. Ethical Standards – covers our policies on the ethical standards independence and scope of practice – to be observed throughout our worldwide practice.
4. Accounting Standards – two volumes (thirty-four chapters) to furnish our worldwide organisation with a comprehensive working tool which summarises the firm's policies on substantially all accounting matters of significance to auditors.

The policies set forth in these and other texts apply to our worldwide practice except where formally modified to cover special conditions and circumstances in a particular country.

National committees on professional standards

While the foregoing material is written with the intent of worldwide use, we have a system whereby formal national consideration is given to how these policies will be applied in a particular country. Each of the major countries has a National Committee on Professional Standards whose primary responsibility is to monitor our worldwide policies on auditing, accounting, ethical and tax matters as set forth in our firmwide literature and to identify any modifications that should be made to these to comply with local laws, pronouncements of the accounting profession or custom in their country. In this regard, as a general rule, we accept practices mandated by law, professional pronouncement or custom in a country where public financial reporting is well established and there is an organised accounting and auditing profession. The national committees are charged with:

1. The continuous review and monitoring of changes in standards and regulations of the local accounting profession and regulatory bodies.
2. Focussing on local business conditions and economic trends that could and should affect our professional policies and practices and reporting responsibilities.
3. Monitoring the quality of services performed by the various practice disciplines, initiating appropriate local review procedures (as supplements to the firmwide Practice Review Programmes), where deemed necessary to determine adherence to worldwide policies, and appropriate country supplements of accounting and auditing.
4. The preparation of national supplements to each chapter of our core literature.
5. The compilation of Country Statements on Accounting and Auditing Matters which cover unique accounting, auditing, financial reporting and scope of practice issues faced in the countries in which we practice as well as approved deviations from our worldwide accounting, auditing and reporting policies.
6. The preparation of other technical series used by countries to disseminate local information.

The foregoing core literature and national publications provide a comprehensive statement of our practice in each country.

Recruiting

Long before our worldwide policies and national policies could be implemented, we needed the right people, dedicated business professionals committed to providing outstanding client service. This brings me to recruiting, training and promotion.

To ensure that we can provide uniformly high calibre personnel, our overall recruiting principles are determined worldwide. We seek to hire the highest calibre university graduate available to the profession in each country, taking into account the relevance of their academic background/qualification to the needs of each national profession. Our principles of recruiting embrace:

1. Academic achievement is important not because of the knowledge acquired but to identify potential achievers.
2. Intellectual quality is important because of the intensely varied demands made upon our people.
3. The notion that we hire 'minds' rather than 'knowledge'.

Recruiting is the lifeblood of our firm and the decisions made today will affect the quality of our practice for decades to come. Accordingly, the choices we make should be of uniformly high quality. We do not lower our standards if the market in any year is what we consider to be below average. We would rather underhire than hire the wrong people. We seek to hire future partners – by this we mean that there should be no barrier other than time and progress that would preclude a person from partnership.

Training

Training is critical to quality control. We spend some 8 per cent of our net fees worldwide on training and this is likely to increase. Training is the responsibility of our professional education division. The function is worthy of special mention because it is an important tie that holds our organisation together in a professional and in a philosophical sense. Each Arthur Andersen professional receives centralised training from our professional education division. A good portion of this is conducted in a small college campus that the firm owns in St Charles, Illinois. In this faculty, where we have invested over £50 million, we have 250 highly specialised educators working on our worldwide training needs.

During the first ten years of a professional's career with us, that individual will receive extensive training designed on a worldwide basis. Additional training occurs after the tenth year, but this is aimed at improving pre-existing skills, and adding new management perspectives. This centrally driven training provides us with a commonality of backgrounds, a common internal culture, it provides us with a commonality of experiences and it provides us with an ability to apply a uniform approach – regardless of client location – to the technical questions that are brought up by our clients.

Firmwide training embraces the major part of the training in basic audit methodology. It involves teaching auditing in simulated client conditions using line personnel as instructors. The schools bring our national personnel into contact with their overseas contemporaries at an early stage.

Local training provides continuous training throughout an individual's professional career. Such training builds on the firmwide schools and, in particular, grafts onto the firmwide programme the many issues requiring special national implementation.

Promotion

Part of our worldwide approach assumes that personnel of a certain grade can function at that grade in any office throughout the world. Such a notion obviously assumes that promotion is based on a common merit approach supported by vigorous, continuous evaluation of performance and achievement. At every level the production of quality work is a key measure of performance. Our standards provide for the evaluation of our personnel after each assignment, and the preparation of annual summaries of performance based on assignments. The standards necessary for promotion at each stage are determined and reviewed worldwide. In this way we ensure our basic common merit approach.

Conclusion

I have ranged over a broad canvas and of necessity have not dwelt for long on any particular issue. In the early part of this chapter I identified certain key challenges facing the international accounting firm. These were how to respond to change and expectations; how to design a management structure that will last; and how to develop a worldwide ethic. In discussing these challenges, I identified the sources of the current impetus for change and in discussing my own firm I have tried to illustrate how we respond to these key challenges. I apologise if the discussion of my own firm appears parochial. I could think of no better way to illustrate these key challenges than to describe how one major firm has endeavoured to respond.

5
International Pressures for the Harmonisation of Accounting

Paul Rutteman

Saatchi and Saatchi sparked off a controversy in the autumn of 1985 when they applied to the courts for a reduction in their share premium account, thereby setting up a non-distributable reserve against which to write off goodwill. The *Financial Times* leader commented that even the stock market appeared to be taking an interest in 'the arcane topic' of how to account for goodwill. Moreover, for an arcane topic, the interest has been a persistent one – technical debates on how to account for acquisitions are at the centre of many takeover battles today.

One thing which the *Financial Times* leader did not comment on was that Saatchi's controversial treatment of goodwill indirectly stemmed from what the City would doubtless regard as an even more arcane topic: the EEC Fourth and Seventh Directives. But it also illustrates how difficult it is, despite the Directives, to achieve comparability between sets of accounts at a national, not to mention an international level. The Saatchi scheme runs contrary to the spirit of the Directives and United Kingdom generally accepted accounting principles (UK GAAP) – but neatly sidesteps the legal formalities, in a way which was not anticipated.

It is now five years since the Fourth Directive was implemented in the United Kingdom. It is interesting to look at the reactions when the Directive was first introduced. There was a general feeling of apprehension that the Directive would restrict United Kingdom accounting standard setters too much. It brought accounting principles and rules within the framework of the law, and the detailed requirements were, in many respects, more prudent than United Kingdom GAAP. They were obviously geared to those member states where the profit and loss account is used for taxation or distribution purposes, rather than as a measurement of performance. But on the face of it, this apprehension was unfounded. A survey of published accounts today shows less conformity with the Fourth Directive accounting principles and rules than there was before it was even introduced into the United Kingdom. The Fourth Directive valuation rules require that all fixed assets having a limited useful economic life should be depreciated over that life, but there is an increasing tendency towards non-depreciation of buildings. Many current devices for accounting for business combinations are questionable. Unrealised gains on foreign currency loans are taken through the profit and loss account, when the Fourth Directive requires that only realised profits should be so treated.

Harmonisation: some of the problems

Why then has the Fourth Directive had less impact than was envisaged? There are several obstacles to effective harmonisation, despite the amount of effort that is being put into it at an international level, particularly within the EEC. These range from the widely differing practices of the EEC member states – which make achieving uniformity within the framework of the directives extremely difficult – to, at the other end of the scale, the difficulty of enforcing standards at a national level in a situation where the standard setting process is largely self-regulating. The fact is that there are so many steps in harmonisation, that it is easy for things to go wrong somewhere along the route.

There are broadly four steps:

1. Adoption of the EEC Directives.
2. Implementation by the United Kingdom.
3. Translation of the requirements into United Kingdom GAAP.
4. Accounts preparation.

It may be instructive to look at some of the problems that arise at each of these stages and then go on to look at possible solutions.

The EEC Directives

The different member states all have different uses for accounts: in the United Kingdom, for instance, the prime function of a company's accounts is as an indicator of performance; whereas in other member states, such as Germany, accounts are more directly linked to distributability of profit and taxation requirements. Because of the widely different uses for accounts, accounting practices differ.

The link with distributability means that more emphasis is placed on prudence in other member states than in the United Kingdom. During the negotiation stage of the Fourth Directive, the Council of Ministers had to seek to accommodate the widely differing needs of the EEC member states. The result was, broadly, a system of compromises. Probably the major concession to the United Kingdom during the negotiation process for the Fourth Directive was the 'true and fair override' – an arrangement which has been more widely used than originally intended.

The Seventh Directive on group accounts also provides an example of how directives can change at the negotiation stage. There are currently widely diverging practices in the different member states. In Luxembourg and Greece, for example, there is no general requirement to prepare consolidated accounts, and in many member states the requirements extend only to listed companies. Moreover, consolidation techniques differ, as does the question of which undertakings should be included in a consolidation. The net effect is that there is little equivalence or comparability between accounts produced in different countries; it is therefore difficult to compare the results of groups based in different EEC countries. There is no doubt, therefore, that there is a need for harmonisation: the question is whether the Seventh Directive will be able to cater for that need adequately. So many member states' options were introduced at the negotiation stage that many divergent practices will be allowed to continue. For instance, there are now different definitions of the parent – subsidiary relationship, some of which are optional. There are several optional exemptions from the requirement to consolidate at sub-group level. Member states may permit merger accounting, given certain conditions apply.

All this is not to say that the Seventh Directive will not go a long way towards achieving comparability. It will undoubtedly have a significant effect when implemented in those member states where group accounts are currently not required at all. But the compromises achieved during negotiation mean that there is still room for significant variation in practice between member states.

Implementation – the United Kingdom Companies Act

It is on implementation that the member states can decide which of the options to bring into their own law, and consequently it is at this stage that variations between practices become most obvious. But practically, problems over interpretation can be initiated at the implementation stage as well. The recent paper issued by the Department of Trade and Industry (DTI) on depreciation and the use of the revaluation reserve illustrates this. The paper dealt with two practices which were developing in United Kingdom accounts which had come in for some criticism. One of these was the practice of writing goodwill off against the revaluation reserve: a practice which was based on a liberal interpretation of S34 (3) to Schedule 4 to the 1985 Act. This states that 'the revaluation reserve should be reduced to the extent that it is no longer necessary *for the purposes of the accounting practices adopted by the company*': a phrase which has been interpreted by some companies as referring to all of their accounting policies and not just those relating to valuation. In fact, the wording of the Fourth Directive implies at least that the revaluation reserve should only be reduced to the extent that it is no longer necessary for the purpose of valuation. The DTI is likely to amend Schedule 4 to reflect this.

The other problem with which the DTI paper is concerned is that of 'split depreciation', whereby some companies, for example Woolworths, were charging part of the depreciation on revalued assets directly to the revaluation reserve, and taking only the proportion that related to the original cost through the profit and loss account. This method arose from an interpretation of para 32 (3) of Schedule 4 of the Act, which states that a company may include under the relevant profit and loss account heading provisions for depreciation based only on their historical cost, provided that the difference between that and the provision for depreciation calculated on the revalued amounts is shown separately – either in the profit and loss account, or in the notes.

The Directive in fact states that this difference should be shown separately 'in the layouts' – that is to say, charged to the profit and loss account. The reference to the notes was introduced into United Kingdom law to allow for items in the profit and loss account being combined and then analysed in the notes – it was not intended to give companies carte blanche to choose whether to charge the difference to the profit and loss account or, in the notes, to the revaluation reserve. The DTI are consequently considering whether an amendment to Schedule 4 is necessary.

UK GAAP

Problems over interpretation can arise, then, in translating the requirements of the Directives into United Kingdom law. But probably some of the most significant problems on the implementation of the Fourth Directive have arisen at the standard-setting stage. The Fourth Directive brought certain accounting principles and valuation rules into the Companies Act, and the intention was that accounting standards would complement, and fill out the detail for, these accounting principles and rules. In fact, this was far from being the case.

The 1981 Companies Act more or less coincided with the issue of two new accounting standards. SSAP 19 on investment properties was issued in November 1981, with effect for accounting periods starting on or after 1 July, 1981. SSAP 20 on foreign currency translation was issued seventeen months later, effective for accounting periods beginning on or after April 1983. Both SSAPs took the same approach to the Fourth Directive's accounting principles and rules: they ignored them. Or at least, they merely paid lip-service to the requirements. SSAP 19, para 17, issued before the implementation date of the Companies Act 1981, stated:

> The application of this standard will usually be a departure, *for the overriding purpose of giving a true and fair view*, from the otherwise specific requirement of the law to provide depreciation on any fixed asset which has a limited useful economic life. In this circumstance,

there will need to be given in the notes to the accounts, particulars of that departure, the reasons for it, and its effect.

The British Property Federation (BPF) were quick to come up with 'suitable wording' for companies complying with SSAP 19 – and not complying with the depreciation rules: 'Depreciation or amortisation is only one of the many factors reflected in the annual revaluation, and the amount which might otherwise have been shown cannot be separately identified or quantified.'

This manoeuvre by the Accounting Standards Committee and the BPF endorsed non-compliance with the Fourth Directive in the case of investment buildings. It is an overt case of non-compliance, since the Fourth Directive requires explicitly that, where the true and fair override is used, the effect must be quantified. One possible solution is to reclassify any investment properties as investments and not tangible fixed assets: thus avoiding the legal requirement for depreciation.

At the time of issue of SSAP 19, the ASC were receiving responses on what was to become SSAP 20 – ED 27 on accounting for foreign currency transactions. ED 27 had been issued in October 1980 and responses were due in by March 1981. Several of the responses picked up on the question of long-term loans. ED 27 stated simply that all monetary assets and liabilities should be translated at the closing rate, or forward rate, with all exchange differences taken to the profit and loss account.

One criticism of this was that it implied that exchange gains on long-term loans should always be taken to the profit and loss account: was this in accordance with the prudence concept of SSAP 20? The more perceptive commentators pointed out that the proposals might also be contrary to the law, since the Fourth Directive, soon to be implemented in the United Kingdom, required that 'only profits made[1] at the balance sheet date shall be included in the profit and loss account'.

The ASC were unsympathetic: the revised draft of December 1981 was not changed and they commented that the treatment did not conflict with the prudence concept 'since the effect of all movements in exchange rate can be determined objectively at the balance sheet date'. They also dismissed the concerns over the Fourth Directive: 'These exchange gains and losses should also be regarded as realised for the purposes of the Companies Act'.

However, when SSAP 20 finally appeared in April 1983, specific mention was made of long-term loans: the amount of the gain would need to be restricted in exceptional cases, where there were doubts as to the convertibility or marketability of the currency in question. Para 65 also acknowledged that this could result in unrealised exchange gains on unsettled long-term monetary items being taken to the profit and loss account: 'the need to show a true and fair view of results is considered to constitute a special reason for departure from the principle' (that only realised profits may be included in the profit and loss account).

Both SSAPs 19 and 20 made use of the true and fair override in order to depart from the requirements of the Fourth Directive. In fact, they did so under different sections of the Act – SSAP 20 departed from the accounting principles of Schedule 4 on the grounds that there were 'special reasons' for doing so, under para 15 of Schedule 4. SSAP 19 made use of the general true and fair override under S228 (5). However, both departures undermined the United Kingdom's credibility with the other member states. This is because the true and fair override was intended to be applied – if at all – only in exceptional circumstances, at the individual company level, and certainly not, in the wider context, at standard-setting level.

It was not just the new SSAPs that were at odds in some respects with the Fourth Directive requirements: existing SSAPs also did not line up with the valuation rules. The most widely publicised divergence was the SSAP 9 treatment of long-term contract work in progress. The valuation rules of the Fourth Directive require that current assets be stated at purchase price, or production cost. Long-term contract work in progress is included under SSAP 9 at cost, plus attributable profits, less progress payments: an obvious departure from the Fourth Directive requirements. The construction industry's immediate reaction was to invoke the true and fair override. It is, of course, a necessary condition of a departure from the Directive's regulations that its effect be quantified in the accounts, which means that the amount of attributable profit included in work in progress has to be quantified. However, several companies took the line that it was not possible to quantify the attributable profit and accordingly did not do so.

The grounds for their argument were that the figure that was required was the profit attributable to the 'net' long term contract figure (i.e. cost less progress payments) which they said could not be quantified (even though the profit included in the gross amount – before deduction of progress payments – can readily be determined).

The Department of Trade and Industry, understandably, had little sympathy for such a line: to such an extent that it was rumoured that a test case might be pending. The result was the establishment of an ASC working party to review SSAP 9. ASC's proposals, in fact, solve the problems quite neatly. They propose that long-term contract work in progress be reclassified, not as stock, but as a debtor. How does this get round the problem? It does so, quite simply, because under the Directive, debtors can include a profit element. The ASC proposals thus resolve the issue without any fundamental changes in the way in which the results of long-term contracts are reported, and incidentally brings United Kingdom GAAP into line with IAS 11.

There are, however, no similar proposals to amend SSAP 20 to bring it into line with the Fourth Directive requirements. Concern over the divergent treatment of foreign currency transactions throughout the member states has resulted in a more detailed review being undertaken in Brussels by the Groupe d'Etudes des Experts Comptables de la CEE at the request of the EEC Commission and, following discussion at the Contact Committee, this could result in specific amendments being introduced to the Fourth Directive to deal with foreign currency translation.

Accounts preparation

SSAPs 19 and 20, then, both provide examples of divergences from the Fourth Directive, at the standard-setting level. SSAPs 22 and 23, on the other hand, broadly comply with the Fourth and Seventh Directive requirements on accounting for goodwill and merger accounting respectively – although, in the former case at least, only after amendments had been made at the exposure draft stage. The problems that are occurring with these standards are arising at the level of accounts preparation, rather than at the standard-setting level.

The Fourth Directive required that goodwill should not be carried as a permanent item in the company's balance sheet – a requirement which the Seventh Directive extends to consolidation goodwill. In conformity with this, SSAP 22 requires immediate write off against reserves, or systematic depreciation 'over useful economic life'.

The Fourth Directive does not deal explicitly with immediate write off against reserves: however, the intention was that it should be against retained earnings. Companies are, however, making use of various schemes in order to 'improve' their accounts in the area of goodwill accounting, and – with the exception of the use of the revaluation reserve mentioned above – they are devices which neither the Fourth Directive nor SSAP 22 cater for. One is the 'negative reserve' route, i.e. setting up a reserve against which to write off goodwill by apportionment from existing reserves. The amount apportioned is zero or a nominal £1: goodwill is then written off against this amount so that the reserve is shown as a negative balance equal to the amount of goodwill written off. The other is the much publicised Saatchi's scheme, referred to above. Both of these seem to be contrary to the spirit of United Kingdom GAAP and the Fourth Directive but the DTI seems to regard them as acceptable.

There is a similar problem with SSAP 23 on merger accounting. When the Seventh Directive was first drafted, merger accounting was simply not permitted. The Directive was, however, amended to permit merger accounting, subject to certain conditions, and SSAP 23 reflected this. The problem is that, as with goodwill accounting, companies have become adept at finding imaginative ways to circumvent the spirit of the requirements. Vendor placings and vendor rights issues are two such cases in point. They both meet the merger accounting criteria because no resources leave the group. From the acquiring company's point of view, there is a 'share for share exchange'. However, the acquired company shareholders sell their shares for cash. An intermediary – the merchant bank – arranges the conversion of the acquiring company's share to cash by arranging a vendor placing or a rights issue. The prevalence of these and similar schemes is embarrassing because, during the negotiations, other member states conceded an option for merger accounting to be included in the Seventh Directive, on the understanding that mergers were a rare phenomenon and that it would be only in exceptional circumstances that a business combination would be merger accounted. Those circumstances were assumed to include a continuity of shareholding interest in the merged group by both groups of original shareholders.

Compliance – or rather non-compliance – with the SSAPs is a topical subject and the problems are not limited to SSAPs 22 and 23. Another major area of non-compliance that is causing concern is the increasing tendency towards non-depreciation of buildings, on the grounds that the maintenance charges incurred on the buildings effectively cancel out the need for depreciation. Such a line would seem to be contrary to both the SSAP 12 requirements and the Fourth Directive valuation rules as well.

When *Financial Reporting 1985-6* was published by the ICAEW, it drew comments from the *Financial Times* because it highlighted increasing non-compliance with SSAPs, and press comment is beginning to question the ability of the accountancy profession to regulate accounting standards.

Alternative strategies

Inevitably, one effect of the EEC harmonisation programme has been to put constraints on standard-setting in the United Kingdom. Originally (pre-1981 Companies Act), the law provided a very broad framework within which accounting could develop. There were no detailed rules.

Implementation of the Fourth Directive brought detailed accounting rules into the law and, whilst the profession was content with those rules when the Directives were negotiated, they have increasingly been seen to be awkward and inflexible constraints. The Accounting Standards Committee had previously developed standards on the basis of best accounting practice, but now it has to consider whether that is compatible with the law and, if it is not, it resorts to artificial solutions – particularly the 'true and fair' override. Departures from the detailed requirements of the Companies Act can only be made when it is necessary to do so in order to show a true and fair view. It is debatable, to say the least, whether the non-depreciation of investment property is *necessary* to show a true and fair view, given the wide definition of investment property.

If the artificial solutions had to be judged only in the United Kingdom, they would be found acceptable, but they have to be judged elsewhere – in Brussels and maybe in the courts in Luxembourg. Will they be found to be acceptable there? That remains to be seen, but there has obviously been some bending of the rules and the solutions are vulnerable to challenge.

Similarly, in the United Kingdom, the merger accounting standard was initially challenged by the Law Society as being in conflict with the detailed Companies Act requirements. The more that is written into law, the less the scope for standard setting.

If the Fourth Directive was necessary to achieve basic harmonisation, at least it is sufficiently general to avoid excessive constraints on standard setting. It is sufficiently flexible to allow further development of accounting but how should that be done – by further Directives? By national standard setters? By other means on a European wide basis? Or by some other means on an international basis?

Reliance on directives

The major problem with harmonisation by means of the EEC Directives is that it is a very slow process. This means that not only are the negotiation stages prior to adoption of the Directive a time-consuming exercise, but more significantly, the Directives are slow to respond to an accounting environment which is essentially dynamic. The recent manoeuvres over goodwill and merger accounting illustrate this. There is no doubt that the devices being introduced by companies to eliminate goodwill without impact on retained earnings – or, indeed, to avoid creating goodwill in the first place – are contrary to the substance of United Kingdom GAAP and the EEC Directives. But they represent developments which were simply not envisaged when the Fourth and the Seventh Directives were negotiated.

Moreover, because of the timescale involved, it would be unrealistic to expect that the situation could be remedied by means of an EEC Directive now. In fact, the Contact Committee in Brussels was set up with a view to monitoring developments in the member states and the implementation of the Fourth Directive. It comprises representatives of the European Commission, plus representatives of the member states' administrations responsible for implementation. Among matters currently under discussion, there is accounting for foreign currency translation. Whilst the idea of such a Committee is obviously sound, its successes to date have been somewhat limited. If Directives are to achieve a higher degree of success in reaching harmonisation, the Contact Committee will have to assume a much higher profile. Only in this way can problems which have arisen over implementing the Directive into United Kingdom Company Law and elsewhere, and on translating its requirements into

United Kingdom SSAPs, be dealt with effectively.

The major criticism of EEC Directives, as with any legislative framework, must be that the procedural aspects are too time-consuming, with the result that the requirements are implemented too slowly in the first place, and that adaptions cannot keep pace with changing circumstances. But their major strength – and one which has probably not been fully appreciated – is that they have the force of law. Member states bring the Directive requirements into their law – itself an important factor, given the low priorities accorded to harmonisation – and, thereafter, any company failing to comply with the Directive requirements is acting illegally.

The importance of this should not be underestimated, given the increasing non-compliance with SSAPs in the United Kingdom today. Whilst the prevailing view within the profession is that accounting standards should largely be regulated by the accountancy profession, there is a growing feeling outside the profession that the accountancy bodies may not be capable of ensuring compliance with SSAPs on their own, so that statutory backing for accounting standards will shortly be needed.

The problem is that without effective monitoring of compliance with standards, there will be less incentive to adhere to them. There has been criticism that the professional bodies have failed to deal with cases of non-compliance with the SSAPs – a factor which has probably contributed to the increase in such cases over recent months. Moreover, although there are proposals to remedy this, to track every case of non-compliance would be a time-consuming task, and resources are limited. Certainly legal penalties for non-compliance would provide a more effective deterrent provided, of course, that enforcement procedures are effective. At present, there is no reason to believe the DTI would wish to take a more active enforcement role and their resources are also limited.

European-wide standards

It seems attractive, therefore, to develop further by means of national standards. They can more easily be agreed; there is an existing system in most member states. But it conflicts with the aim of a wider harmonisation. National standard-setters write new laws, which then require new directives to overrule them in the interests of European harmonisation. It is tempting, then, to suggest European-wide accounting standards but that raises the question as to who would set them, and how? If the Directive approach is too slow a process, is there an alternative? Decisions and Regulations of the EC Council of Ministers are not the answer but the Contact Committee and the Groupe d'Etudes des Experts Comptables provide a framework for another approach. If the Contact Committee provides the Forum for governmental representatives to meet, and the Groupe d'Etudes is the body representing the accounting bodies and which advises the Commission on accounting matters, could not the two tackle specific issues on a basis whereby standard-setters, such as ASC in the United Kingdom and governmental agencies elsewhere, agree to implement the solutions agreed in Brussels in national accounting standards? (That solution, incidentally, would probably sound more attractive in Continental Europe than in the United Kingdom or Ireland.) Any solution based on the accountancy profession alone agreeing standards throughout Europe is doomed, by virtue of the different roles of the profession in standard-setting in the individual member states.

International accounting standards

Another alternative to relying on Directives to achieve comparability at an international level is to do so by means of international accounting standards. Of course, we already have international accounting standards promulgated by the International Accounting Standards Committee (IASC). Those standards are widely acknowledged to be well thought out and technically competent. Moreover, in so far as the United Kingdom is concerned, they are reflected in our SSAPs. For instance, the 'substance over form' concept which is currently topical in the United Kingdom, and on which SSAP 21 (lease accounting) is based, as well as the recent Technical Release (TR 603) from the Institute of Chartered Accountants in England and Wales on 'off balance sheet' finance, is a concept which has found its way into United Kingdom GAAP from the International Accounting Standards. The United Kingdom Stock Exchange requires that all overseas companies coming for a listing should comply with International Accounting Standards.

But despite the respect accorded to IASs, their success in achieving comparability has been limited. Professional organisations in all the EEC member states are members of the International Accounting Standards Committee. In fact, accountancy bodies in five EEC countries have been members since its foundation in 1973. But this did not of itself achieve harmonisation: for example, during the period when the Seventh Directive on group accounts was at the negotiation stage, there were still substantial differences in group accounts practices throughout the member states. This was in spite of the fact that the IASC had already issued two standards dealing with consolidated accounts and accounting for business combinations.

An interesting example of the attitude to International Accounting Standards taken by the EEC Commission emerged from a problem in implementing the Seventh Directive in Holland. The Seventh Directive permits member states to grant exemption from the requirement to produce consolidated accounts at an intermediate group level if the parent is itself a subsidiary of another company which prepares and files group consolidated accounts on a basis equivalent to those required by the Seventh Directive. What constitutes equivalence is an open question and the EEC Commission accepts that this needs clarification. However, the Dutch Government in implementing the Seventh Directive decided that, provided the overall consolidated accounts comply with International Accounting Standards, that would be sufficient to satisfy the equivalence rule. This decision met with disfavour from the Commission, who consider International Accounting Standards to be much more permissive than the Directive, and so not 'equivalent'.

The Commission is reported to have commented that 'reference to professional standards over which we have no control should not immediately make the accounts equivalent'. This statement sums up the difficulty with International Accounting Standards and explains why their impact has been so limited. The problem is that the International Accounting Standards Committee, as a private sector body, cannot be given delegated powers. It is also widely felt to be too strongly influenced by US and United Kingdom practice.

This is a pity, since accounting standards at an international level could overcome many of the problems that have arisen with the Directives. They could conceivably eliminate two of the stages discussed earlier – i.e. implementation of international policies into United Kingdom law, and thence into United Kingdom SSAPs.

There would be three immediate advantages to this. Firstly, implementation would obviously be much quicker. Secondly, cutting out the two intervening stages would prevent any problems of misinterpretation occurring at these stages, such as the confusion over the use of the revaluation reserve, or the misuse of the true and fair override. Finally, loopholes could, theoretically, be closed quickly, without the drawn-out debates as to whether problems should be tackled by the ASC or the DTI, and how to reconcile any amendments with EEC Directives.

To make any system of international accounting standards effective, however, the standard-setting body would have to be one which is recognised internationally by governments, in a way in which the IASC is not. It would also need effective systems to ensure compliance. Within the EEC, the Fourth and Seventh Directives could then be seen as a framework enacted in law. The international standards, which are, in my view, not in conflict with the Fourth and Seventh Directives even now, could be used to refine the detailed accounting rules. Ideally, governments would be prepared to give the necessary enforcement powers, in the United Kingdom to the professional bodies (but elsewhere, perhaps, to bodies more broadly representative of preparers and users of financial statements). The international standards themselves could perhaps be further refined to narrow the range of permitted practice.

Conclusion – the need for harmonisation

Whatever the best solution, there can be no doubt that there is a growing need for harmonisation. The problems during the negotiations stages of the Seventh Directive illustrate just how fundamental the differences in accounting practice can be between different countries. It is obviously a disadvantage when shareholders, creditors and potential investors cannot easily compare the results of different companies, and the problem has been made more pressing recently because of the increasing internationalisation of the capital markets.

At the EEC level, this is evidenced by the recent adoption of a draft capital markets directive. The proposed directive would make it possible for residents of one EEC country to take capital stakes in unlisted companies in another country; allow enterprises based in one member country to issue securities on other national capital markets; and, finally, allow financial institutions throughout the EEC to issue commercial credits to non-residents for more than five years. If adopted, this directive will put pressure on member states, notably France and Italy which do not allow free movement of capital, to extend recent capital liberalisation moves.

This marks a step towards the idea of a European Stock Exchange, where European companies' shares would be treated as a domestic issue, but there is already an increasing internationalisation of the securities markets.

It is in the interests of both European companies and European investors that harmonisation of accounting standards is global, rather than just European. In developing the Fourth and Seventh Directives, the EEC Commission has moved the harmonisation process forward a long way in Europe but the risk now lies in developing these further in isolation (i.e. as if standards elsewhere are of no importance). It would be sad if the EEC Commission moves in one direction, the United States Financial Accounting Standards Board in another and Japanese authorities in yet another. The result might be yet broader international accounting standards, permitting all these practices.

Realistically, it is time for all standard-setting bodies to recognise that they should not be producing standards in isolation; that there is a need for joint development and of an appropriate forum for such development.

Currently, the EEC Commission is active in the committees of the OECD and UN, where transnational reporting is discussed but, whilst it shows the willingness of the Commission to take into account international developments, it does little to achieve international harmonisation.

What is needed is a forum for standard-setting bodies to meet and agree international standards. IASC was intended to achieve just that but, in practice, in very few countries does the accounting profession actually set the standards. Would it then be a solution to transform IASC into a forum where the real standard-setters meet (and that implies a mixture of governmental organisations and private bodies)? International standards proposed by such an organisation could more easily be directly implemented in each country.

Such a solution would not be reached without first overcoming significant obstacles such as:

1. Who would represent individual EEC countries? (would it be the EEC Commission for all, as they would claim is implied in the Common Market law, or would it be the ASC for the United Kingdom, etc.?).
2. Would application of standards be direct or indirect? (most countries would probably insist on interpreting the international standards in local standards or local law, with all the variations that implies).
3. Would the standards be enforced in the same way? (in some countries, standards would be seen as strict law; in others, mere statements of good practice).
4. Would countries be prepared to delegate standard-setting to an international body? (not yet, but eventually it must come).
5. Are standard-setters prepared even to meet as a mixed body to agree action, even though some are government agencies and other professional organisations? (IASC comprises solely professional organisations, UN and OECD solely governmental representation – albeit assisted by advisory bodies from the private sector. The standard-setters have met under the auspices of OECD on one occasion for a gentle testing of the water but there are no signs of a mass plunge).

The likelihood of overcoming these obstacles in the short term is small but, if the need for global harmonisation is accepted, should moves not be started in that direction?

Note

1. 'Made' means the same as 'realised' in this context. The Companies Act (para 12 of the Fourth Schedule CA 1985) therefore refers to 'realised profits'.

Some Illustrative Examples

6

Financial Reporting by Interlisted European Companies: Issues in Transnational Disclosure

Simon Archer and Stuart McLeay

In the past few years, many European-based multinational companies have experienced or, indeed, successfully encouraged an increase in the international trading of their equity securities. For instance, Volkswagen's survey of stockholders, carried out in September 1985 revealed that:

> Foreign stockholders have 19.73% of our capital compared with 6.83% in 1977. The increase is mainly attributable to buying from Switzerland, the United Kingdom and the US. Almost half of the foreign holdings are in countries where Volkswagen shares are traded on the local stock exchanges (the Benelux countries, Austria and Switzerland).(Volkswagen Annual Report 1985, page 26).

A general movement towards deregulation of the capital markets in the 1980s and new conditions allowing free trading by foreigners in domestic equities may have contributed to this growth in the volume of international transactions in listed securities (Ayling, 1986). Of course, a quotation on one or more foreign exchanges may or may not be accompanied by new issues aimed at the international capital market – foreign exchanges offer an enlargement of secondary as well as primary markets for securities. This is well illustrated by the case of Volvo:

> Volvo shares have been traded on the Stockholm Stock Exchange since 1935 and on the London Stock Exchange since 1972. In 1974 the shares were listed on the exchanges in Frankfurt, Hamburg and Dusseldorf, and in 1979 on the Oslo exchange. Since the autumn of 1984, Volvo shares have been traded on the Paris Bourse and, via American Depositary Receipts (ADRs), in the over-the-counter market in the United States through the NASDAQ electronic quotation system. New listings were added in Brussels and Antwerp, in 1985. (Volvo Annual Report, 1985. page 56).

A few multinational groups are structured in a way that entails a dual or multiple listing. Royal Dutch Shell and Unilever are well-known examples of groups whose affairs are reflected in stock exchange quotations in the two countries where the parent companies are registered. But, in addition, their shares are listed in several other countries. In the case of Unilever:

> The shares or certificates (depositary receipts) of Unilever N.V. are listed on the stock exchanges in Amsterdam, London, New York, and in Austria, Belgium, France, Germany, Luxembourg and Switzerland.

and

> The shares of Unilever PLC are listed on The Stock Exchange in the United Kingdom and Ireland and, as American Depositary Receipts, in New York. (Unilever, 1985 Annual Report and Salient Figures, page 39).

In fact, many European multinationals are listed on stock exchanges throughout Europe. In the literature there is evidence that access to a variety of capital markets would reduce their costs of capital (Choi, 1973), including the facilitation of borrowings by local subsidiaries. Furthermore, Switzer (1975) provides some evidence that a new additional listing is associated with positive anticipatory abnormal returns in the home market, which would indicate an expectation of reduced capital costs. Thus, a listing in the United States by non-US companies appears to be viewed favourably by investors, notwithstanding the nontrivial costs involved in meeting the related disclosure requirements.

Additionally, it seems that listing in a foreign country, together with the related production of an annual report (full or abridged) in the language of that country, may be seen by some multinationals as a valuable form of public relations in that particular national market, thereby facilitating such matters as product sales and staff recruitment. Indeed, these latter factors may be of considerable importance in offsetting costs of foreign language annual reports, for a number of multinationals produce versions of their reports in Spanish without being listed on any exchange in a Spanish speaking country.

Language *per se*, however, is but one of the more tractable of a number of obstacles which transnational financial reporting must cross, if the reader is not to be confronted with major pitfalls in attempting to interpret transnational financial statements. Another obstacle is the need to cope with currencies that are not merely as different in unit value as the Italian Lira and the Pound Sterling, but which are also subject to changes in parity. For the latter reason, this obstacle cannot adequately be dealt with by restatement into the currency unit of the reader's country (so-called 'convenience translations'), since such matters as sales growth rates are distorted by the parity changes.

More intractable, however, is the obstacle constituted by the prevalence of differing sets of accounting conventions in different countries. These conventions, in turn, may be the reflections in accounting practice and terminology of institutional differences, the import of which cannot be conveyed by mere translation, with or without currency restatement. One expedient employed by some companies to minimise this obstacle is the restatement of the financial statements, or of key extracts, using the accounting conventions prevalent in the reader's country (e.g. US GAAP). Some writers, however, criticise this practice on the basis of the so-called 'single domicile viewpoint', according to which:

> Financial statements can present only a single representation of financial decisions and results of operations – only for a given time, under a given set of rules, and for a given purpose. When business decisions are made under these conditions, they ought to be reported only in terms of the same conditions (Choi and Mueller, 1984, page 265).

Taken to its logical conclusion, this latter view casts doubt on the interpretability and validity of worldwide consolidated financial statements *per se* when prepared by multinational groups (as opposed to the domestic consolidations favoured by German-based multinationals). At least one writer (Nobes, 1986) has indeed expressed such a doubt. Perhaps, however, this represents a *reductio ad absurdum* of the case against transnational financial reporting. For while multinational consolidated financial statements indeed contain many pitfalls, and 'segmental reporting' at lower levels of aggregation is a prerequisite of serious financial analysis, such segment information is arguably best seen as providing a necessary qualification and amplification of, rather than a substitute for, the overall picture presented by the consolidation.

In any event, European multinationals are evidently not deterred by purist considerations, and exhibit a multiplicity of devices intended to aid foreign readers of their financial reports. These are reviewed below; in general, we have adopted the perspective of the professional user of published financial statements. At the same time, the European Community is achieving some degree of harmonisation of the accounting conventions of the member states by the expedient of harmonising companies legislation. This is, however, a slow process; as our analysis will show, the disparity between the reporting practices of European companies from different countries seems equally great whether or not they belong to EC member states.

Transnational financial reporting[1] poses particular challenges for the independent auditor. The wave of British overseas investment that carried British accountants as auditors to the United States and elsewhere between 1840 and 1914 (Choi and Mueller, 1984, page 330) led to the development of the first transnational accounting practices. More recently, the growth of multinationals has led to the development of mammoth international accounting firms or groups of firms. For the most part, it is these firms which have the resources that are necessary to carry out audit assignments spanning the numerous countries in which a multinational client operates, leading not only to the preparation of audit reports on the accounts of subsidiaries located in different environments but also to a final opinion on the accounts of the group as a whole. Furthermore, the likelihood that financial statements of multinational groups are directed towards an audience that is itself international can provide an added dimension to the opinion that is expressed by the auditor. As Stamp and Moonitz (1978, page 146) put it:

> The need [for effective and credible auditing] is all the greater in the case of multinational enterprises since management is separated from the outsiders by greater differences in culture, political and economic systems, geographical boundaries, etc.

One of the issues which we consider below is the response of the auditing profession to the development of transnational financial reporting.

The purpose of the present analysis is threefold. First, to set the scene, we review the existing financial reporting practices of a sizeable sample of European multinationals (excluding, in the present study, British ones; also, we have not included in our review employee or 'social responsibility' reporting). Second, we examine the ways in which their auditors have reported on the scope and conclusion of their examinations, with particular attention to references (or the lack of them) to accepted auditing standards and accounting principles, so as to consider the implications of these for the foreign reader of the financial statements. Finally, we wish to consider tentatively some implications of these practices for the likely development of transnational financial reporting. The next section describes the approach used in the study. We then comment on salient features of the transnational financial reporting practices of the companies included in the review. A taxonomy of such practices has already been presented in the literature (Choi and Mueller, 1984, Chapter 7), but we have found it helpful to introduce some additional categories. Thereafter an analysis is made of the related audit practices as apparent from auditors' reports included in the financial statements of the companies studied. Some tentative conclusions follow.

Salient features of transnational reporting practices

The approach used in this study

For this study, we focussed on companies which are listed on more than one European stock exchange and which, therefore, are likely to prepare financial reports in more than one language. For this initial review, we have not included British companies and we have restricted our sampling frame to European companies with a second listing on London, Paris, Frankfurt or Amsterdam.

We obtained financial reports in more than one language from forty-two European groups, of which twenty-eight have holding companies incorporated in the EEC and fourteen outside the EEC (predominantly in Sweden). Table 6.1 gives further details of the countries involved and a full list of these companies ('positive respondents') is given in the Appendix.

Table 6.1 The number of companies in the sample, by country (positive responses)

Sweden	12
Germany	8
Holland	5
Belgium	4
France	3
Italy	3
Denmark	2
Switzerland	2
Finland	1
Luxembourg	1
Norway	1
	42

In addition, three companies informed us that they do not prepare any supplementary information for foreign investors, preparing only one report drawn up in accordance with local requirements ('negative respondents'). In fact, these three companies (two German and one Swedish) each has just one additional listing, that being in Amsterdam. Furthermore, eleven companies falling within the sampling frame did not forward the information requested. The overall response rate was thus 80 per cent.

Given the restriction to companies whose financial report is originally in a language other than English, this initial study does not deal with the extent to which British-based groups listed on other EEC exchanges provide for the information needs of investors dealing in those markets. On the other hand, a number of groups in our sample also had a listing in the United States and, therefore, it has been possible to draw some inferences about the United States influence on international financial reporting by European companies.

In analysing the reports which we have received, our immediate need was for some basis for classifying them according to the type of information presented for foreign or 'transnational' readers. An initial basis was provided by Choi and Mueller (1984, Chapter 7). These writers distinguished five main approaches:

1. Convenience linguistic translations – 'a modest concession to multinational audiences-of-interest [whereby] companies translate at least the language portion of their reports into the national idiom of major groups of addressees' (*op. cit.*, page 261).
2. Convenience currency translations – where 'in addition to language translations monetary amounts are translated as well' (*op. cit.*, page 262).
3. Special information – wherein 'a small number of multinational companies have made an effort to explain to readers in other countries the particular accounting standards and practices forming the basis of their reporting' (*ibid*).
4. Limited restatements – 'for instance, in addition to language translations, the Philips Company estimates what earning adjustments would be required if accounting principles generally accepted in the United States rather than the Netherlands were followed' (*op. cit.*, page 263).
5. Primary – secondary statements – 'Primary financial statements [following the IASG's recommendations] would be prepared according to financial accounting principles in a company's country of domicile and in that country's language and currency .... Secondary financial statements would be prepared specifically for financial reporting audiences-of-interest in other countries. [They] would have one or more of the following characteristics:
   (a) The reporting standards of a foreign country would have been followed.
   (b) The statements would have been translated into a foreign currency, [and/or]
   (c) Into a [foreign] language.
   (d) The independent auditor's report would be expressed in [a foreign language] in a form not commonly used in the reporting country's country of domicile' (*ibid*).

Our analysis revealed a number of interesting variants of the 'special information' category, and for this and other reasons we thought it preferable to characterise the reports in terms of the following eight attributes, some of which may co-exist in the same report:

1. A straightforward linguistic translation of the official, original language annual report into a foreign language without any other changes.
2. A condensed foreign language version of, or extract from, the official

original language annual report.
3. A 'convenience currency translation'.
4. A note explaining to the reader the particularities of the domestic accounting principles used.
5. A lexicon or glossary of technical expressions used in the financial statements.
6. A 'limited restatement' of key figures, perhaps accompanied by a reconciliation, to reflect differences between domestic accounting principles and US GAAP.
7. A statement to the effect that group accounting policies applied in preparing the financial statements conform to International Accounting Standards.
8. Secondary financial statements, based on different accounting principles from those used for the main or primary statements.

A summary of our findings appears in Table 6.2. We found that the majority of companies (thirty-four of the forty-two positive respondents) produced a straight linguistic translation (category 'A'). In all cases, such reports were produced in English, and in a number of instances in one or more other languages (French, German, Italian, Portuguese or Spanish) as well. Amongst these, there were four companies which published straight translations into English and abridged reports in one or more other languages.

Abridged foreign language versions (category 'B' above) were less popular with our respondents, as only twelve of forty-two produced these. These, however, ranged from lengthy reports containing a great deal of the information given in the original annual reports, to extracts only a few pages long, in some cases confined to a set of consolidated financial statements. We consider linguistic translations, and the issues they raise, in more detail below.

'Convenience currency translation' (category 'C') was even less popular. Only six respondents appeared to use it. These, however, included Unilever and Royal Dutch Petroleum, groups which seem to be highly sophisticated financial communicators. We comment further on the issues of currency translation below.

All translated and some condensed reports contained explicit statements of the accounting principles used in the preparation of the financial statements; but, in the case of a few German and Swedish groups, additional explanations were offered of the accounting principles or terminology used. We found that six of the forty-two companies produced special notes to assist the foreign reader (category 'D', above) and two companies included glossaries or lexicons in their annual report (category 'E'). Perhaps more helpful to the reader (at least if he or she is familiar with US GAAP or International Accounting Standards) are category 'F' disclosures, providing restatements of key figures from domestic to US

Table 6.2 Categories of disclosures in transnational
financial reporting

		Number of companies
1.	A straightforward linguistic translation of the original annual report	34
2.	An abridged foreign language version only	8
Total		42
3.	A convenience currency translation	6
4.	Special notes for the foreign reader	6
5.	A lexicon or glossary of financial terminology	2
6.	A restatement of accounting results using alternative accounting principles	11
7.	A statement that the accounts are prepared in conformity with international standards	2
8.	Preparation of a full set of secondary financial statements	2

GAAP (or, in one case, to IASC standards) and sometimes reconciliations between them. Among our 'positive' respondents, eleven of the forty-two produced such information. Only two groups, on the other hand, informed the reader that their 'primary' financial statements had been prepared in accordance with standards laid down by the IASC. Finally, full sets of 'secondary' financial statements (category 'H') were rare; only two respondents appeared to prepare this information. These various disclosures (categories 'D' to 'G') are discussed below.

Linguistic translations

In the introduction we recalled the 'single domicile viewpoint', which holds that financial statements can present only a single representation of financial decisions and results of operations as they occurred in a given national socio-economic context, and that the statements ought therefore to report these occurrences in terms of that context. Such a proposition can, of course, be interpreted in a number of ways, one of which, as already noted, would seem to rule out the validity of any worldwide (as opposed to German-style domestic) consolidations.

Without adopting such an extreme stance, we would nevertheless like to draw attention to a problem which the 'single domicile' school have failed to emphasise: if the particular national socio-economic context is so crucial to the validity of accounting representations, does this not raise major problems as regards the preparation of foreign language versions? For the terminology employed in the statements and notes will contain expressions, the import of which is tied up with a whole socio-linguistic nexus of meanings in the host country. How are these to be communicated to 'foreigners' in a translation? According to the Italian proverb '*traduttori traditori*', the translator betrays the integrity of what he or she translates. If this is a valid observation regarding literature in general, the 'single domicile viewpoint' should remind us that it is likely to be valid for accounting reports in particular.

On the other hand, the development of multinational firms whose decision processes are no longer rooted in a purely national context, and whose managements include a substantial proportion of internationally-orientated individuals, constitutes a countervailing influence. Moreover, while reflecting the local context, accounting terminology possesses an important aspect of professional technique which, to a considerable extent, transcends national borders. For instance, the French 'fonds de roulement' and the English 'working capital' or the French 'disponibilité' and the English 'liquid funds' imply in each case parallel levels of aggregation. Nevertheless, underlying any financial term is a host of contextual signals that convey meaning which is culture-bound. There is, for instance, the question of how a French company deals with discounted and undiscounted bills – which are far more prevalent in countries like France or Italy than, say, the United Kingdom – when it reports on 'liquidity'.

Moreover, new terms in accounting and finance are both being created by financial innovations and being transmitted with varying degrees of difficulty across linguistic borders as part of the internationalisation of capital markets. The process of terminological innovation may be compared to the way Faraday created a new terminology for electricity because the old terminology implied ideas that he had disproved. On the face of it, this should not be a problem in translation. However, financial terms tend to be fairly idiomatic and, in the same way as the translator finds that the French prefer to speak of 'intensité' (current) and the Germans prefer 'Spannung' (tension) when referring to voltage, we also find that French accountants prefer to use the term 'autofinancement' when referring to 'funds generated from operations' whilst Germans use the borrowed term 'cash-flow' even though the context in which it generally appears is that of working capital flows. Clearly, then, there are a number of problematic issues in translating financial terms, since the concepts may differ between countries.

Yet, whilst financial language is highly idiomatic, it is at the same time made explicit by generally accepted rules. Even so, connotation is of great importance and differences in economic situation leave their imprint on the language. So, whilst ambiguity may be reduced by the fact that accounting definitions can be operationalised and because their meaning is shared by a wide financial community, there is one important issue which is a particularly problematic one in financial translation – that, even ignoring international differences in accounting method, financial statements are culture-bound.

At the present time, we are unaware of any substantial research into financial translation[2] and the present analysis does not dwell on linguistic issues. In effect, we have considered what is the scope of linguistic translation in transnational financial reporting and what issues arise in practice from these translations.

Figure 6.1 Secondary reporting languages

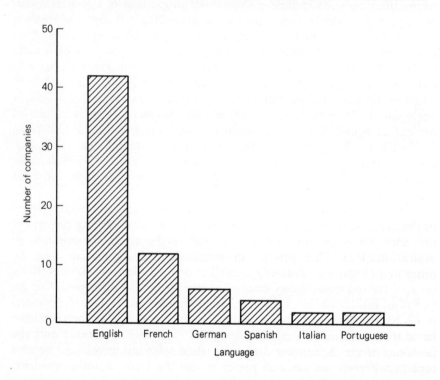

Not surprisingly, English is the predominant second language (see Figure 6.1). Indeed, all forty-two companies prepared an English language version of their report, including some companies which are listed neither in London nor in the United States. Nevertheless, sixteen of the forty-two companies reported in three or more languages and, for some, this was clearly an extensive operation, viz.

> The full version of this report is available in German and English. The abridged version is also available in German, English, French, Italian, Portuguese and Spanish. (Hoechst Annual Report 1985, inside front cover).

Not all companies make reference in their reports to the existence of alternative language version(s). Furthermore, it would be useful if more companies were to provide a clear statement of the nature of the 'translation', given the range of comments that we have observed in the published reports. For instance:

> This Annual Report is an unabridged translation from the Swedish original (AGA Annual Report 1985, page 1).

or

> This is the English version of the Dutch original Annual Report for the financial year ended March 31, 1985 (KLM Annual Report 1984/85, page 2).

or

> Free translation of the Italian Text (Montedison Group Facts and Figures 1985, page 113).

might each be interpreted as translations (although differing degrees of precision are intimated), but in the following comment there is some indication that the English-language and German-language reports may differ in some more substantial way:

> adapted from the original German report (Swissair 1985, inside front cover).

In this respect, some companies give explicit warnings about the problems of semantic equivalence that may arise in translating financial reports, for example:

> Translation. In the event of a conflict in interpretation, reference should be made to the Dutch version of this Annual Report. (Akzo Annual Report 1985, inside front cover).

or

> The German version of this report is authoritative (Hoechst Annual

Report 1985, inside front cover).

or

> This version of our Annual Report is a translation from the
> German original. The German text is definitive. (Volkswagen
> Annual Report 1985, inside front cover).

As regards auditors' reports, careful wording is no doubt something that
one would expect. Moreover, in order to define with precision the
information that is covered by the opinion, it is usual for an auditor to
refer to the specific financial statements to which the audit report relates.
In international financial reporting, such precision is again evident. Take
this example from the English-language version of the annual report
published by Bayer, for instance:

> The auditors' report applies to the German version of the Financial
> Statement and Business Report of Bayer AG (Bayer Business
> Report 1985, page 62).

Here, it is interesting to compare the following translations, one in the
English-language version and the other in the French-language version of
the report of a Danish company:

> Our examination was made in accordance with generally accepted
> auditing principles as applied in Denmark and included such
> auditing procedures as we considered necessary.

> Notre vérification a été effectuée conformément aux normes
> professionnelles généralement admises. Les contrôles et sondages
> jugés opportuns ont également été effectués.

> (Great Nordic Annual Report 1985, page 12 and Rapport et
> comptes de 1985, page 12)

The phrase 'as applied in Denmark' is a pertinent addition to the English
version, but the same notion is neither in the French nor the original
Danish reports. Now, whilst there may be a general convergence across
linguistic and cultural barriers in the technical translation of financial
terminology, in cases such as this we still observe the absence of 'cultural
overlap'. Perhaps it is assumed that the English-language reader would
be exposed to greater ambiguity because of the more common use of an
extant set of auditing standards in, say, the United States or the United
Kingdom.

Currency translations

Most of the groups in our sample have international operations such that
the currency mix of their revenues will not necessarily match the currency
mix of their costs. For instance, consider briefly the case of an oil

company like Royal Dutch Shell. In 1985, commodity prices and currency movements had a considerable effect on results: not only did Shell's manufacturing costs decline because of reductions in oil prices but this was enhanced in local currency terms by the weakening dollar. This is reflected in Fig. 6.2 in which the US dollar (the oil pricing currency) is indexed against the 'Shell currency basket', a cocktail comprising the currencies of fourteen major countries weighted by the sales proceeds of Shell group companies outside North America. However, this was the only instance that we noted of a departure from the usual conventions of currency translation and, of course, this was just an illustrative addition to the review of operations and not part of the financial report.

Figure 6.2 Extract from the Royal Dutch Shell Annual Report

Movement of US dollar against Shell currency basket*

Quarterly average; index base 100 = January 1983

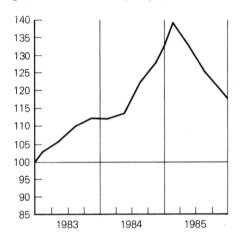

* The Shell currency basket comprises the currencies of 14 major countries weighted by the sales proceeds of Group Companies outside North America

Indeed, for the most part, the companies in our sample have not attempted to represent the multi-currency nature of their operations in their financial report and, with the exception of Unilever and Royal Dutch, the few instances of alternative currency reporting were restricted to translations into United States dollars. Only six out of forty-two companies included translated figures in their reports, either in the form of multi-column financial statements, *or* translated highlights, *or* special supplements, *or* in one case a separate report translated into US dollars. Perhaps it is the SEC's position on 20-F filings which has had some influence here, viz:

> Present regulations of the Securities and Exchange Commission do not permit the conversion of figures as presented in the original Dutch KLM Annual Report from guilders to U.S. dollars (KLM Annual Report 1984/85, page 2).

Nevertheless, when convenience currency translations are included in the financial report, this is another area of international financial reporting which attracts appropriate caveats: .

> All the amounts in the annual accounts which are stated in US$ have been translated from Danish kroner at the exchange rate ruling on 31 December, 1985 (US$1–Dkr8.969), if not otherwise stated. The US$ amounts are presented solely for the purpose of convenience (Novo Annual Report 1985, page 47).

For the purposes of consolidation of their worldwide operations into the domestic currency, the companies in our sample adopt a variety of different translation methods. The same can be said to apply to 'convenience translations'. Indeed, in the case of the latter we observed the use of (i) average rates for income statement items and year-end rates for assets and liabilities, (ii) year-end rates for all amounts (iii) average rates for all amounts and (iv) just one rate applied not only to the current year but also to comparatives.

The effect of exchange rate changes on 'convenience translations' can be seen in Table 6.3 which reproduces highlights included in some of Unilever's reports. Consider, for example, the turnover figures of the combined group when restated in United States Dollars:[3]

(in millions)	1984	1985	%
N.V. (Dutch Guilders)	42,592	40,790	-4.2%
PLC (Sterling Pounds)	5,859	6,496	+10.9%
Combined:			
in Dutch Guilders	66,791	66,771	-0.03%
in Sterling Pounds	16,172	16,693	+3.2%
in US Dollars	18,760	24,205	+29.0%

Table 6.3 Extract from the Unilever Annual Report

Salient figures in various currencies

1985 above 1984	Sterling Pounds	Dutch Guilders	Austrian Schillings	Belgian Francs	Franch Francs	German Marks	Swiss Francs	US Dollars
Rates of	4.00	24.95	72.60	10.90	3.55	2.99	1.45
exchange £1 = [a]	4.13	25.67	73.23	11.20	3.66	3.01	1.16

In millions of currency

	Sterling Pounds	Dutch Guilders	Austrian Schillings	Belgian Francs	Franch Francs	German Marks	Swiss Francs	US Dollars
Turnover	16 693	66 771	416 487	1 211 902	181 952	59 260	49 912	24 205
	16 172	66 791	415 137	1 184 280	181 127	59 190	48 678	18 760
Operating profit	949	3 797	23 683	68 912	10 346	3 370	2 838	1 376
	930	3 841	23 875	68 110	10 417	3 404	2 800	1 078
Profit on ordinary activities before taxation	953	3 814	23 788	69 219	10 392	3 385	2 851	1 382
	925	3 823	23 765	67 795	10 369	3 388	2 787	1 073
Profit on ordinary activities after taxation	556	2 223	13 863	40 340	6 056	1 973	1 661	805
	537	2 218	13 787	39 332	6 015	1 966	1 617	622
Profit on ordinary activities attributable to shareholders	516	2 064	12 876	37 467	5 625	1 832	1 543	748
	503	2 078	12 918	36 851	5 636	1 842	1 515	583
Ordinary dividends	179	718	4 482	13 042	1 958	638	537	260
	165	684	4 248	12 120	1 854	606	498	192
Profit of the year retained	333	1 330	8 296	24 139	3 624	1 180	994	482
	308	1 270	7 899	22 535	3 447	1 126	926	357

In units of currency

Earnings per share	Sterling Pounds	Dutch Guilders	Austrian Schillings	Belgian Francs	Franch Francs	German Marks	Swiss Francs	US Dollars
Per F1.20	919.71p	36.79	229.50	667.67	100.24	32.66	27.53	13.33
of capital	895.56p	37.01	230.00	656.15	100.37	32.78	27.01	10.39
Per 25p	137.96p	5.52	34.42	100.15	15.04	4.90	4.13	2.00
of capital	134.33p	5.55	34.50	98.42	15.06	4.92	4.05	1.56
Ordinary dividends [b]								
N.V.–per F1.20	370.50p	14.82	92.45	268.97	40.38	13.16	11.09	5.37
of capital	341.65p	14.11	87.69	250.18	38.27	12.50	10.30	3.96
PLC–per 25p	38.62p	1.54	9.64	28.04	4.21	1.37	1.15	0.56
of capital	35.52p	1.47	9.12	26.01	3.98	1.30	1.07	0.41
Shareholders' equity per share								
Per F1.20	5 949.40p	237.92	1 484.23	4 318.00	648.29	211.22	178.02	86.20
of capital	6 008.69p	248.14	1 542.18	4 399.59	673.00	219.80	181.12	69.70
Per 25p	892.41p	35.69	222.63	647.70	97.24	31.68	26.70	12.93
of capital	901.30p	37.22	231.33	659.94	100.95	32.97	27.17	10.46

(a) Rates of exchange are respective year-end rates used in translating the combined figures in the various currencies.

(b) The value of dividends received by shareholders in currencies other than sterling or guilders will be affected by fluctuations in the rates of exchange after the year-end.

Movements between 1984 and 1985 will vary according to the currencies in which the figures are expressed.

Clearly, the dollar translation effect is exceptionally large in these
'convenience translations', being considerably greater than the currency
translation effects which normally occur in the process of consolidating
the accounts of diversified multinationals. In fact, Unilever provide a
clear statement on the interpretation of 'convenience statements' in the
introduction to a version of their report that is translated into US dollars:

> Movements in exchange rates have a significant influence on the
> figures: when expressed in guilders or sterling, the yearly per-
> centage changes are different from those in dollars. The Report is
> written on the basis of the guilder and sterling results and what is
> said therein may not correspond with the comparison and trends
> in dollars (Unilever Annual Report and Salient Figures 1985
> Translated into US Dollars, page 1).

But this does raise an important issue: how is the reader to interpret and
use the United States $ figures? In fact, Unilever also provides similar
information relating to Earnings per Share, whose significance to a
United States investor is far more obvious:

(Per F1.20 of capital)	1984	1985
in Dutch Guilders	37.01	36.79
in Sterling Pounds	8.96	9.20
in US Dollars	10.39	13.33

Finally, we note that there were no instances amongst those companies
which provided 'convenience translations' of any reference to these
statements by company auditors. Indeed, where there has been some
mention of currencies, it has been done in order to point out that the
scope of the opinion is restricted to the local currency financial statements
only:

> We have examined the accounts expressed in guilders of Unilever
> N.V. ... (Unilever in 1985 Annual Accounts English Version in
> Guilders, page 2).[4]

Explaining accounting policies and their effects

The accounting policies used in financial reports may be divided into
three categories:

1. Those reflecting particular features of the national institutional
   environment, company law or tax law,
2. Those imposed by national accounting standards bodies,
3. Those which are the reporting entity's own choice.

The second two categories tend to concern choices between different methods of treating certain perennial accounting issues such as inventory valuation, tooling costs, foreign currency translation, goodwill on consolidation, and so forth. In this connection, the international reader may be concerned to know the effects of such policies when these differ from those to which he or she is accustomed. But in the case of the first category, some further background explanation may be called for. Thus, while linguistic translation and currency translation may help to further the international readership of a company's report, there are other ways to assist the foreign reader. This may be done by including some information on the nature of local accounting principles and how they contrast with those to which the foreign reader may be more accustomed. But there is another and perhaps more fundamental barrier to achieving cross-national equivalence of financial reports. For the user, an essential precondition to placing any company's behaviour in context is an appreciation of the key features of its operating environment and, even in the case of multinationals, it is perhaps the domestic financial systems, laws and tax regulations of the principal country or countries of operations that will most condition both its financial representations and the knowledge required to understand them properly.

Let us consider an example here. In Italy, for instance, we find that deferred remuneration is a significant item in company financing. This is because of the legal requirement to pay, at current rates of remuneration, a leaving indemnity of one month's salary for each year on the payroll to an employee who retires or whose contract is terminated in some other way. But not only is it useful for an analyst to know how the amount reported in the balance sheet has been determined, it is also important to appreciate that, unlike the French participation scheme or a typical company pension scheme in the United Kingdom, it is not usual for an Italian company to place such funds in earmarked investments or with financial institutions. Consequently, cash must be generated internally to meet future payments which will depend both on employee age structure and wage inflation. It is in contexts like this that the foreign reader may benefit not only from some indication of the accounting treatment of an item such as provisions (as we may expect from notes to the accounts), but also from some background information on similarly idiosyncratic aspects of the company's operations.

Consider also the position of Swedish companies which are likely to include restricted deposits in the Central Bank amongst their assets, and untaxed reserves amongst liabilities and shareholders' equity. The fuller implications of accounting for this aspect of corporate reporting in Sweden are described below:

> Transfers up to 50% of profit before tax may be made to an investment reserve and excluded from taxable income. A blocked interest-free deposit is then required in the Bank of Sweden. With

the approval of the works councils and appropriate authorities, the reserve may be used for accelerated depreciation of certain types of fixed assets and the deposit released. If not used for the approved purposes, releases from the reserve are included in taxable income and a tax surcharge is levied (Special note in the foreign-language version of the Swedish Match Annual Report 1985, page 42).

The inclusion of special notes or explanatory supplements for the foreign reader seems to be a Swedish innovation. For instance, Volvo publishes supplementary 'Reader's Guides' to the foreign language editions of its Annual Report, including a short tutorial on Swedish accounting (see Fig 6.3).

But there are alternatives. Some companies include a glossary or lexicon, providing background information that may be of some use to the uninformed reader. Volkswagen is one such company. It precedes its 'Explanations of Certain Financial Terms' as follows:

Since our Annual Report is intended to be read by as wide a circle as possible, and some of the technical terms used in it are subject to varying definitions, we should like to explain them. We make no attempt to be comprehensive, nor do we claim scientific exactitude. Rather we wish to indicate the interpretations current within the Company (Volkswagen Annual Report 1985, page 81).

For instance, there are issues of accounting method where practices differ and where harmonisation has yet to occur:

Added value: The increase in value by a company in a period (added value) is calculated at Volkswagen AG as follows: Gross performance as shown in the statement of earnings + other income minus expenditures (predominantly material costs) minus depreciation and losses from disposals... (Volkswagen Annual Report 1985, page 81).

In other words, like other German companies, it is VW's practice to disclose Net Value Added in Production rather than Gross Value Added in Sales, as is the convention is the United Kingdom (McLeay, 1983). Likewise, there are particular features of German legislation which can benefit from explanation, such as the requirement for a Reserve for Treasury Stock, the latter being defined as:

Treasury stock: This represents that part of the capital stock of a company which the company has acquired itself and is shown in the current assets with the acquisition costs or the possibly lower stock exchange value. The Corporation Law makes the acquisition of treasury stock dependent on the existence of certain preconditions and limits it to 10% of the capital stock (Volkswagen Annual Report 1985, page 84).

Figure 6.3 Extract from the Volvo 'Readers' Guide'

The annual reports of listed Swedish companies today generally adhere to high international standards of financial reporting. They are characterized by openness and willingness to provide comprehensive information.

The interest of various parties in the content of annual reports has grown. As a result, the reports have become increasingly detailed.

The trend is particularly applicable to Volvo. The Company has sought, with the aid of readership studies, to structure the style and content of its Annual Report to make it useful to the widest possible audience. As a result the information presented has increased over the years and the Company is today offering substantially more information than is prescribed by law or recommended by various groups in the financial community.

Volvo also publishes "Financial and Operating Statistics", a statistical yearbook for those who wish to follow trends in a longer perspective.

Accounting in Sweden is regulated by the Swedish Accounting Act, which is supplemented in the case of limited companies by the Swedish Companies Act.

Accounting practice is also regulated by recommendations and instructions issued by various organizations, as well as by the companies themselves. The most important organizations are the Swedish Authorized Public Accounts Association (FAR) and the Swedish Accounting Standards Board, a government body.

Since it began operations nearly 60 years ago, Volvo has been foremost among those working for the establishment of generally accepted accounting principles in Sweden.

This supplement is designed to enhance an understanding and interpretation of Volvo's financial statements. A detailed description of the accounting policies applied by Volvo appears on pages 35 and 36 in the 1985 Annual Report.

Figure 6.3 Extract from the Volvo 'Readers' Guide' (cont'd)

Deferred Taxes for Untaxed Reserves —Example

Let us assume that, in year 1, a company has the following condensed income statement:

Income before allocations and taxes	1,000
Allocations to untaxed reserves (in this case, the General inventory reserve)	(400)
Income before taxes	600
Taxes	(250)
Net income	350

The balance sheet shows, among **Untaxed reserves,** a General inventory reserve of 400.

In year 2 the company shows the following condensed income statement:

	Alternative A	Alternative B
Income before allocations and taxes	100	100
Withdrawal from General inventory reserve	300	-
Income before taxes	400	100
Taxes	(186)	(30)
Net income	214	70

Under Alternative A, the company elects to withdraw 300 from the General inventory reserve to show a higher net income. It may wish, for example, to show a net income that is high enough to maintain its dividend at a desired level. However, the amount withdrawn from the General inventory reserve becomes subject to taxation and the tax charge for the year thereby increases in the amount of 156 (52 percent of 300).

The company may, if it wishes, show an income statement based on Alternative B, which produces a net income of 70.

Utilizing the untaxed reserves to increase the taxed **net income** is not common. Instead, it is more usual for a company to reduce untaxed reserves in order to avoid reporting a net loss, which is illustrated by the following example:

	Alternative A	Alternative B
Loss before allocations and taxes	(300)	(300)
Withdrawal from General inventory reserve	300	-
Income (loss) before taxes	0	(300)
Taxes	0	0
Net income	0	(300)

In this case, the withdrawal from the reserve does not result in any direct tax consequences.

As the company indicates elsewhere in its glossary, a German company is required by law (i.e. the Aktiengesetz) to set up a reserve equal to the book value of any of its own shares which it has acquired. This is not necessarily the accounting convention in other countries, nor is the acquisition of Treasury shares even a common commercial practice. Perhaps this illustrates more forcefully the idea that, in international financial reporting, it is not only accounting method that is variable; so too are financial practices, laws and taxes.

The effect of differences in accounting method

Some companies point to the main way or ways in which the application of a different set of accounting principles might affect their published figures:

> Special note for the English edition: AGA's Financial Statements are prepared in conformity with Swedish law and accounting principles generally accepted in Sweden. In most respects, Swedish accounting principles comply with international accounting standards. The differences that arise are mainly due to the Swedish method of assessing income tax... (AGA Annual Report 1985, pages 46-7 – not in Swedish-language version)

This may be restricted to a simple note indicating the main differences but without quantifying their effect (as above) or, in some cases, alternative financial statements are prepared in accordance with a second set of accounting principles. Amongst these secondary reports issued by companies in our sample were financial restatements prepared by certain companies with a listing on the London Stock Exchange, and 20-F filings with the SEC which are restated in accordance with accounting principles generally accepted in the United States.

But not all companies preparing these secondary accounts include the restated figures in their published financial report. For instance, Unilever simply notes that:

> Unilever's Annual Reports on Form 20-F filed each year with the SEC contain profit figures prepared in accordance with United States generally accepted accounting principles, expressed in sterling and guilders (Unilever Annual Report and Salient Figures 1985 Translated into US Dollars, page 32).

Elsewhere Unilever informs the report user of the availability of this secondary report. Nevertheless, in our sample, eleven out of forty-two companies published some accounting information restated in accordance with an alternative set of accounting conventions in their annual report, ten using Generally Accepted Accounting Principles in the United States as the reference set and one using International Accounting Standards.

Fig 6.4 (pages 96-7) shows the approach taken by the Finnish company Wärtsilä.

In the research literature, there has been some investigation of the accounting numbers produced under alternative sets of accounting regulations. Gray (1980) has provided some evidence that European financial analysts 'normalised' earnings figures to reveal a tendency for understatement in the original accounts of French and German companies and an overstatement for British companies. In a study of Japanese companies, Choi *et al.* (1983) found that accounting restatements do have some effect on observed financial ratios but that, in most instances, differences in accounting policy explain only a minor portion of observed ratio differences. For instance, it is the nature of the Japanese financial system that explains an average Total Debt/Total Assets ratio of 84 per cent, not accounting differences.

Nevertheless, when we look in detail at the effects of applying US GAAP, we find that usually European companies are led to comment on not a few but several significant differences between their accounting practices and those generally accepted in the United States. As an illustration, Table 6.4 shows the reconciliation between net income in accordance with Swedish accounting principles and net income in accordance with US GAAP for four Swedish companies. In fact, these companies provide fairly detailed explanations of each reconciling item, i.e.

> Volvo generally expenses tooling costs as incurred. Industry practice in the United States is to capitalise all significant tooling costs. Accordingly, for U.S. GAAP purposes, costs are capitalised and amortised over a period of 3 to 5 years (Volvo Annual Report 1985, page 41).

In Table 6.4, it can be seen that the differences are related not only to fiscal effects or the specific practices of particular industries but to aspects of consolidation and the timing of revenue recognition as well as to such items as the accounting treatment of leases and associates and to foreign currency translation. Indeed, there are even important differences of definition:

> In Swedish practice, earnings per share is usually based on earnings before extraordinary items and appropriations, and not on net earnings reported for the year. Under U.S. GAAP, net earnings must be used to calculate earnings per share. Under U.S. GAAP, outstanding warrants and convertible bond loans must be considered when calculating earnings per share assuming full dilution (SCA Annual Report 1985, page 49).

Finally, as far as we were able to determine, and with the exception of one Danish company (Novo) and one Swedish company (Volvo), these

Table 6.4 Restatement of income and equity using US GAAP: A comparison of four Swedish companies

(in millions of Swedish kroner)	ASEA 1985	ASEA 1984	ERICSSON 1985	ERICSSON 1984	SKF 1985	SKF 1984	VOLVO 1985	VOLVO 1984
Net income in accordance with Swedish GAAP	422	370	837	444	898	1000	2546	1565
Allocations to untaxed reserves	1509	1540	-371	683	183	61	3330	4384
Deferred taxes	-809	-749	-158	-596	189	-173	-1975	-3276
Currency translation			165	29	-421	-308	-808	510
Equity accounting for investments	179	153			10	1	122	-3
Capitalisation of interest expense	-24	-3	39	22	-4	24		
Revaluation of assets	32	16	53	79	48	29		
Business combination adjustments			-12	24			192	-85
Other items:								
Tooling costs							323	302
Oil and gas activities							0	486
Early retirement pension					54	46		
Sale of property			8	-41				
Miscellaneous	62	-44					35	9
Tax benefits of loss carry-forwards			168	93				
Tax effects on intercompany transactions			6	-18				
Tax on undistributed earnings of associates			-31	-183				
Minority interests in adjustments	7	-39					744	471
Net income in accordance with US GAAP	1383	1244	735	719	559	680	4478	4100
Shareholders' equity:								
in accordance with Swedish GAAP	4148	4244	8092	7811	6708	6772	8798	7356
in accordance with US GAAP	7874	6898			8495	8255	17804	13496
Ratio of Income to Equity:								
based on Swedish figures (%)	10.17	8.72	9.08	9.21	13.39	14.77	28.94	21.28
based on US figures (%)	17.56	18.86			6.58	8.24	25.15	30.38

Figure 6.4 Extract from the Wärtsilä Annual Report

Group Financial Statements in Accordance with International Accounting Standards

The Finnish accounting practice differs considerably from the one generally applied in Anglo-Saxon countries. I.e. tax laws have a great impact on the financial statements of Finnish companies as nearly all the items that are considered in calculating the taxable income must also be shown in the financial statements. Considering the extensiveness of Wärtsilä's international operations and the fact that Wärtsilä shares apart from Helsinki are also listed on the Stockholm and London Stock Exchanges, Group financial statements are here presented in a more familiar form for the international reader. The accounting policies applied correspond with International Accounting Standards (IAS).

IAS is a set of instructions prepared and published by the International Accounting Standards Committee (IASC) in order to conform to the international accounting practice and thus promote the comprehensibility and correspondence of financial statements prepared in different countries.

On the next page are shown the principal adjustments made in deriving the financial position and results of the Group in accordance with IAS from the financial statements produced in accordance with Finnish law and practice.

The principle adjustments include:

1. VALUATION OF INVENTORIES

According to Finnish law and practice only the direct acquisition value of products is included in the inventory values. In consequence, work in progress and finished goods are at a low value in the balance sheet.

According to IAS also the attributable indirect costs of production are included in the inventory value.

2. ASSOCIATED COMPANIES

Wärtsilä has a considerable minority share in the Finnish Ovako Oy Ab (38.3%) and the Norwegian Sterkoder Mek. Verksted A/S (44.9%). According to Finnish law and practice only dividends from these companies are included in Wärtsilä's income statement each year. In the balance sheet only the original acquisition costs of the shares are shown. In the financial statements according to IAS the companies in question are included applying the equity accounting method. This means that instead of dividends Wärtsilä's share of the profits of these associated companies is shown in the income statement. In the balance sheet the acquisition cost of these shares is replaced by Wärtsilä's share of the companies' equity capital. The occuring difference is included in the non-restricted shareholders' equity.

3. TAX RESERVES

The Finnish tax legislation allows companies to decrease the taxable income by creating tax reserves in the financial statements (see Accounting Policies and notes 4 and 15). According to Finnish taxation practice these reserves should also be created in the books of account.

Profit for the financial year according to IAS has been calculated before appropriations to tax reserves. In the balance sheet the reserves have been included in the non-restricted shareholders' equity.

4. TAXES

Mainly due to the above tax reserves the taxes in the income statement are small in relation to profit for the financial year according to IAS. The latent tax in appropriations to tax reserves – the going tax rate in Finland is approx. 50% from the beginning of 1986 – has been disregarded as in the Group managements' opinion it will not fall due for payment in the future.

Group Income Statement

(MFIM)	1985	1984
Net sales	5,546	6,243
Expenses	(4,938)	(5,350)
Depreciation	(208)	(183)
Operational profit	**400**	**710**
Financial income and expenses	18	(2)
Share of profits in associated companies	47	51
Profit before extraordinary items	**465**	**759**
Other income and expenses	(225)	(13)
Profit before tax	**240**	**746**
Direct taxes	(13)	(29)
Minority interest	2	6
Profit for the financial year	**229**	**723**

Group Statement of Source and Application of Funds

(MFIM)	1985	1984
Funds generated by operations	530	800
Decrease in fixed assets	60	39
Share issues		382
New long-term funds	222	161
Total source of funds	**812**	**1,382**
Decrease in minority shares		16
Amortisation of long-term debts	159	107
Investments	496	367
Total applications of funds	**655**	**489**
Increase in net working capital	157	893
Delivery credits, net	+ 26	(301)
Inventories		+ 117
Other current assets	+ 31	(288)
Advance payments received and construction-time loans	(226)	(524)
Other current liabilities	+ 12	+ 103
Increase in net working capital	157	(893)

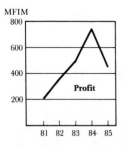

MFIM

Profit

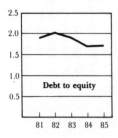

Debt to equity

Figure 6.4 Extract from the Wärtsilä Annual Report (cont'd)

Group Balance Sheet

Assets (MFIM)	1985	1984	Liabilities and shareholders' equity (MFIM)	1985	1984
Cash and bank receivables	1,345	1,508	Current debt	2,665	2,474
Other receivables	1,899	1,915	Long-term debt	1,237	1,157
Inventories	2,514	2,499	Long-term refinancing loans for delivery credits		
./. Advance payments received	(864)	(1,390)		2,483	2,572
	4,894	4,532	Total liabilities	6,385	6,203
			Minority interests	8	3
Long-term receivables	2,696	2,993	Shareholders' equity		
			restricted	927	943
			non-restricted	2,885	2,728
Fixed assets	2,615	2,352	Total shareholders' equity	3,812	3,671
	10,205	9,877		10,205	9,877

Adjustments to Income Statement

	1985	1984
Profit for the financial year in accordance with IAS	**229**	723
Adjustments to change in inventories to include appropriate proportion of overhead expenses	**(61)**	6
Difference between historical cost depreciation and recorded depreciation	**(136)**	(111)
Other appropriations to inventory and other reserves	**209**	(411)
Share of profits in associated companies	**(40)**	(51)
Movement in provision of warranty costs	**5**	5
Profit for the financial year in accordance with Finnish law and practice	**206**	161

Adjustments to Shareholders' Equity

	1985	1984
Shareholders' equity in accordance with IAS	**3,812**	3,671
Inclusion in inventories of appropriate proportion of production overhead expenses	**(389)**	(327)
The accumulative difference between recorded and historical cost depreciation	**(589)**	(453)
Reclassification of inventory and other reserves	**(1,297)**	(1,508)
Restatement of investments in associated companies at appropriate proportion of adjusted net assets	**(106)**	(66)
Provision of expected liabilities in connection with warranties to customers	**70**	65
Shareholders' equity in accordance with Finnish law and practice	**1,501**	1,382

Key Figures Based on IAS

		1981	1982	1983	1984	**1985**
Net sales	MFIM	3,058	3,864	5,419	6,243	**5,546**
Profit for the financial year before extraordinary items	MFIM	208	362	499	736	**544**
Earnings/share[1]	FIM	31	53	63	80	**47**
Dividend/share[2]	FIM	3.33	4.48	4.97	7.80	**7.80**
Net assets per share[3]	FIM	250	277	323	377	**391**
Return on shareholders'equity[4]	%	12	19	20	23	**6**
Debt to equity ratio		1.9	2.0	1.9	1.7	**1.7**

1 Average number of shares during the year, adjusted
2 Proposal of the Board of Directors
3 Number of shares at the end of each year, adjusted
4 Profit for the financial year per average Shareholders' equity
  Key figures per share are adjusted to share issues.

accounting restatements did not fall within the scope of the audit report even though they appeared in several cases amongst the notes to the accounts. The auditors of Novo and Volvo were alone in stating explicitly that their opinion extended to the notes to the accounts which included figures stated on a 'US basis'. We note, however, that for the companies restating in accordance with US GAAP, the effect of applying this alternative set of accounting principles is usually reported as an 'approximate' effect, with terms such as 'estimated value according to US GAAP' or 'Approximate net income in accordance with US GAAP' being adopted.

Audit reports

Choi and Mueller (1984, page 327) comment that 'sensitivity to the attest function is probably higher in multinational settings than it is in single country situations'. While that is indeed a reasonable proposition, our review indicates that the audit report is a problematic aspect of transnational financial reporting, so that if foreign readers are supposed to be more 'sensitive' to the attest function than domestic readers, in many instances this sensitivity is hardly catered for.

It is true that the International Auditing Practices Committee (IAPC) has developed a number of International Auditing Guidelines (for an account of its work, see Jones (1986)). But these have so far included only an Exposure Draft (ED No.12) on the structure and wording of audit reports, and these continue to vary considerably from country to country (see below). Moreover, not one of the seventy audit reports appearing in the English language reports which we received made any reference to International Auditing Guidelines, although thirteen mentioned 'generally accepted auditing standards' without indicating where or by whom they were generally accepted. In addition, one report (BASF) referred to 'auditing standards' generally accepted in Germany and the USA', one (Great Nordic) referred to 'generally accepted auditing standards as applied in Denmark' (the mention of Denmark being omitted from the French language version, as already noted!); another (Wärtsilä) referred to 'generally accepted auditing standards in Finland', the auditors of one Italian company (SNIA) stated that their examination was made in accordance with the auditing standards 'approved by the Consigli Naxionali dei Dottori Commercialisti e dei Ragionieri...'; and, last but not least, another Italian company (Olivetti) stated in the report on the parent company's accounts that the 'examination was made in accordance with the principles and standards set forth in the auditing principles approved by the National Councils of Public Accountants', and in the report on the consolidated accounts that it had been made 'in accordance with established auditing standards'.

What is the sensitive international reader to make of all that?

Another aspect of audit reports of potential concern to the international reader is whether there is a reference to the accounting principles to which the financial statements do (or do not) conform. Again, there is considerable variation. Moreover, there are instances where the audit report states that the financial statements 'fairly present' or 'give a true and fair view', without any reference to the accounting principles in terms of which the alleged 'fair presentation' has been provided. Yet it is widely recognised in professional and academic accounting circles that the representations made in financial statements depend on sets of accounting conventions or 'principles', between which considerable choice exists, and that the choice made may significantly affect the content of the representations. It is not clear, therefore, how a set of financial statements can simply be declared (as seems to be customary in the Netherlands) to present a 'true and fair view' in some unspecified sense without reference to the accounting principles used. On the other hand, in some countries (e.g. the Federal Republic of Germany) the usual form of audit report makes no reference to 'fair presentation'. What is the international reader to understand regarding the attestations being made by the auditors in such cases?

Apart from national practices in the respondent's home country and (in theory at least) the pronouncement of the IAPC, the style of audit report could be influenced by the particular predilections of the audit firm (especially, perhaps, in the case of the so-called 'Big Eight' major international practices), and perhaps by the exchanges on which the respondent's shares are listed. As far as possible, we have attempted to observe any such influences; so far as we could tell, however, neither of the latter two was a major factor.

In the remainder of this Section, we first review the contents of audit reports on a country-by-country basis. Some of those to which we refer are reprinted in Figs 5-10. We then briefly consider the extent to which the influence of the major international accounting firms or groupments, notably the so-called 'Big Eight', is discernible as an influence towards harmonisation of audit reporting style or the provision of more useful information to the international reader. Our country-by country review considers first the EC member states represented among our respondents, and then the other countries.

A review of audit reports by country: The European Community

Belgium

Four of our respondents were Belgian-based. In one case (Vieille-Montagne), the English language report was a supplement (category 'B') which contained no audit report. In none of the three remaining cases

Figure 6.5 Extract from the Intercom Annual Report

Rapport des commissaires-réviseurs

Mesdames, Messieurs,

Conformément aux dispositions légales et statutaires, nous avons l'honneur de vous faire rapport sur l'exécution, au cours de l'exercice social 1984, de notre mandat.

Dans le courant de l'exercice, nous avons examiné en détail la situation semestrielle, effectué des visites d'inspection dans les centrales et dans les magasins, procédé aux contrôles souhaités par le Comité de Gestion des Entreprises d'Electricité.

Les vérifications auxquelles nous avons procédé nous ont permis de constater l'efficacité du service de contrôle interne ainsi que le fonctionnement adéquat des services de comptabilité.

L'organisation administrative est garante d'un enregistrement correct et fiable des opérations.

En fin d'exercice, nous avons examiné les comptes annuels conformément aux normes belges.

A l'issue de nos contrôles, nous avons pu constater que la présentation des comptes annuels de 1984 respecte le principe de continuité par rapport à l'exercice précédent, étant entendu que les comptes annuels de l'exercice 1983 ont été redressés, pour la comparabilité avec ceux du présent exercice, en vertu de l'arrêté royal du 12 septembre 1983.

L'annexe mentionne ces redressements sous la rubrique XXII.

La présentation des règles d'évaluation a été adaptée en fonction de l'arrêté royal précité.

En matière d'évaluation l'annexe mentionne une modification relative aux amortissements des équipements de traitement de l'information administrative y compris le matériel de bureau pour tenir compte de la recommandation du Comité de Contrôle de l'Electricité et du Gaz. Le taux d'amortissement passe de 10 à 20% en 1984.

Cette modification entraîne une charge supplémentaire de 36.448 milliers de F.

Nous remercions les membres de la direction et du personnel qui nous ont toujours apporté les concours nécessaires au bon accomplissement de notre mission.

En conclusion, nous estimons que les comptes annuels, dont le total du bilan exprimé en milliers de F se chiffre à 186.587.526 et dont le résultat de l'exercice se chiffre en milliers de F à 7.739.330 ont été dressés correctement et de bonne foi, qu'ils traduisent de façon sincère et complète la situation patrimoniale à la date de clôture, les résultats de l'exercice 1984 ainsi que les engagements de la société.

Bruxelles, le 9 avril 1985   Les commissaires-reviseurs did the auditors appear to be members of international practices, although since Belgian auditors sign in their own names, not that of the firm, we could not be sure.

The form of audit report appearing in the three English language versions (EBES, Intercom, Solvay) varied considerably. The usual form of a Belgian independent auditor's report, as exemplified in the French or Dutch language originals, employs a somewhat flowery and verbose wording and includes an opinion on the client's internal control and accounting procedures, as well as an attestation as to whether the financial statements fairly present ('traduisent bien' or 'een getrouw beeld geeft van') the financial position and results. In the English language versions, for Solvay the audit reports for both the parent company and the group were direct translations from the French or Dutch of the originals; but in the other two cases, shorter forms were used.

In one case (Intercom), the auditor attested that the group accounts 'give a true and fair view in accordance with United Kingdom requirements'. As the English language report contained no statement of accounting policies, and we saw from the French language version that proportional consolidation (not accepted in the United Kingdom) had been used in some cases, we compared the consolidated financial statements in the English and French versions and saw evidence that the offending proportional consolidation had indeed been replaced by global consolidation, and that, more generally, the statements have been recast for the English language version.

Denmark

Among our respondents were two Danish groups. The two audit reports used rather different wordings. One refers to 'generally accepted auditing standards as applied in Denmark' and, as well as the Danish standard reference to conformity with the law and the company's articles, attests that the statements 'fairly present' the position and results. The other makes no reference to 'generally accepted auditing standards' and, in addition to the standard reference to legal compliance, attests that 'the financial statements contain the information necessary to evaluate the financial position as at [the balance date]'. This is, perhaps, a paraphrase for 'fair presentation'.

France

Our respondents included three French groups. All include among their auditors members of the 'Big Eight' accounting practices. One (CFP-Total) has its shares listed on the London Stock Exchange, another (Lafarge-Coppee) has a major subsidiary Corporation (52.82 per cent owned) whose shares are listed in New York, Montreal and Toronto. The third (Elf-Acquitaine) is listed on a number of exchanges in Continental Europe, but not elsewhere.

Again, the audit reports differed considerably. One (Elf-Acquitaine consolidated statements) contained a reference to 'generally accepted auditing standards' and attested that the consolidated financial statements 'fairly present the ... position ... and results ... in conformity with the accounting principles described in note 1...'. (Note 1 indicated among other things that the group employs the *monetary–nonmonetary* method of foreign currency translation.) Another (Lafarge-Coppee) contains a similar reference to fair presentation in conformity with accounting principles described in the notes (from which it is evident that the *current–noncurrent* method of currency translation was used), with the auditors expressing an exception on the treatment of deferred taxation; but there is no reference to 'generally accepted auditing standards'.

In the third case (CFP-Total consolidated statements), there is a report from the auditors (part of one of the 'Big Eight') in the usual French form, including the usual reference to a 'true and fair view' (image fidèle). But this is accompanied by a long form report by a major British accounting firm (not part of the same international practice or indeed of any of the 'Big Eight') which states that 'in connection with the listing of the Company's shares on the Stock Exchange in London we have reviewed the audited accounts....We comment below on the more significant variations which would arise if the accounts were prepared in accordance with United Kingdom accounting requirements'. (These variations appeared to relate to issues of presentation and disclosure rather than to measurement conventions.)

Here we can see clearly the influence of listing considerations but again the variations in the style and content of the audit reports are not trivial.

Germany

We received replies from ten German groups, but two of these prepared no foreign language reports. Of the remaining eight, two included no audit report in the English language abridged version of their report. We therefore had six sets of audit reports to examine.

Most German-based multinationals seem to publish three sets of financial statements: parent company, domestic consolidation and world-wide consolidation. It is evidently the latter which are deemed to be of interest to the international reader, since two groups (BASF and Volkswagen) did not include the domestic consolidated statements in their English language reports, while two others (Bayer and Hoechst), had a special form of audit report on their worldwide consolidation (as did BASF, but not Volkswagen).

Thus, the auditors of three of the six groups abandoned the hyperlaconic German standard short-form audit report ('The Financial Statements and the Annual Report were duly verified and found by us to comply with the law'), in favour of a lengthier wording in the case of the worldwide consolidation. One of these (on BASF) has already been

---

Figure 6.6 Extract from the AEG annual report

The Consolidated Financial Statements and the Annual Report were duly
verified and found by us to comply with the law.

DWT Deutsche Warentreuhand-Aktiengesellschaft
Wirtschaftsprüfungsgesellschaft, Steuerberatungsgesellschaft

Dr. Jacob   Neukirchen
Wirtschaftsprüfer   Wirtschaftsprüfer

Berlin and Frankfurt, April 16, 1986

---

mentioned above. The other two differ from it and (although both were
produced by the same 'Big Eight' member firms) from each other. In the
case of Bayer, the auditors attest that the financial statements 'drawn up
in accordance with the principles described in the Explanatory Report,
have been audited by us. In conjunction with the Explanatory Report,
they fairly present the financial and earnings position of the consolidated
companies'. (The Explanatory Report states that the group accounts are
'prepared in accordance with uniform guidelines based on generally
accepted accounting principles'.)

In the case of Hoechst, there is a much longer audit report, stating that
'our examination was made in accordance with generally accepted
auditing standards' and attesting that the statements 'fairly present the
consolidated financial position ... and results ... in conformity with the
accounting policies set out in the Annual Report which correspond in all
material respects to the German Stock Corporation Act and generally
accepted German accounting principles, except for the deferral of income
taxes on consolidation entries, which corresponds to internationally
accepted accounting principles.'

Consideration of these German examples contributes to the impression
that, as European multinationals try different methods to cope with the
problems of multinational financial reporting, so different forms of audit
report are thought appropriate. However, variations in the clients'
methods are not the only source of audit report diversity and, given the
great number of different styles that we have observed, we are led to
conclude that the reader would have great difficulty in interpreting the
many signals that are included.

Italy
Our respondents included three Italian groups. One audit report (on
Montedison) refers to 'generally accepted auditing standards' and attests
that the financial statements 'present ... in conformity with correct
accounting principles, the most significant of which are described [in the

notes]...'. One other (Olivetti consolidation), refers to 'established auditing standards' and attests that the statements 'present ... in accordance with the accounting principles established or adopted (International Accounting Standards) by the Italian Accounting Profession...'. In the third case (SNIA), the accounting principles to

Figure 6.7 Extract from the SNIA Annual Report

SNIA BPD S.p.A and subsidiaries

Report of the Auditors on the consolidated financial statements as at 31st December 1985
(Translation of the original Italian Certificate)

To the Shareholders of SNIA BPD S.p.A.

1 In performing the engagement conferred on us, we have examined the consolidated financial statements of SNIA BPD S.p.A. and subsidiaries for the year ended 31st December 1985 comprising the balance sheet, the profit and loss account, the source and application of funds and the statement of movements in Group capital and reserves, together with the Directors' report and the supplementary schedules and notes.

2 Our examination was made in accordance with the auditing standards approved by the 'Consigli Nazionali dei Dottori Commercialisti e dei Ragionieri' (Nos 1 to 17) and, accordingly, included such audit tests of the accounting records and of the Companies' assets and liabilities that we considered necessary to comply with our engagement. We have applied our professional judgement in evaluating the system for recording transactions in the books of account and their presentation in the consolidated financial statements (taking account of the necessary consolidation adjustments and eliminations) and also in determining the nature and extent of our tests of the books and records, in order to enable us to express an opinion, with due care and on the basis of adequate documentary support, on the consolidated financial statements taken as a whole. The selection of audit tests was determined as a result of an analysis of the degree of reliability demonstrated by the accounting procedures and by the internal controls within the consolidated Companies and a subsequent evaluation of the degree of risk that the consolidated financial statements, taken as a whole, could be materially affected by errors, irregularities or fraud.

In expressing our opinion on the consolidated financial statements of SNIA BPD S.p.A and subsidiaries, the accounting principles referred to are those issued by the 'Consigli Nazionali dei Dottori Commercialisti e dei Ragionieri' and, in absence thereof, those issued by the International Accounting Standards Committee (I.A.S.C.).

3 The above mentioned forming an integral part of our opinion, we certify that the consolidated financial statements of the SNIA BPD S.p.A. and subsidiaries at 31st December 1985 and for the year then ended are in agreement with the accounting records (taking account of the necessary consolidation adjustments and eliminations) and conform to the results of audit procedures performed and to the regulations concerning the format and content of financial statements and that the underlying transactions are accurately recorded in the above mentioned accounting records on the basis of correct accounting principles.

Milan, 28th May 1986
**Reconta Touche Ross
di Bruno Gimpel & C. S.a.s.
(Giuseppe Roccasalvo, partner)**

which the auditors refer in expressing their opinion are 'those issued by the Consigli Nazionali dei Dottori Commercialisti e dei Ragionieri and, in the absence thereof, those issued by the International Accounting Standards Committee...'. It is not obvious to what extent these three reports are saying the same things.

The differences in wording between the Olivetti parent company and consolidation audit reports has already been noted above. In the case of SNIA, the audit report in the English-language version of the consolidated financial statements was presented as a 'Translation of the original Italian Certificate' but our attempts to square this translation with the audit report appearing in the Italian published financial report were unfruitful as the latter only related to the accounts of the parent company. Indeed, in the Italian-language audit report on the parent company there was something of an *apologia* for the absence of consolidated statements, which, however, did not prevent the auditor from reaching an opinion on the parent's accounts ('l'attuale indisponibilita del documento in questione non comporti impedimento al rilascio della presente certificazione'). Nevertheless, it is worth noting that the Italian-language audit report contains a comment on accounting treatment (of the proceeds from the disposal of mining concessions) which the auditors deemed worthy of mention in the parent company context but which does not appear in the English language report on the Group as a whole. Presumably there was some change in accounting policy, or perhaps the item in question was immaterial in a group context, but one is left wondering what the international reader will make of statements like 'translation of the original certificate'.

Luxembourg
We received one reply from the Grand Duchy. The report contained no independent auditor's report, but only one from the Board of Auditors.

The Netherlands
We received responses from five Dutch groups, two of these, however, being the Dutch parts of the Anglo-Dutch groups, Royal Dutch Shell and Unilever.

As noted earlier in this chapter, Unilever issue a number of complementary financial reports. The annual report of the Dutch parent contains an auditor's opinion on the accounts expressed in guilders of Unilever N.V. which include 'the accounts of the N.V. Group, the PLC Group and the combined N.V. and PLC Groups'. It seems that the audit report on N.V. resembles more a standard United Kingdom audit opinion than a standard Dutch opinion. Yet it is interesting to note that, unlike the auditors' report to the members of the British parent, there are no statements in the N.V. report as to whether the audit was carried out in accordance with approved auditing standards nor whether the accounts comply with the law. Here again one is left wondering whether this is an example of the way in which the coded language of the auditor is 'culture bound', so that the inclusion or exclusion of a term has significance in one country but not another. Also of interest is the approach taken in the Unilever reports which are directed towards an international readership (the 'Annual Report and Salient Figures' series), which are translated into languages other than English and Dutch and also re-expressed in US$. These publications contain no audit report, but merely a statement by the auditors to the effect that they had issued an unqualified report.

In the case of Royal Dutch Petroleum, there is again no mention in the audit report on the Dutch holding company of either auditing procedures or accounting policies; whilst, in the auditors' report on the Royal Dutch Shell Group of companies, there is reference to 'generally accepted auditing standards' and an attestation that the statements are 'presented fairly ... in accordance with the accounting policies described on pages...'. The other three (AKZO, KLM and Philips) all had standard Dutch short-form audit reports (which attest to 'fair presentation').

Figure 6.8 Extract from the AKZO Annual Report

Auditors' Report

We have examined the foregoing 1985 financial statements of Akzo N.V., Arnhem.

In our opinion, these financial statements present fairly the financial position of Akzo N.V. at December 31, 1985, and the results of its operations for the year then ended.

Arnhem, March 7, 1986

KMG Klynveld Kraayenhof & Co.

Non European Community countries

Finland

There was one Finnish respondent, Wärtsilä. This group included in its report a set of consolidated financial statements restated from the Finnish statutory form so as to comply with International Accounting Standards. (The shares are listed on the London Stock Exchange, as well as in Helsinki and Stockholm.) However, the auditors' report refers only to the statutory Finnish statements, and, having stated that the examination was made in accordance with generally accepted auditing standards in Finland, attests simply to legal compliance.

Norway
Again, there was one Norwegian respondent, Norsk Hydro. The audit report refers to 'generally accepted auditing standards' and, as well as attesting to compliance with the law and with generally accepted accounting principles in Norway, attests that the statements 'give a true and fair view'.

Sweden
Swedish companies constituted the largest national group (twelve) among our respondents. One of them, however, prepared no foreign language report. There is a standard Swedish short form of audit report, which attests to legal compliance and proposes the discharge of the directors from liability for their administration, and which was used in all of the twelve reports we received, but with some variations. In the cases of eight groups (AGA, Electrolux, LM Ericsson, Esselte, Sandvik, SKF, Svenska Cellulosa and Swedish Match), there was also a reference to 'generally accepted auditing standards', or 'recognised auditing practice'. The report on Ericsson also refers to presentation being 'in accordance with good accounting practice in Sweden'. In the case of Volvo, there is a reference to 'a true and fair view'.

There appear to be differences in the scope of the audit attestation as well, at least in the English language versions. The auditors of two companies (PLM and SKF) stated that it is the parent company's 'annual report' and the consolidated 'annual report' which have been prepared in accordance with the Swedish Companies Act; in five other cases (AGA, Electrolux, LM Ericsson, Swedish Match and Perstorp), this attestation related again to the parent company 'annual report' but was restricted to the consolidated 'financial statements' (or 'accounts'); and in the remaining five cases (ASEA, Esselte, Sandvik, Svenska Cellulosa and Volvo) the auditor's opinion on compliance with the law is restricted to the parent company 'financial statements' and the consolidated 'financial statements'. But these seem to be problems of translation, since in Swedish it is the annual report, i.e. 'arresdovisningen', or 'koncernredovisningen' (Report on the Group) that is mentioned in the original audit reports. Only in Volvo's case was there a more explicit recognition of audit scope where the opinion that 'the financial statements on pages 32 through 50 give a true and fair view...' could be seen to cover not just the financial statements of the group and the parent but also the notes to the financial statements. Even in this seemingly unique case, we are left with some doubt as to whether the 'true and fair view of the income for the year 1985, and of the financial position at December 31, 1985' can in any sense extend to the approximate figures that have been restated in accordance with US GAAP as set out in one of the notes to the accounts.

It is important to emphasise here that what we have observed are variations on the standard Swedish short-form rather than departures from it, and the Swedish respondents on the whole exhibit less variability in the wording of audit reports than any other group. Nevertheless, it is hard to know what to make of the variations. In fact, they pose a dilemma: either they can be disregarded as having no meaning (but in that case, one is saying that phrases such as 'generally accepted auditing standards' and 'true and fair view' are to be treated as having no meaning ; or else one can take them seriously (but in that case, were generally accepted auditing standards not followed in four of the cases, and a true and fair view only given in the case of Volvo?). We return to this dilemma below.

Switzerland

There were two Swiss respondents, Nestlé and Swissair. Both reports followed a Swiss short form, which attests to the propriety of the accounting and compliance with the law, with a Swedish-style recommendation in the case of Nestlé that the directors be discharged from their liability. In each case, however, the audit report related to the parent company, not the consolidated statements. For Swissair, no consolidation had been presented, on the grounds that the subsidiaries were not material. But that was not at all the case with Nestlé.

The international accounting firms

Of the seventy audit reports which we read, we were able to identify forty as the work of one of the 'Big Eight' international accounting practices. (A number of others possibly were also, since most of the largest national firms in Germany and Sweden are part of one of the 'Big Eight' organisations, and also auditors sign in their own names rather than in the names of their firms, which may not be mentioned.) In general, the wording of these audit reports conformed to the normal practice in the country concerned. As will have been apparent from our comments above, however, in most countries the style of report appears to vary. Variations between countries are also considerable. There was no evidence to suggest that the 'Big Eight' constitute an influence towards greater harmony in the style of audit reports ostensibly intended for the international reader.

Conclusion

It should be clear from the evidence reviewed above that the 'greater sensitivity' to the attest function alleged by Choi and Mueller to exist in multinational settings is not generally reflected in the existence of any form of audit report which would assist the international reader in

Figure 6.9 Extracts from the ASEA and Nestlé Annual Reports

Auditors' Report

We have audited the accounts for the year, the consolidated accounts, other accounts and the administration of the Board of Directors and of the President.

Parent Company

The accounts for the year 1985 have been prepared in accordance with the Swedish Companies Act.

We recommend that the Annual Meeting
approve the profit and loss account and the balance sheet as at December 31, 1985,
approve the disposition of the profits as proposed in the report of the Board of Directors,
and discharge the members of the Board of Directors and the President from responsibility
for the period covered by the Annual Report.

ASEA Group

The consolidated accounts for the year 1985 have been prepared in accordance with the Swedish Companies Act.

We recommend that the Annual Meeting approve the consolidated profit and loss account and the consolidated balance sheet.

Västerås, March 6, 1986
Gunnar Widhagen
Authorized Public Accountant

Torbjörn Hanson   Gunnar Hambraeus   Stig Schenning
Authorized Public Accountant

Auditors' Report
to the General Meeting of Nestlé S.A. on 15th May 1986

To the Shareholders,

In accordance with the duties with which we have been entrusted, we have audited the balance sheet and profit and loss account of Nestlé S.A. for the year ended 31st December 1985 and we have examined the report dated 21st March 1986 prepared by Messrs Peat, Marwick, Mitchell & Co., London, independent Chartered Accountants, in accordance with article 723 of the 'Code des Obligations'. We have obtained all the information and explanations which we required from these accountants and from the officers of the Company.

The balance sheet at 31st December 1985, the total of which amounts to Fr. 7 631 499 006, and the profit and loss account, showing a net profit for the year 1985 of Fr. 592 853 274, are in agreement with the books of account. The earned surplus available for appropriation amounts to Fr. 594 549 701.

We have satisfied ourselves that the books are correctly kept and that the presentation of the financial situation and of the result of the year is in accordance with legal requirements.

We propose that you should approve the balance sheet and profit and loss account presented to you, and also the Directors' proposals for the appropriation of profit, which are in accordance with the legal and statutory provisions, and that the Board of Directors and the Management should be given their release with the thanks of the Shareholders.

The Auditors:
A. PESTALOZZI
Cham and Vevey, 9th April 1986.   J. ITEN
D. von SCHULTHESS
W. de RHAM

deciding how best to interpret the financial statements to which the audit report relates. We did note a few cases (e.g. in Germany) where the auditors had produced special styles of report intended for international readers, but these styles all differed. The international reader is left with the dilemma we noted when discussing Sweden, concerning the significance of the presence or absence in audit reports of phrases like 'generally accepted auditing standards' and 'present a true and fair view'. We suggest that this should be of some concern to the IAPC.

Some tentative conclusions

Our review of some of the salient features of transnational financial reporting by Continental European Multinationals has shown how a great variety of different techniques are employed by these companies to communicate with foreign report readers. We have highlighted the reservations that a number of companies have expressed about mere linguistic translations, some going as far as to state that the original language report is the definitive version or even that the audit report refers strictly to the original language version of the financial statements. We have shown that 'convenience currency translations' are uncommon and, indeed, a minefield of accounting contradictions. We have also shown how accounting differences can largely reflect institutional differences in host countries, differences which cannot be ironed out except to the extent that the institutions themselves (and the legal and fiscal regulations that support them) can be harmonised. To some extent, this is being done for the member states of the EC, but the process is very slow and one is hard pressed to find greater harmony between member states than between non-members such as Switzerland and Sweden. Some companies make particular efforts to provide supplementary information to help the international reader to appreciate the company's domestic environment.

From the international reader's point of view, we would suggest that the very diversity of these types of transnational reporting is likely to militate against their communicative effectiveness. Accounting reports are full of coded language, and lack of consistency in the codes used makes it much harder for the reader to penetrate them. Yet to some extent, companies may find themselves impelled towards one type of transnational reporting rather than another. For example, listing requirements do differ between countries. For instance, it would seem that the COB in France requires: (a) audited accounts from foreign listed companies; (b) that reports of the general shareholder meetings be translated into French; (c) publication of interim reports in the French financial press; and (d) that the French market be provided with all other information provided to other foreign stock markets throughout the world. No mention, however, is made of the use of French or international accounting principles. In the United Kingdom, the Stock Exchange expects: (a) accounts to be prepared in conformity with the international accounting standards published by the International Accounting Standards Committee; and (b) disclosure and explanation of any significant departure from, or any non-compliance with, the applicable standards. In the United States, on the other hand, the SEC requires companies to restate certain items using principles generally accepted in that particular country.[5]

In certain cases, the need to meet listing requirements on foreign exchanges is referred to by the companies themselves:

> As a result of the registration of American Depositary Shares (ADS) with the United States Securities and Exchange Commission, the Company prepares a reconciliation of the effect on shareholders' funds and net income of the application of US generally accepted accounting principles in lieu of Danish principles (Novo Annual Report 1985, page 48).

On the whole, there is little (to us, surprisingly little) apparent use of International Accounting Standards. One of the exceptions is the Finnish engineering group Wärtsilä:

> Considering the extensiveness of Wärtsilä's international operations and the fact that Wärtsilä shares apart from Helsinki are also listed on the Stockholm and London Stock Exchanges, Group financial statements are here presented in a more familiar form for the international reader. The accounting policies applied correspond with International Accounting Standards (IAS) (Wärtsilä Annual Report 1985, page 40).

Another aspect which surprised us is the apparent lack of impact of the major international accounting firms. To be sure, their influence over institutional harmonisation, insofar as it is occurring, cannot be large; nor do they choose the accounting policies adopted by their clients. But two areas where they could possess considerable influence are international auditing standards and the style and wording of audit reports. We cannot comment on progress on the former, but it will be clear from the review presented in this chapter that, in spite of the IAPC's ED No.12, little or nothing has been done towards harmonising the latter.

Yet audit reports are a particularly clear instance of the use of coded language, where terms like 'generally accepted auditing standards' or 'a true and fair view' do not possess an unequivocal, context-free meaning. What meaning is the reader to attach to the presence or absence of such phrases, when the wording of audit reports varies so widely? In addition, a more uniform style of audit reporting might act as a spur to harmonisation of the institutional factors which affect accounting conventions, since it would throw discrepancies in the latter into greater relief.

In any event, neither the behaviour of preparers nor that of auditors of transnational financial reports seems explicable in terms of a systematic concern with user needs. It remains an open question just what the responsible individuals in the reporting entities and in the accounting firms are trying to achieve in their choices of type of report, what assumptions they make about user needs and about their own interest in meeting these needs. Agency theory suggests that the provision of an optimal level of 'monitoring' minimises agency costs. It is hard to believe that the present level is optimal; and Choi and Mueller and Stamp and Moonitz seem to suggest that there is room for improvement. On the other hand, it would be premature to draw such a conclusion without knowing more about how professional users of transnational reports actually do use them. How much attention do they pay to audit reports, for example? These various issues clearly call for further research.

Notes

1. We use the term 'transnational financial reporting' to refer to the production of financial reports for readers in foreign countries.
2. With the exception of the CONCORDANCE project that has been initiated at the University of Lancaster and which has as its aim the creation of an on-line financial lexicon in a number of European languages.
3. The exchange rate current at each year end has been used in combining the N.V. and PLC accounts, i.e.

	1984	1985
£1 = Guilders	4.13	4.00
£1 = US$	1.16	1.45
$1 = Guilders	3.56	2.76

4. It is worth noting in more detail the extensive reporting operation of the Unilever group. The annual accounts of Unilever N.V. are published in the original Dutch with currency figures expressed in guilders. There is an English translation of the report (again in guilders) and, as the company points out,

> there is also an English version issued by PLC with currency figures expressed in pounds sterling and containing the Unilever PLC Annual Accounts...together with the Auditors' Report thereon; it is identical with (the Unilever N.V. Annual Accounts) except for the difference in currency and for certain details which are required only in the United

Kingdom or in the Netherlands and which are therefore not included in the N.V or PLC versions respectively (Unilever in 1985: English Version in Guilders of the Annual Accounts, page 1).

In addition, Unilever publish another series of reports (Unilever in 1985 Annual Report and Salient Figures which contain extracts from the combined consolidated accounts along with a Directors' Report). These are available (i) from PLC in pounds sterling in English and (ii) from N.V. in guilders in Dutch, (iii) in German translation, (iv) in English translation or (v) in French abridged translation as well as (vi) an English version with currency figures translated into US dollars. Finally, both N.V. and PLC make filings with the SEC in the form required by United States legislation.

5. The various requirements of different stock exchanges are not presented here in full, but in sufficient detail to demonstrate the varying stipulations on accounting policies.

Appendix

Details of positive respondents

Company	Country of origin	European Inter-listings[1]	Reporting languages
AEG-Telefunken AG	Germany	(2)	German, English, French, Spanish,
AGA AB	Sweden	3	Swedish, English
AKZO	Netherlands	7	Dutch, English, German
Arbed	Luxemburg	(4)	French, German, English
ASEA	Sweden	3	Swedish, English
BASF	Germany	(4)	German, English, French
Bayer	Germany	(4)	German, English, French, Spanish
CFP-Total	France	2	French, English
EBES	Belgium	(2)	French, English
Elf-Aquitaine	France	5	French, English
Electrolux	Sweden	4	Swedish, English, French, Italian
Ericsson	Sweden	6	Swedish, English
Esselte	Sweden	(2)	Swedish, English
Great Nordic	Denmark	(2)	Danish, English, French
Hoechst	Germany	(4)	German, English, French Italian, Spanish, Portuguese
Intercom Belge	Belgium	(2)	Dutch, French, English
KLM	Netherlands	3	Dutch, English

Lafarge Coppee	France	2	French, English
Mannesman	Germany	(2)	German, English
Montedison	Italy	(2)	Italian, English
Nestlé	Switzerland	(4)	German, French, English
Norsk Hydro	Norway	(4)	Norwegian, English
Novo Industri	Denmark	2	Danish, English
Olivetti	Italy	(3)	Italian, English
OY Wärtsilä	Finland	3	Finnish, English, Swedish
Perstorp	Sweden	2	Swedish, English
Philips	Netherlands	9	Dutch, English, German, French
PLM	Sweden	3	Swedish, English
Royal Dutch Petroleum NV	Netherlands	8	Dutch, English, French, German
Sandvik	Sweden	(2)	Swedish, English
SKF	Sweden	4	Swedish, English
SNIA Viscosa	Italy	(2)	Italian, English
Solvay	Belgium	5	French, English
Svenska Cellulosa	Sweden	4	Swedish, English
Swedish Match	Sweden	6	Swedish, English, French, Spanish, German
Swissair	Switzerland	(2)	German, English
Thyssen	Germany	(3)	German, English
Unilever NV	Netherlands	8	Dutch, English, German, French
Veba	Germany	(2)	German, English
Vieille Montagne	Belgium	(2)	French, English
Volkswagen	Germany	6	German, English, Spanish
Volvo	Sweden	6	Swedish, English, French

[1] *Number of European countries where the company's equity securities are listed, as reported in the 1985 annual report. The figures in brackets indicate the number of European listings which we have been able to identify in the absence of information to that end in the company's report.*

References

Ayling, D.E., *The Internationalisation of Stock Markets* (Aldershot: Gower Press, 1986).

Choi, F.D.S., European disclosure: the competitive disclosure hypotheses, *Journal of International Business Studies* (Fall 1974), pp. 15-23.

Choi, F.D.S. and Mueller, G.G., *International Accounting* (Englewood Cliffs, N.J.:Prentice Hall, 1984).

Gray, S.J., The impact of international accounting differences from a security-analysis perspective: some European evidence, *Journal of Accounting Research* (Spring 1980), pp. 64-76.

Jones, M.E., The relevance and use of research in the development of international auditing guidelines, *Symposium on International Financial Accounting Research 1985*. University of Glasgow Discussion Paper, 1986, pp. 29-45.

McLeay S.J., Value added: a comparative study, *Accounting Organisations and Society* (1983), pp. 31-56.

Nobes, C.W., Financial reporting by multinational groups: a few of the questions, and fewer answers, *Symposium on International Financial Accounting Research 1985*. University of Glasgow Discussion Paper, 1986, pp. 49-76.

Pinchuck, I., *Scientific and Technical Translation* (London:Andre Deutsch, 1977).

Stamp, E. and Moonitz, M., *International Auditing Standards* (Hemel Hempstead:Prentice Hall, 1979).

Switzer, L., Is there a premium for listing on major stock exchanges? – evidence for Canadian based stocks interlisted in the US Paper presented at the EIASM Research Symposium in Stock Pricing Anomalies, Brussels, December 1985.

7
Voluntary Information Disclosure and the British Multinationals: Corporate Perceptions of Costs and Benefits[1]

Sidney J. Gray and Clare B. Roberts

The power of multinational corporations to control and co-ordinate resources internationally gave rise to increased pressures in the 1970s for extensions in public accountability and control (Choi and Mueller, 1984; Gray, 1984). Information was perceived to be a key factor in this 'age of regulation' as a necessary means of monitoring the multinationals. The 1980s promise to be more of an 'age of understanding' as nations endeavour, with the help of the multinationals, to emerge from recession and move into a recovery and growth phase. While the climate for multinationals is currently more tolerant, this does not mean that the further regulation of information disclosure is now unlikely. Pressures for investor protection or employee communication may well increase in a more favourable economic environment. Further indications of likely pressures are provided by recently witnessed corporate scandals, giant takeover battles, and increasingly internationalised financial markets.

Purpose of the research

Although multinationals tend to support the existence of a minimum regulatory framework and moves towards international harmonisation, mainly on the grounds of cost effectiveness, there would appear also to be some concern at the number and variety of international standard-setting agencies involved, e.g. OECD, UN, IASC, and fear that the demand for further extensions in information disclosure will impose significant net costs on business operations.

Insights into these issues may be gained by investigating the attitudes of multinationals to voluntary information disclosures (i.e. information

[1] The authors gratefully acknowledge the financial support of the Economic and Social Research Council (ESRC).

in excess of legal requirements/accounting standards/stock exchange rules) and to proposals involving the disclosure of more information about their operations. Related to this is the issue of whether further regulation is necessary or feasible if a voluntary or self-regulatory framework cannot meet external demands.

What then are the costs and benefits of disclosing additional information and to what extent are net benefits perceived to exist? Further, what is the extent of voluntary disclosure already practised and what are the major factors underlying the decision to disclose, or not disclose, additional information beyond existing regulations? These are the research questions explored in this chapter.

These are important questions because corporate voluntary disclosures by multinationals have yet to be assessed in this problem context. Prior research has investigated differences in attitudes to disclosure by corporate executives and financial analysts in the US context (Mautz and May, 1978). More recently, an assessment of differences in the perceptions of costs and benefits by these groups with reference to disclosures by US multinationals has been carried out (McKinnon, 1984). But these studies of cost-benefit perceptions have not fully explored the specific nature of the relevant influences, the costs and benefits involved and the impact of such factors on the voluntary disclosure or non-disclosure of information. This study should, therefore, help to improve our understanding of disclosure behaviour in practice and should be of interest to all parties concerned with multinational accountability and regulation.

Voluntary corporate disclosure

It has been suggested that disclosure choices tend to be determined by managerial assessments of the costs and benefits of proposed alternative disclosures (Kelly, 1983). Following this approach, disclosure choices would be made by multinationals on the basis of their cash flow implications. Voluntary disclosures can also be seen as the outcome of market and political pressures (Watts, 1977; Watts and Zimmerman, 1986). This is a complex interactive process where corporate management is both influenced by and seeks to influence the sources of such pressures. Voluntary disclosures are also likely to be influenced by managerial expectations of positive share price effects, in terms of higher returns and/or reduced risk (Jensen and Meckling, 1976).

However, disclosures in excess of requirements may not always be beneficial. They may lead to investor forecasts of reductions in future cash flows or to perceptions of increased riskiness depending on the nature and significance of the disclosures about multinational operations (Ronen and Livnat, 1981). At the same time, there are costs directly associated with voluntary disclosures such as data collection, processing, production and auditing costs. There are also indirect costs such as competitive disadvantage. Disclosure may encourage the involvement of competitors and reduce the ability to generate cash flows expected from inventive and innovative activities. Investment decisions by managers may also be affected to the extent that disclosure is perceived to increase the risks of claims, e.g. by employees/trades unions or taxation authorities. However, such direct and indirect costs may well be lower in the case of large firms, in that disclosures are more easily produced and likely to be less revealing compared to small firms. Further, the fact that large firms are more visible in the market, and more widely traded, than small firms, seems likely to be an important pressure for disclosure.

There is also the impact of the political process on future cash flows to be taken into account, e.g. through taxation, intervention in takeovers/mergers. In the case of multinationals, political pressures are likely to be particularly significant and more so in respect of large companies, with substantial market power, and those in sectors such as energy and defence which are of national concern or in the publicity limelight. Voluntary disclosures may also be encouraged by expectations of positive effects in terms of host country attitudes towards foreign investment, e.g. as a result of complying with the OECD disclosure guidelines for multinationals or IASC standards. But beneficial effects are unlikely if disclosures reveal situations of monopoly advantage, tax anomalies or social inequality which encourage political intervention.

In summary, it seems likely that multinationals will be sensitive to market and political pressures to the extent that future cash flows are likely to be impacted. Voluntary disclosures may be expected, therefore, where there is a perception of net benefits. In calculating such net benefits, if any, the constraints of both direct and indirect costs will intervene and place limits on the extent of disclosure. In this situation it may be expected that the positive effects of voluntary disclosures will tend to be more appreciated by companies under market pressure to improve their image and performance and also by those with 'good news' to report. But for the larger multinationals operating in sectors of public and political concern disclosure could well be a 'mixed blessing'. A combination of market and political pressures seems likely, therefore, to encourage but at the same time place some constraints on voluntary information disclosures.

Methodology

In order to explore the research questions identified and to examine the nature of market and political pressures on multinationals, an empirical study involving questionnaires and interviews was carried out. This focussed on British multinationals to keep the research within manageable bounds, to facilitate in-depth analysis and to minimise the problem of cultural differences.

A total population of 212 British multinationals was identified for the purposes of the study. A multinational was defined, following the UN, to include all companies with foreign operations in two or more countries. Additional criteria required the companies identified to be stock exchange listed and to have total revenues in excess of £100 million.

A questionnaire survey of these companies was carried out in early 1984 as a prelude to more in-depth field research involving interviews conducted later in the year. A survey of actual reporting practices was also carried out but is the subject of a separate report, as this chapter is concerned primarily with corporate attitudes to information disclosure. The questionnaire and interviews (both strictly confidential as to the source of responses) were designed to assess attitudes to voluntary disclosures with specific reference to the types of benefits and costs involved, the major factors influencing disclosure, and the effects of disclosing specific items of information which are voluntary/discretionary or controversial in nature. Respondents were also invited to add items not covered by the questionnaire and to contribute comments. The specific disclosure items included in the questionnaire were selected on the basis of proposals/guidelines from the UN (1977), OECD (1976) and IASC (1977, 1983), prior research, current issues of corporate and professional concern and voluntary corporate disclosure behaviour in practice (see Appendix for the full list).

In constructing the questionnaire, a series of questions using Likert-type scales were developed to assess perceptions and attitudes, with scores ranging from 1 to 5 (see Tables 7.1-8) except in the case of assessment of the net costs or benefits from disclosure (see Tables 7.9-11) where this was increased from 1 to 7 so as to provide for a wider range of opinions about both net costs and net benefits.

A total of 116 multinationals or 55 per cent of the population responded to the questionnaire survey. These respondents comprised a broad cross-section of companies. An analysis of the size and industry of the responding companies indicated that the only significant difference from the total population of 212 multinationals was in respect of the standard deviation of turnover, i.e. the very largest companies were relatively over-represented in the replying companies. The effect of this is the possibility of a slight bias in the overall results towards more positive attitudes to voluntary disclosure. Interviews were subsequently carried out with financial executives at a senior level, i.e. Finance Director, Controller, or Chief Accountant, in thirty multinationals. A representative sample of companies was selected for this purpose, comprising a variety of attitudes to voluntary disclosure, while ensuring a mixture of companies of different size, extent of multinationality, and industrial activity. Considerable emphasis was placed on the interviews as a means both to validate and extend insights gained from the questionnaires.

Naturally, the limitations of opinion research of this kind must be recognised, e.g. respondents may well not reveal their true opinions and may act differently in practice. The results of the survey must, therefore, be treated with some caution. It should also be noted that the opinions surveyed were those of financial executives only.

Results

Given the extent to which regulation in the United Kingdom has increased during the 1970s and early 1980s, both in terms of Company Law requirements, Stock Exchange rules and Accounting Standards, it is noteworthy that 71 per cent or 83 of the 116 multinationals responding to the questionnaire stated that they made voluntary information disclosures (see Table 7.1). From this group, eleven companies perceived themselves to be making extensive voluntary disclosures.

Table 7.1 Voluntary information disclosure
by British multinationals

	No. of companies	
Very large extent	4	(3%)
Large extent	7	(6%)
Medium extent	38	(33%)
Small extent	34	(29%)
None	33	(29%)
	116	(100%)

Clearly, the disclosure policy-making process involves a number of participants, and in this regard it was evident that the preparation of the corporate report was viewed as an increasingly important and major exercise in financial communications. For most companies it was an ongoing activity. The Finance Director was the executive most closely concerned with voluntary disclosure decisions but the Chief Executive and/or Chairman usually had a major influence on the philosophy and style of the report as well as on specific accounting and disclosure policy issues (see Table 7.2). In addition, there was usually heavy participation by the Chief Accountant or Controller. These conclusions are confirmed by the results of the Wilcoxon matched-pairs signed-ranks tests which are used here, and also in Tables 7.3-8, to assess the significance of differences between the rankings of the various influential factors identified in the study.

Table 7.2 British multinationals' organisational influences on annual report disclosures

Rank	Mean (n = 116)	Coefficient of variation (%)	Wilcoxon test prob.
1 Finance Director	4.85	8	
			0.0000
2 Chief Executive	4.18	25	
			0.1431
3 Chief Accountant/Controller	4.03	27	
			0.8668
4 Chairman	3.96	27	
			0.0000
5 Board of Directors	3.31	29	
			0.0007
6 Public Relations	2.49	45	
			0.3310
7 Investor Relations	2.21	55	
			0.0000
8 Marketing	1.72	54	
			0.0428
9 Divisional Accountants	1.70	52	

Range = 1-5
1 = no influence
5 = large influence

It was interesting to note from the interviews that positive attitudes towards regulation and accounting standards tended to be related to the extent to which the finance team was professionally qualified. Public and investor relations experts, both internal and external, were also usually involved to some degree providing advice on design and communications techniques.

Market and political pressures

While the Corporate Report was considered by most companies making voluntary disclosures as likely to be of interest to a wide range of users, it was clear from both the questionnaire and interviews that, despite the range of views, the primary users of voluntary disclosures were perceived to be the 'experts' i.e. financial analysts and institutional investors (see Table 7.3). Other important influences included potential investors, private investors and the financial press. Taken overall, there was a strong stock market orientation with voluntary disclosures dominated by market considerations. This was both in terms of influencing and being influenced by stock market perceptions. This included recognition of the need for effective public relations (see Table 7.4) with a view to enhancing the company's image and reputation with consequent effects on share prices and investor assessments of risk (see Table 7.5). This emphasis was supported by the perceived need for equity/loan finance and the threat of takeover, though this latter influence was of major significance for only 12 per cent of the companies surveyed.

As regards political pressures, the perceived influences of domestic governmental agencies, including taxation authorities, and international inter-governmental organisations such as the OECD and UN, was relatively less important for most companies. However, EEC proposals of forthcoming directives were, not surprisingly, more influential owing to their potential legal impact.

At the professional level, the IASC was somewhat more influential than the OECD and UN but of relatively minor significance overall. More important were proposals by the United Kingdom accounting profession, which were apparently responded to in anticipation of forthcoming standards. Proposals by the company's auditors were also relatively important. Social responsibility considerations were also perceived to be important and in fact were ranked ahead of EEC influences. Perhaps not surprisingly, proposals by academics were of fringe interest – but ranked ahead of the UN nevertheless.

The perceived benefits of voluntary disclosures centred on market considerations, as already indicated, with the emphasis on improving the image and reputation of the company (see Table 7.5). While it was suggested that voluntary disclosures would lead to better investment decisions, fairer share prices, and more accurate assessments of risk, it was interesting to note that improved accountability to shareholders also ranked highly. Accountability to society, in contrast, was ranked relatively low.

From the interviews, it was apparent that a major impetus for voluntary disclosure tended to arise from a situation where multinationals perceived themselves to be 'misunderstood' or unfairly assessed by financial analysts and the stock market in general. This perception was most prevalent where there were changes in corporate strategy affecting the range and balance of activities or where there was expectation of an upsurge in company fortunes. Successful, i.e. more profitable, companies tended, in any case, to be 'high profile' companies from a voluntary disclosure perspective. Companies in this category under threat of

Table 7.3 British multinationals: The influences of user groups on voluntary information disclosure

Rank		Mean (n = 116)	Coefficient of variation (%)	Wilcoxon test prob.
1	Financial Analysts	3.86	27	
				0.4662
2	Institutional Investors	3.78	27	
				0.0000
3	Potential Investors	3.24	35	
				0.2675
4	Private Investors	3.12	31	
				0.8697
5	The Financial Press	3.05	34	
				0.4378
6	Employees	2.93	35	
				0.1757
7	Bankers	2.71	43	
				0.0000
8	General Public	1.84	48	
				0.0429
9 =	Creditors	1.58	47	
				0.8109
9 =	Consumer Groups	1.58	56	
				0.5521
11	Domestic Government Agencies	1.51	52	
				0.5014
12	Foreign Government Agencies	1.46	59	
				0.4342
13	Domestic Taxation Authorities	1.39	57	
				0.1614
14	Foreign Taxation Authorities	1.33	55	

Range = 1-5
1 = no influence
5 = large influence

Table 7.4 British multinationals: Additional
factors influencing voluntary information disclosure

Rank	Mean (n = 116)	Coefficient of variation (%)	Wilcoxon test prob.
1 Public Relations Consideration	3.06	37	
			0.5117
2 Proposals by the UK Accounting Profession	2.89	38	
			0.0012
3 Equity/Loan Finance Requirements	2.37	53	
			0.6958
4 Proposals by Auditors	2.31	42	
			0.7007
5 Social Responsibility Considerations	2.26	40	
			0.7122
6 EEC Proposals/New Directives	2.24	48	
			0.0238
7 International Accounting Standards	2.01	52	
			0.9753
8 Threat of Takeover	1.98	56	
			0.0789
9 USA Regulations/ Standards	1.74	57	
			0.2388
10 OECD Disclosure Guidelines	1.60	55	
			0.0131
11 Proposals by Academics	1.37	43	
			0.3314
12 UN Proposals for Information Disclosure	1.30	48	

Range = 1-5
1 - no influence
5 = large influence

Table 7.5 British multinationals' benefits of voluntary information disclosure

Rank	Mean (n = 83)	Coefficient of variation (%)	Wilcoxon test prob.
1 Improved image/ reputation of company	3.59	28	
			0.0982
2 Better investment decisions by investors	3.34	35	
			0.4916
3 Improved accountability to share holders	3.23	38	
			0.1904
4 More accurate risk assessment by investors	3.07	38	
			0.4909
5 Fairer share prices	2.98	35	
			0.4092
6 More accurate forecasts of earnings	2.88	35	
			0.4092
7 Lower risk assessment by investors	2.52	50	
			0.0552
8 Higher share prices	2.31	45	
			0.5156
9 Improved accountability to society	2.22	49	
			0.0997
10 Lower cost of capital	1.94	58	
			0.0109
11 More efficient resource allocation in the economy	1.56	53	

Range = 1-5
1 = not at all
5 = large extent

takeover were especially concerned to communicate more effectively to the market. On the other hand, poor performers tended to adopt a 'low profile'. In the same category were companies with a 'minimum disclosure' or 'secrecy' philosophy, stemming from relatively recent growth from 'family business' origins. This approach was pertinent to a number of what are now very large companies.

Costs of disclosure

A variety of costs, both direct and indirect, serve to constrain voluntary corporate disclosure. An assessment of *all* respondents' views indicates (Table 7.6) that multinationals are particularly sensitive to the cost of competitive disadvantage and that this was perceived, or at least purported, to be the major constraint. While this is clearly significant, the extent to which competitive disadvantage is likely to be damaging in practice is difficult to assess, especially if all companies are required to comply with respect to a specific item of disclosure. Important but not so significant was the cost of data collection and processing and the cost of auditing. The possibility of claims from employees/trades unions also ranked relatively high, as did the threat of takeover, which appears both to motivate and constrain voluntary disclosure depending on the situation of the company. Political pressures in the form of intervention by government agencies/taxation authorities or claims from political/ consumer groups were not so significant taken overall, though 12 per cent of the companies surveyed expressed major concern.

Analysis of the impact of costs was taken further by assessing the attitudes of *all* respondents to 34 specific items of information disclosure which are voluntary/discretionary or controversial in nature in the context of United Kingdom Company Law, Stock Exchange rules and Accounting Standards. While there was a wide range of views, Table 7.7 shows that disclosures especially sensitive to the costs of competitive disadvantage included, most importantly, future-orientated information quantifying forecasts of sales and profits, and segmental information relating to sales and profits where lines of business or geographical areas were narrowly defined e.g. by individual country.

As regards the cost of producing additional information, including the cost of data collection, auditing and publication, the most significant items were inflation adjusted profits and quarterly interim reports followed by segmental information on a narrowly defined basis, employment information, quantitative forecasts of sales and profits, and amounts of transfers between segments (see Table 7.8).

Having identified specific costs and benefits, an assessment of the overall net costs or benefits of voluntary/discretionary disclosures indicated that each of the disclosure items was perceived to give rise to

Table 7.6 British multinationals' cost factors constraining voluntary information disclosure

Rank	Mean (n = 116)	Coefficient of variation (%)	Wilcoxon test prob.
1 Cost of competitive disadvantage	3.68	35	0.0000
2 Cost of data collection and processing	2.78	45	0.0033
3 Cost of auditing	2.36	49	0.7048
4 Possibility of claims from employers/trade unions	2.27	45	0.7600
5 Threat of takeover	2.24	54	0.2765
6 Cost of publication	2.12	50	0.7811
7 Technical processing problems	2.07	51	0.4025
8 Possibility of intervention by government agencies	1.96	58	0.1462
9 Possibility of claims from political/consumer groups	1.83	51	0.7890
10 Possibility of intervention by taxation authorities	1.80	57	

Range = 1-5
1 = not at all
5 = large extent

Table 7.7 British multinationals' information disclosure items involving major competitive disadvantage

Rank		Mean (n = 116)	Coefficient of variation (%)	Wilcoxon test prob.
1	Quantitative forecasts of sales and profits	4.01	29	
				0.1632
2	Profits by line of business (narrowly defined)	3.81	33	
				0.3013
3	Company objectives, plans, policies for next year	3.69	34	
				0.2195
4	Profits by geographical area (narrowly defined)	3.50	40	
				0.3714
5	Sales by line of business (narrowly defined)	3.42	41	
				0.0000
6	Description of major patents	3.06	52	
				0.0000
7 =	Plans for future capital expenditure	3.04	44	
				0.8789
7 =	Description of major legal proceedings	3.04	44	
				0.6778
9	Sales by geographical area (narrowly defined)	2.97	48	
				0.9864
10	Statement of company prospects in qualitative terms	2.95	44	

Range = 1-5
1 = not at all
5 = large extent

net costs from the perspective of a majority of companies. However, this was the view taking *all* respondents together, i.e. including both voluntary and non-disclosing companies. In fact, there was a substantial range of views with net benefits perceived by a significant number of companies for most items.

The top ten items perceived to give rise to the highest net benefits, or lowest net costs, included (in rank order): the description of major new products, the description of organisational structure, segmental information provided on a broadly defined basis, and qualitative information about prospects and capital expenditure projects in progress (see Table 7.9). On the other hand, the top ten disclosure items apparently giving rise to the highest net costs, or lowest net benefits, included (in rank order): segmental information on a narrowly defined basis, quantitative forecasts of sales and profits, information about major legal proceedings, inflation adjusted profits, amounts of transfers between segments, description of major patents, and quarterly interim reports (see Table 7.10).

A further analysis of the perceived net benefits of additional disclosures is necessary to assess the extent to which multinationals purporting to make voluntary disclosures (eighty-three companies) take a different view from the non-disclosers (thirty-three companies). In this way, items which may be susceptible to voluntary disclosure can be identified. A series of t test and chi-square tests were carried out to assess differences between the two groups for all thirty-four items of information disclosure ranked in terms of perceived net benefits. The chi-square tests were also used as an alternative to t tests in recognition of the possibility of measurement weaknesses which could make the results of t tests unreliable. From these tests it is evident that while the differences are all in the expected direction, there are also some areas of information disclosure where broadly similar views are held. Table 7.11 shows the responses and results in respect of items where there is *disagreement* about the perceived net benefits/costs of disclosure.

A major finding is that there is disagreement about the relative advantages of disclosing segmental information even on a broadly defined basis, with non-disclosing multinationals showing significantly less enthusiasm. Other items of disagreement, in order of perceived net benefits, relate to the description of major new capital expenditure projects in progress, the amount of exchange differences from translation, value added statements, the amount of research and development expenditure, plans for future capital expenditure, foreign short-term debt analysed by currency, and the amount of lease commitments. While there are some further differences in perception, it would seem that the overall view of the net costs involved may not necessarily suggest significant differences in disclosure behaviour in practice. These items in rank order are: the amount of foreign assets subject to high political risks, quarterly

Table 7.8 British multinationals information disclosure items involving major production costs

Rank	Mean (n = 116)	Coefficient of variation (%)	Wilcoxon test prob.
1 Inflation adjusted profits	3.67	31	
			0.2079
2 Quarterly interim reports	3.46	36	
			0.0018
3 Profits by line of business (narrowly defined)	3.03	44	
			0.1031
4 Sales by line of business (narrowly defined)	2.96	44	
			0.4347
5 Employment information	2.87	35	
			0.6982
6 Quantitative forecasts of sales and profits	2.86	51	
			0.2931
7 Profits by geographical area (narrowly defined)	2.80	48	
			0.4940
8 Amount of transfers between lines of business	2.75	48	
			0.1515
9 Sales by geographical area (narrowly defined)	2.70	46	
			0.7567
10 Amount of transfers between geographical areas	2.67	46	

Range = 1-5
1 = not at all
5 = large extent

Table 7.9 British multinationals, top ten disclosure items involving lowest net costs/highest net benefits

	1 Major net costs	2	3	4 Matching of costs and benefits	5	6	7 Major net benefits
1 Description of major new products	5%	21%	26%	16%	20%	11%	1%
2 Description of organisational structure	4	11	36	30	11	6	2
3 = Sales by geographical area (broadly defined)	4	15	40	25	7	7	2
3 = Description of major new capital expenditure projects in progress	4	24	29	18	12	12	1
5 Sales by line of business (broadly defined)	3	20	40	18	9	6	4
6 Profits by geographical area (broadly defined)	8	15	39	21	7	8	2
7 Profits by line of business (broadly defined)	7	22	34	19	7	7	4
8 = Description of major environmental projects	2	22	38	24	9	3	2
8 = Statement of prospects in qualitative terms	14	18	28	14	13	12	1
10 Amount of exchange differences from translation	2	17	50	26	4	0	1

interim reports, the description of major patents, segmental profits on a narrowly defined basis, and inflation adjusted profits.

These results indicate the kind of disclosures items which are more likely to be considered relatively beneficial by multinationals. They also indicate those items which would be more easily accepted in a regulatory framework, if considered desirable, and those which would meet with the most opposition. The least controversial items, as shown in Table 7.9, include the description of major new products, the description of organisation structure, the description of major new capital expenditure projects in progress, the description of major environmental projects and employment information. In contrast, as shown in Table 7.10, segmental information narrowly defined, quantitative forecasts of sales and profits, the description of major legal proceedings, the amounts of transfers between segments, and the description of major patents are items likely to arouse substantial opposition from multinationals.

Further explanations of disclosure behaviour

The differences in perceptions between disclosing and non-disclosing multinationals concerning the net costs or benefits of voluntary disclosure are confirmed by reference to the awareness of benefits by disclosing companies in the context of market and political pressures and by perceived differences in the costs of disclosure with special reference to competitive disadvantage and production costs.

But are there any major corporate factors underlying these differences which might help to confirm or add to our understanding of voluntary disclosure behaviour? To what extent are variables such as corporate size, profitability, capital structure, multinationality, and industrial sector important explanatory variables? In an attempt to explore these questions the companies were initially divided into two groups; those that reported no voluntary information at all (thirty-three companies) and those that reported at least some voluntary information (eighty-three companies). The Mann-Whitney U test was then applied to these two groups to assess differences in terms of the variables identified. The results are reported in Table 7.12, from which it appears that size, as measured by both turnover and tangible assets, is significantly and positively associated with the disclosing companies. However, trading profit/turnover representing profitability is also significant, but only at the 0.102 level, while the debt/equity ratio representing capital structure is significant at the 0.046 level. Both of these variables are positively associated with the companies making voluntary disclosures. However, none of the variables reflecting the extent of multinationality, i.e. percentage of foreign turnover and index of geographical diversification are significant. These results are largely supported by those using the

Table 7.10 British multinationals' top ten disclosure items involving highest net costs/lowest net benefits

Rank		1 2 3 Major net costs			4 5 Matching of costs and benefits		6	7 Major net benefits
1	Profits by line of business (narrowly defined)	32%	34%	22%	5%	4%	3%	0%
2	Quantitative forecasts of sales and profits	32	32	24	5	5	1	1
3	Description of major legal proceedings	19	42	32	6	1	0	0
4 =	Sales by line of business (narrowly defined)	25	38	27	3	5	2	0
4 =	Inflation adjusted profits	27	49	11	2	4	6	1
6	Amount of transfers between lines of business	20	36	35	9	0	0	0
a7	Profits by geographical area (narrowly defined)	27	35	21	11	3	3	0
8	Description of major patents	17	34	40	7	2	0	0
9	Amount of transfers between geographical areas	14	37	37	12	0	0	0
10	Quarterly interim Reports	24	41	16	8	5	5	1

Table 7.11 British multinationals' disagreements about
perceived net benefits of information disclosures

Overall ranking of net benefits	Item	Voluntary disclosers mean (n = 83)	coeff. of var. (%)	Non disclosers mean (n = 33)	coeff. of var. (%)	t prob.	X^2 prob.
1	Description of major new products	3.7108	48	3.3030	48	0.127	0.0039
2	Description of organisational structure	3.5663	38	3.2424	42	0.125	0.0223
3 =	Sales by geographical area (broadly defined)	3.5422	40	3.0606	45	0.049	0.0137
4	Description of major new capital expenditure projects in progress	3.4337	46	3.1212	47	0.164	0.0047
5	Sales by line of business (broadly defined)	3.6506	43	2.9091	46	0.009	0.0095
6	Profits by geographical area (broadly defined)	3.4217	45	2.8788	40	0.034	0.0007
7	Profits by line of business (broadly defined)	3.5301	49	2.8182	47	0.017	0.0000
10	Amount of exchange differences from translation	3.2651	34	2.8182	37	0.025	0.0000
11	Value added statement	3.3494	44	2.6970	53	0.015	0.0078

Table 7.11 Continued

Overall ranking of net benefits	Item	Voluntary disclosers mean coeff. (n = 83) of var. (%)		Non disclosers mean coeff. (n = 33) of var. (%)		t prob.	X² prob.
13 =	Foreign LT debt analysed by currency	3.2892	36	2.5455	38	0.001	0.0543
13 =	Amount of R & D expenditure	3.4940	50	3.0000	33	0.029	0.0001
15	Plans for future capital expenditure	3.1084	51	2.9697	51	0.335	0.0058
17	Foreign ST debt analysed by currency	3.1325	39	2.6061	52	0.041	0.0016
18	Amount of lease commitments	3.0723	40	2.6364	36	0.034	0.0052
22	Amount of foreign assets subject to high political risks	2.7349	50	2.3636	45	0.082	0.0010
25	Quarterly interim reports	2.5542	64	2.0909	61	0.073	0.0011
27	Description of major patents	2.7831	66	2.6061	39	0.256	0.0185
28	Profits by geographical area (narrowly defined)	2.2892	58	2.2424	46	0.428	0.0012
30	Inflation adjusted profits	2.2771	53	2.0606	50	0.185	0.0016
34	Profits by line of business (narrowly defined)	2.2771	53	2.0606	50	0.185	0.0016

Range = 1-7
1 = major net costs
7 = major net benefits

Table 7.12 British multinationals' voluntary disclosure behaviour:
analysis of explanatory variables

	Mann-Whitney z value	probability	Chi-Square X^2 value	probability
Turnover	2.365	0.009	27.366	0.003
Tangible Net Assets	2.002	0.022	20.808	0.026
Trading Profit /Turnover	1.267	0.102	19.167	0.042
Debt/Equity Ratio	1.677	0.046	13.061	0.182
Percentage Foreign Sales	0.136	0.446	6.395	0.447
Geographical Diversification Index	0.054	0.478	10.615	0.281
Industry	-	-	16.924	0.076

chi-square test. The advantage of this test is that it compares not just the two groups of companies used in the Mann-Whitney test but facilitates grouping the companies into five groups reflecting the extent of voluntary information disclosure that the companies perceive themselves to make. The independent variables were classified into four quartiles. The test results are also reported in Table 7.12. Again, the variables that appear to have major discriminating power are the two size variables. The debt/equity ratio is no longer significant. However, trading profit/turnover becomes relatively more significant at the 0.042 level. As regards industry influences, the industry classification used was a four-way classification of capital goods, consumer goods, other groups and commodity groups, based upon the Stock Exchange Index. Industrial sector did appear to be a significant factor based upon this form of sectoral analysis, indicating that the capital goods sector is positively associated with more disclosure, but only at the 0.076 level.

The significance of corporate size, supported to a lesser extent by profitability, industrial sector, and capital structure, as variables to explain voluntary disclosures would seem to support the evidence from the survey of opinions about the influence of market and political pressures. The importance of size is consistent with the idea that larger firms attempt to reduce political costs (e.g. Watts and Zimmerman 1978), that they are more visible in the market and so more exposed to pressure especially from financial analysts, and that they have both lower competitive disadvantage costs and lower information production costs. While the lack of significance of the extent of multinationality is, perhaps, surprising in the light of pressures from international organisations for extensions in disclosure it is nevertheless consistent with the stock market emphasis of financial communications evident in most companies.

Conclusions

This empirical study of corporate perceptions of the costs and benefits of voluntary disclosure by British multinationals provides confirmation of the existence of market and political pressures as major factors, which both encourage and constrain voluntary disclosure behaviour in a complex interactive process, where corporate management influences and is influenced by its environment.

Taken overall, stock market pressures would appear to dominate political pressures in encouraging voluntary disclosures. Such disclosures are designed primarily to project a company's image and enhance its market reputation. However, a number of cost constraints are involved in limiting disclosures. In particular, the indirect costs of competitive disadvantage would appear to weigh heavily in the disclosure policy decision.

This analysis is supported by an examination of major corporate factors underlying disclosure policy. Perhaps the most important variable is corporate size, with profitability and industrial sector also influential in the disclosure process. The extent of multinationality does not, however, help to explain differences in disclosure behaviour. It would seem, therefore, that British multinationals are not, in general, sensitive to the international dimension. This is supported by the perceived lack of importance of the IASC, OECD and UN in relation to other factors in formulating policy and influencing voluntary disclosures in practice.

The results of the study also provide insights into the specific items of information likely to be disclosed voluntarily and the reasons for doing so in terms of the perceived balance of costs and benefits involved. In particular, it is clear that certain kinds of information disclosure, e.g. quantitative forecasts and segmental information narrowly defined, are generally perceived to give rise to major net costs. An appreciation of these cost-benefit perceptions should help all interested parties to better understand voluntary disclosure behaviour in practice and to predict the likely response to proposals to extend disclosure regulation.

Appendix: British multinationals' information disclosure items in questionnaire survey

Inflation adjusted profits	Amount of transfers between geographical segments	Value added statement
Description of major patents with expiry dates	Amount of transfers between product or line of business segments	Description of major new products
Amount of R & D expenditure	Sales disaggregated by line of business (broadly defined)	Description of major new capital expenditure projects in progress
Amount of advertising expenditure		Plans for future capital expenditure
Amounts of lease commitments	Sales disaggregated by line of business (narrowly defined)	Description of major organisational structure
Amount of exchange differences from translation	Profit disaggregated by line of business (broadly defined)	Description of major environmental projects
Amount of exchange differences from transactions	Profit disaggregated by line of business (narrowly defined)	Description of major legal proceedings
Amount of foreign assets analysed by individual country	Sales disaggregated by geographical area (broadly defined)	Company objectives plans and policies for next year
Amount of foreign assets analysed by continent or grouping of countries	Sales disaggregated by geographical area (narrowly defined)	Statement of company prospects in qualitative terms
Amount of foreign assets subject to high political risks	Profit disaggregated by geographical area (broadly defined)	Quantitative forecasts of sales and profits
Amount of foreign LT debt analysed by currency	Profit disaggregated by geographical area (narrowly defined)	Interim reports on a quarterly basis

| Amount of foreign ST debt analysed by currency | Employment information e.g. training, pensions, safety |

References

Choi, F.D.S. and Mueller, G.G., *International Accounting* (Prentice Hall International, 1984).

Gray, S.J., with McSweeney, L.B. and Shaw, J.C., *Information Disclosure and the the Multinational Corporation* (John Wiley and Sons, 1984).

Jensen, M.C. and Meckling, W.H., Theory of the Firm: Managerial Behaviour, Agency Costs and Ownership Structure, *Journal of Financial Economics* (October 1976) pp. 305-60.

Kelly, L., The Development of a Positive Theory of Corporate Management's Role in External Financial Reporting, *Journal of Accounting Literature* (1983) pp. 111-50.

Mautz, R.K. and May, W.G., *Financial Disclosure in a Competitive Economy* (Financial Executives Research Foundation, 1978).

McKinnon, S.M., A Cost-benefit Study of Disclosure Requirements for Multinational Corporations, *Journal of Business Finance and Accounting* (Winter 1984) pp. 451-68.

Ronen, J, and Livnat, J., Incentives for Segment Reporting, *Journal of Accounting Research* (Autumn 1981) pp. 459-81.

Watts, R.L., Corporate Financial Statements: A Product of the Market and Political Processes, *Australian Journal of Management* (April 1977) pp. 53-75.

Watts, R.L. and Zimmerman, J.L., Towards a Positive Theory of the Determination of Accounting Standards, *The Accounting Review* (January 1978) pp. 112-34.

Watts, R.L. and Zimmerman, J.L., *Positive Accounting Theory* (Prentice Hall International, 1986).

Comparative Experiences

8
The United Kingdom Response to International Pressures for Accounting Change

Geoffrey B. Mitchell[1]

In many areas the United Kingdom has achieved a significant influence over the affairs of the world. This is also true of accountancy where United Kingdom practitioners, and lately academics, have been very influential and in the forefront of developments. The United Kingdom has been and is an active player in accounting change, and so any discussion of the United Kingdom's role must be seen in the context of the United Kingdom's input to that change as well as its response to any external pressure for change.

In the fifteenth and sixteenth centuries, the United Kingdom received and adopted the simple and straightforward double entry method of accounting from the Italian states. As United Kingdom influence increased throughout the world in the eighteenth and nineteenth centuries, accounting and, more importantly, United Kingdom accountants were exported to record and help watch over investments. The influence was greatest in those countries in which there was a common language or where there were political ties. The United Kingdom can reasonably claim to have been the major influence in Canada and the United States in the nineteenth century and in the rest of the Commonwealth in the first sixty years of the twentieth century. But, with some delay, political independence was also followed by independence of thought and action.

In more recent times, when formal United Kingdom influence has fallen significantly in the United States and in the Commonwealth, a new area for United Kingdom influence has been established through membership of the European Economic Community. The United Kingdom Government, fully supported by the profession, has set out to influence the development and content of the EEC Directives which directly affect the United Kingdom accountancy profession (Fourth, Seventh and Eighth Directives on Company Law).

In addition, the United Kingdom Profession has had significant

---

[1]Geoffrey B. Mitchell is Technical Director at the ICAEW; the views expressed are his own.

influence on the major accounting standards coming from the International Accounting Standards Committee (IASC), even though they have not all been taken up in the United Kingdom.

These more recent influences have occurred during a time of change in accounting policy-making in the United Kingdom. New institutional structures have emerged which have provided a context in which international pressures might also be able to influence United Kingdom accounting.

In the late 1960s, United Kingdom accountants were under attack for permitting major companies a wide choice of accounting policies. After some public debate and controversy, the Accounting Standards Committee (ASC) was formed in 1970. The pressures were internal to the United Kingdom and the solution chosen was to form an 'independent' and professional group of experts to set down best practice and to require auditors to note the departures from that best practice which were not otherwise explained.

Such institutional developments were not confined to the United Kingdom however. In 1973, in the United States the Financial Accounting Standards Board (FASB) was formed to replace the Accounting Principles Board (APB), and internationally, the IASC was formed to replace the Accountants International Study Group (AISG). Also in that year the United Kingdom joined the EEC, which meant that United Kingdom professionals would join with their European colleagues to agree a Fourth Directive. (The Fourth Directive was finally implemented in the United Kingdom by the Companies Act 1981.)

The following discussion focusses on the period since the formation of the Accounting Standards Committee. It looks at accounting change in the United Kingdom through the development of accounting standards by the ASC, and considers the extent to which these statements have been influenced by international factors.

Overview of the United Kingdom standard setting process

Accounting practice in the United Kingdom is determined by company law and accounting standards. The ASC produces standards, which represent best accounting practice, through a process of public consultation and open debate aimed at achieving consensus and public acceptance.

The ASC is a private sector body, financed by the six United Kingdom accountancy bodies, charged with the responsibility of acting in the public interest. There is a fine line between achieving a consensus and reflecting best practice, and providing leadership and allowing innovation. The ASC sees itself as having an educational role leading to improved financial reporting. Also, the ASC often has to persuade its many constituencies that what it proposes is in fact an improvement on the status quo. The ASC receives input from preparers and users of financial statements, from government and other regulators, from academics and other interested observers and from overseas and international standard-setting bodies.

The ASC comprises, in the main, professional accountants appointed for their experience in practice. They include preparers from both the public and private sectors, auditors and academics. Recently, non-accountants have been appointed representing users from the banking and investment management industries. In addition, several non-voting observers sit at the table and freely join in the debates. They include representatives from Government, the Auditing Practices Committee (APC) and the United Kingdom and Irish representatives who sit on international committees.

The ASC has a full-time staff of four professional accountants who act as secretaries for the small working parties who are given the responsibility to prepare outlines and drafts. A working party reports to the ASC several times during the life of a project – with a discussion paper, a preliminary exposure draft, an exposure draft and a proposed standard. The exposure draft is published and comments are invited from all interested parties and the general public; the comments are on public record.

Before it can be approved, a standard must receive the votes of at least three-quarters of the members of the ASC. Finally, it must also be approved by each of the six sponsoring bodies.

The ASC is also permitted to publish, without the direct approval of its sponsoring bodies, non-mandatory material such as discussion papers, handbooks and Statements of Recommended Practice (SORPs). SORPs are issued on subjects which are not considered appropriate for an accounting standard at the time, or which relate to specific industries or sectors, including the public sector. SORPs cannot contradict or extend the scope of an existing accounting standard. They are intended, rather, to be indicative of the treatment which should be adopted in situations not specifically covered by accounting standards.

True and fair

The Companies Act requires that financial statements give a 'true and fair view'. The term is not defined and has no precise meaning. The law prescribes certain requirements and leaves it to other means, such as accounting standards, to fill in the detail, although law makers do not necessarily accept that accounting standards are conclusive in determining a true and fair view.

The United Kingdom approach relies on judgement. First comply with the specific requirements of the Companies Act, second provide such additional information as is necessary in order to show a true and fair view, and then, if the results still do not show a true and fair view, make such changes as are necessary in order to present a true and fair view, and disclose the changes and their effects.

The existence of prescribed practices is essential for comparability, but is not the overriding objective. Rather, the overriding requirement is that the accounts present a true and fair view. Therefore, a departure from an accounting standard is not just desirable, but essential in particular circumstances. Where a company necessarily departs from an accounting standard in order to give a true and fair view and this is disclosed and the auditor concurs, there is no need for the auditor to refer to this departure in his report.

Even though accounting standards are not conclusive as to the presentation of a true and fair view, they are nevertheless highly influential and persuasive in that respect. There is a presumption that accounts which depart from accounting standards will not give a true and fair view. This is why it is necessary for the company to justify any departure from accounting standards in the notes.

Unjustified non-compliance with accounting standards by a member of an accountancy body may be acted upon through the various investigation and disciplinary procedures of the particular body.

UK accounting standards

In this section each of the SSAPs and SORPs issued by the ASC as at 30 September 1986 will be considered with a view to identifying the influences which led both to the need for the development of the standard and to the choice of the solution within the standard. There may be more than one influence in each situation. The major influences can be classified as:

1. Internal to the United Kingdom – matters (other than changes in law) which have led to public debate and concern which, in turn, have led to their consideration by ASC.
2. United Kingdom law – changes in United Kingdom law which have required guidance from ASC.
3. External – a development outside the United Kingdom which was of itself, or largely of itself, sufficient to lead the ASC to start work on the topic.

The major influences on the solutions adopted are: current United Kingdom practice; United Kingdom developed practice, i.e. developed specially for the particular topic in question; and foreign or international standards.

SSAP1 – Accounting for associated companies (effective 1/1/71)

The ASC's first standard was a statement on equity accounting. Of all the possible standards that a new standard setting body might wish to issue as its first, few would have chosen equity accounting. The selection was made because various treatments had grown up in the United Kingdom and had become the subject of controversy in the late 1960s. The solution agreed was consistent with the approach being developed in the United States at the same time (APB18 paragraph 17 and SSAP1 paragraphs 13–15 are very similar). The standard introduced the concept of 'significant influence' and provided a quantitative guide for its measurement (20 per cent or more of the equity voting rights of a company). It stands as one of the few standards with a quantitative guide for measurement.

The content of SSAP1 was then largely picked up in IAS3, 'Consolidated Financial Statements', which included the 20 per cent rule for significant influence. In doing this the United Kingdom acted as an intermediary by absorbing a US practice at a time of need and then, quite shortly after, participating in the transfer of that knowledge through the IASC.

SSAP2 – Disclosure of accounting policies (1/1/72)

Some commentators have argued that there is really a need for only one accounting standard – that the accounting policies used in the preparation of a set of financial statements be fully disclosed. Unlike APB22, which merely requires disclosure of accounting policies, SSAP2 identifies four fundamental accounting concepts (going concern, accruals, consistency and prudence), which are assumed to be observed unless there is a clear statement to the contrary. It also identifies accounting bases as methods developed for applying fundamental accounting concepts and accounting policies as the specific bases selected and used by a particular enterprise.

IASC followed but with only three fundamental assumptions (omitting prudence) and three basic concepts (prudence, substance over form and materiality). SSAP2 is currently being revised and consideration is being given to including a reference to substance over form. The United Kingdom does not seem to have absorbed the US concept of 'representational faithfulness'. The FASB has said that this concept 'leaves no room for accounting representations that subordinate substance to form' and that 'substance over form is a rather vague idea that defies precise definition' (FASB Statement of Concepts No.2 para. 160). I suggest that before 1970 the United Kingdom profession's view on issues, in which there was a choice, was to take a stand nearer to 'prudence' than to 'substance over form' than would have been taken in the United States.

But subsequent experience, and in particular the United Kingdom's joining the EEC, has moved thinking and it may now be acceptable to include 'substance over form' as a fundamental accounting concept to counter the growing view that 'prudence' should be the sole or dominant fundamental accounting concept.

SSAP3 – Earnings per share (1/1/73)

Taking an overview, one is also surprised that earnings per share (EPS) was dealt with at such an early stage by ASC. Like equity accounting, it set out to prescribe an acceptable approach to reduce the differences in practice which were current at the time. The calculation and display of earnings per share is capable of manipulation. The standard, although simple in concept, generated a considerable amount of debate, as a similar standard had done in the United States. IASC chose not to take up the topic because the information was not seen as being fundamental to general purpose financial reports. Rather, EPS is seen as a useful guide to performance and, especially in those countries with an active capital market, IASC believes that local guidance may be needed in those countries.

SSAP4 – The accounting treatment of government grants (1/1/75)

This standard was issued to provide guidance following the Industry Act 1972. It provided that capital-based grants should not be accounted for on the flow-through method. Rather, they should be taken to revenue over the expected useful life of the asset, either as a reduction in the cost of the asset or by the creation of a deferred credit (which was not to be treated as part of shareholders' funds). Again, the reason for the standard was internal to the United Kingdom and the solution achieved was simple and straightforward. The ASC did not suffer from the degree of political interference that was experienced in the United States on this subject. The APB had to issue APB4 in 1964 to reverse APB2 which was similar to SSAP4 and, further, in 1971 the US Congress vetoed a proposed US standard on accounting for investment credits which would have prohibited the flow-through method.

SSAP5 – Accounting for value added tax (1/1/75)

Again, this is a straightforward standard with the aim of achieving uniformity of accounting treatment for VAT. The standard was needed following the United Kingdom's admission to the EEC and the introduction of VAT. While there was thus an indirect European influence in the sense that the subject appeared on the ASC's agenda due to the tax change, the choice of standard accounting practice was internal to the United Kingdom.

SSAP6 – Extraordinary items and prior year adjustments (1/1/75)

This standard revisits the theme of setting down uniform procedures in an area in which there is a strong incentive for management systematically to use any lack of guidance to their advantage. SSAP6 conforms with APB9 (1966) and APB30 (1973).

Subsequently, IASC was not persuaded to adopt a profit and loss presentation format which required calculation of profit before extraordinary items; rather, IAS8 requires the identification of 'unusual' items which form part of the calculation of net income (IAS8, para.18).

SSAP7 – (Provisional)–Accounting for changes in the purchasing power of money (withdrawn January 1978)

A provisional standard was released in 1975 recommending a general purchasing power approach to accounting for changing prices. The standard was pre-empted by the Sandilands Committee whose views were very influential in the preparation of SSAP16 (see below).

SSAP8 – The treatment of taxation under the imputation system in the accounts of companies (1/1/75)

This standard provided guidance for companies following a change in the method of collecting corporation tax and the introduction of advance corporation tax (ACT). The standard required that irrecoverable ACT be written off immediately. The need for the standard came from the change in United Kingdom laws.

SSAP9 – Stocks and work-in-progress (1/1/76)

The standard requires that stocks and work-in-progress be recorded in a balance sheet at the lower of cost or net realisable value. This differs from the USA requirement in APB43 that stocks and work-in-progress be recorded at the lower of cost or current replacement cost. SSAP9 discourages LIFO but does not prohibit it.

Under SSAP9, work-in-progress was included in inventories in the balance sheet. If profit is taken reflecting the proportion of the work carried out, then part of the balance of work-in-progress will include this profit, i.e. the amount will be recorded above cost. This is clearly not in accordance with paragraph 22 of Schedule 4 of the Companies Act 1985 which says that, under historic cost accounting, 'the amount to be included in respect of any current asset shall be its purchase price or production cost'. However, as the amounts for debtors usually include a profit element and this is generally accepted (some say that paragraph 90 of Schedule 4 provides the necessary justification for this), the logical answer seems to be for any profit element to be shown as debtors and not as work-in-progress. Some companies in the construction industry are not happy with this proposal. They see a possibility that the Inland Revenue will want to tax them in the year that profit is recognised for accounting purposes, rather than in the year that the cash is received. They also believe that they will lose if stock relief is ever reintroduced.

Paragraph 91 of Schedule 4 makes it clear that profits can be realised, even if no cash has been received. Realised profits are 'such profits of a company as fall to be treated as realised profits for the purpose of those accounts in accordance with the principles generally accepted with respect to the determination for accounting purposes of realised profits'.

The problem of including profit in work-in-progress was created by the enactment of the Fourth Directive. The proposed solution satisfies the legal requirements, but without substantive changes, i.e. the totals for current assets and reported profits have not been changed.

SSAP10 – Statement of source and application of funds (1/1/76)

SSAP10 codified established practice. It does not apply to enterprises with a turnover of less than £25,000 per annum. This exemption is made possible because a statement of source and application of funds is not a requirement of the Companies Act.

SSAP11 – Accounting for deferred taxation (withdrawn October 1978)

Refer to the discussion under SSAP15 below.

SSAP12 – Accounting for depreciation (1/1/78)

SSAP12 was the first major standard to be issued by ASC following the issue of a standard on the same topic by IASC (IAS4). There was some concern in the United Kingdom about the relative timing and at first IAS4 was not readily available in the United Kingdom.

However, the standards are very similar. Both clearly stated that buildings should be depreciated. This led to representations from the investment property industry in the United Kingdom and eventually to SSAP19 'Accounting for investment properties', which created the first major difference between SSAPs and IASs.

At first the United Kingdom delegates to IASC found themselves in a minority of one on investment properties. Nevertheless, they continued to ask over a period of several years that investment properties be considered as a topic by IASC. Eventually they succeeded and investment properties have been dealt with in IAS25, 'Accounting for investments'.

SSAP13 – Accounting for research and development (1/1/78)

SSAP13 and IAS9 produced another difference. Although both required research to be written off as incurred and permitted the capitalisation of development costs, IAS9 required the disclosure of the total of research and development costs charged as expense and the movement in and the balance of any unamortised development costs, thus allowing the amount spent in the year to be calculated. SSAP13 only required the disclosure of movements of unamortised development expenditure during the year.

The ASC is at present (September 1988) considering whether it should require additional disclosures. The Government supports disclosure of research and development expenditure because it believes that substantial and sustained research and development expenditure is needed for long-term growth in the United Kingdom and disclosure would provide an incentive to research and also make it less likely for companies to reduce research and development expenditure merely to increase short term profits.

The response from industry has been mixed. Some argue that to disclose research and development expenditure may be damaging to commercial confidentiality. More companies seem to be writing off research and development as incurred (L.C.L. Skerratt and D.J. Tonkin, Financial Reporting 1985–86, ICAEW 1986, page 158) although over half the listed companies either do not say what they do or their accounts do not show any signs of research and development activity.

There is a view that the City discounts research and development expenditure and marks down companies that have a high research and development spending which makes them vulnerable to takeover. Another view is that high research and development, with a track record for profitable exploitation, is a good sign of future growth and should increase a company's rating.

There are also arguments of detail concerning the definition and measurement of research and development. In most other countries, and in international forums such as the OECD and the United Nations, the disclosure of research and development expenditure is not a controversial item. Here the United Kingdom profession has not taken the international view. Perhaps the Government will eventually feel that it must act and amend Schedule 4 of the Companies Act.

SSAP14 – Group accounts (1/1/79)

Group accounts have been required in the United Kingdom since 1948 and are largely governed by the Companies Act. The preamble to SSAP14 says that because of this, there had been no urgent need for a United Kingdom standard on the subject. However, with the issue of IAS3, the need was felt for a standard to clarify some of the issues.

In order to make progress, the EEC Fourth Directive did not apply to group accounts, which were made the subject of the Seventh Directive. The existence of SSAP14 and IAS3 provided a reference point for the discussions leading up to the Seventh Directive, which in the event was agreed in a form which will largely accommodate existing United Kingdom practice.

The international influence has, therefore, been largely outward, particularly towards the rest of the EEC through the Seventh Directive. Also, the 1948 Companies Act, including the provisions for group accounts, was followed by many Commonwealth countries.

SSAP15 – Accounting for deferred tax (1/1/79)

SSAP11 had originally provided for comprehensive tax allocation along the lines of APB11 although both the liability and deferral methods were permitted. The build up of large provisions for deferred taxation worried many United Kingdom companies. What, they asked, would happen if a Government said that these balances really represented future tax due to the Government but, because the commitment was deferred, the Government would take the value in shares in the companies instead of cash! Also, there was concern that the balances were rising very fast and, in many cases, becoming the largest number in the balance sheet and upsetting the norms for evaluation. Others argued that the benefits of lower tax charges, which under usual assumptions were resulting in deferred tax balances which would never have to be repaid, were not being properly reflected in the profit and loss account. The result of these discussions was to introduce, through SSAP15, the partial method of accounting for deferred tax.

The pressures were internal to the United Kingdom. SSAP15 had unfortunate consequences for larger firms who had to comply with both US and United Kingdom accounting standards. The differences, both in the profit and loss for a year and in the balance sheet numbers, could be significant.

At the suggestion of the United Kingdom, the IASC set up a working party to consider the issues, made up of representatives from the FASB, the Dutch standard-setting body and the ASC, under an independent chairman from France. No standard-setting body wishes it to be thought that it reacts to pressure from another standard-setting body. Nevertheless the FASB has put the topic of deferred taxes back onto its list for consideration. There are early signs that the FASB will amend APB11 to require accounting for deferred taxes on a comprehensive basis but using the liability method. Some observers believe that if the FASB does this they will have to allow partial allocation at some future time. The argument is based on the definition of liabilities in Concept Statement No. 2. ('Liabilities are probable future sacrifices of economic benefits arising from present obligations of a particular entity to transfer assets or provide services to other entities in the future as a result of past transactions'. Concept Statement No. 3 para. 28.)

SSAP16 – Current cost accounting (1/1/80)

SSAP16 replaced the provisional standard based on a general indexing approach (SSAP7) and was the result of a major effort by the United Kingdom profession. This was the first occasion on which many academics played a major role in the development of a standard, both in the generation of ideas and in the public debates on the various proposals.

The United Kingdom profession took the 'lead' internationally with SSAP16. The pressure to reject SSAP7 and produce a standard on current cost accounting (CCA) came first from the Government but became self-generating within the profession. The enthusiasm for accounting for the effects of changing prices was also marked by vocal opposition and resulted in two extraordinary meetings of members of the ICAEW, each producing a result by a narrow margin – one in favour of mandatory reporting of the effects of changing prices and one against.

In the end, SSAP16 failed because it did not provide universal answers for (a) determining the current cost depreciation charge in times of rapid technological (or other) change and (b) the monetary adjustment.

The mood has so turned against SSAP16 that it is doubtful if any statement in favour of reporting the effects of changing prices would now get support from preparers, auditors or Government. But conditions change quickly. Who can predict what the mood will be in a year's time?

It is likely that, if the topic is reconsidered again in the near future, consideration will be given to a simplified and more objective approach, at least as an alternative.

SSAP17 – Accounting for post balance sheet events (1/1/81) and

SSAP18 – Accounting for contingencies (1/1/81)

Again, these standards were needed to prevent companies from exploiting any doubts or uncertainties in existing practice. The standards conform with IAS10 and FAS8.

SSAP19 – Accounting for investment properties (1/7/81)

This standard represents a United Kingdom development and resulted from pressures from the investment property industry following their dissatisfaction with SSAP12. The concept of 'investment properties' has been exported internationally through IAS25.

SSAP20 – Foreign currency translation (1/4/83)

Many United Kingdom companies had tried to absorb the standard US practice from FAS8, the temporal method. It seemed to follow logically from historical cost accounting. However, following the large movements in foreign currency exchange rates which occurred in the 1970s, many companies found that they were reporting consolidated results which were counter-intuitive and not in accordance with the underlying economic conditions. Further, because the temporal method was not mandatory in the United Kingdom, some companies were not using it and therefore disclosing vastly different results in the United States and the United Kingdom. In addition, some US companies, which did not have any choice, started to engage in foreign currency speculation, which they would not otherwise have done, in order to protect their reported profits.

The ASC, the Canadian Institute of Chartered Accountants (CICA) and the FASB, together with IASC, jointly considered the question and reached an accord on the closing rate/net investment method. Each proceeded to write up a standard in its own way. The result was a major event in harmonisation of accounting standards.

This accord created problems, however. The representatives from some European countries were concerned about not being included in the discussions. This could have led to the break-up of IASC. Fortunately, the IASC Board agreed that its members should not hold bilateral, or multilateral, discussions without the presence of an IASC observer (unless, of course, they share common legislation) and the problem was resolved.

The pressures for change in the United Kingdom and the United States came from European multinational companies. They were supported by many US companies who saw the advantages of the closing rate/net investment method, especially during a period in which the US dollar was gaining ground. The ASC was an active agent in promoting the change and largely achieved what it wanted. SSAP20 represents a high point in the technical output and influence of the ASC. FAS52 and IAS21 were published at approximately the same time as SSAP20.

SSAP21 – Accounting for leases and hire purchase contracts (1/7/84)

SSAP21 followed FAS13 and was introduced because of the large increase in the value of leasing business written in the United Kingdom. SSAP21 and IAS17 were prepared at the same time and the working parties which prepared the draft for ASC and IASC had the same Chairman (Mr Paul Rutteman). As a controlled experiment, any differences must reflect the different approaches of the two committees.

IAS17 is simple and straightforward. A finance lease is 'a lease that transfers substantially all the risks and rewards incident to ownership of an asset; title may or may not eventually be transferred'. It is left to the judgement of the preparer and auditor to decide each particular case.

SSAP21, on the other hand, continues the definition to say 'It should be presumed that such a transfer of risks and rewards occurs if at the inception of the lease the present value of the minimum lease payments, including any initial payment, amounts to substantially all (normally 90 per cent or more) of the fair value of the leased asset'. This effectively leaves the choice to the lessee!

SSAP22 – Accounting for goodwill (1/1/85)

The United Kingdom has adopted, as preferred policy, the idea that purchased goodwill should be written off immediately against reserves. Alternatively, companies can amortise goodwill through the profit and loss account. Needless to say, most companies prefer the immediate write-off option, which is not available in the United States (APB17). The pressures leading to this solution were largely from United Kingdom companies.

SSAP23 – Accounting for acquisitions and mergers (1/4/85)

United States practice had permitted pooling of interests for some time (APB16, 1970), and its application had been without controversy. Pooling had not been a common practice in the United Kingdom, but the Companies Act 1981 provided for 'merger relief' where at least 90 per cent of a company was acquired for shares (Companies Act 1985, Section 131).

The ASC was faced with a dilemma. Should it prohibit pooling, or should it set out proper rules, given that pooling appeared to be permitted under the Companies Act? The latter view held. But, before the ink was dry on SSAP23, merchant banks were promoting schemes for taking advantage of its provisions. (Vendor placings is a typical device.)

The pressure for a standard was internal within the United Kingdom and generated by legislation. The approach adopted was similar to the US approach, which is also permitted by IAS22.

SORP1 – Pension scheme accounting (1/5/86)

This statement, which is non-mandatory as far as the accounting bodies themselves are concerned, was prompted partly by the impending Social Security Act 1985. The regulations to that Act require the inclusion of a note to Pension Scheme accounts explaining whether or not the accounts have been prepared in accordance with parts 2 to 4 of the SORP (the sections on definitions and recommended practice).

The SORP differs from IAS 26 'Accounting for retirement benefit plans' because it does not require the quantification and disclosure of the present value of promised future benefits. The United Kingdom approach is to leave the actuary to say whether or not the plan is properly funded and, if it is not, to state his advice on how to make good the deficiency (e.g. to specify the increased contributions needed, as a percentage of wages and salaries). Internationally, the IAS and US views are that the liability should be quantified and disclosed so that the reader can make his own judgement.

Other international influences

The Appendix lists the standards produced by the IASC where there is no United Kingdom standard and offers a brief explanation in each case.

Summary of influences on United Kingdom standards

The influences described in the above consideration of individual standards are summarised in Tables 8.1 and 8.2 (pages 160-1). Table 8.1 identifies influences which led the ASC to consider particular topics and Table 8.2 identifies sources of influence on the choice of standard accounting practice.

Conclusion

The overall impression, if one accepts the classifications in Tables 8.1 and 8.2, is that there has been little external influence on ASC's agenda or even on the methods finally adopted by the ASC.

Six accounting standards have been developed as the result of legislation and three in conjunction with the IASC, one of which was also in conjunction with the FASB. The rest have resulted from internal United Kingdom pressures for guidance. Interestingly, the solutions have been, more often than not, a codification of best existing United Kingdom practice or have been developed in the United Kingdom with little or no reference to external standards. Where a standard has followed a foreign standard it has usually also represented best United Kingdom practice at the time. The foreign standards that have been followed are APB Statements, International Accounting Standards and surprisingly few FASB Standards.

Does this mean that the United Kingdom has been unaware of the FASB's programme or that the FASB's work has mainly been concentrated on questions which are specific to the United States? The FASB inherited from the APB a rich collection of basic accounting statements which has left it free to tackle the major problems of the day, as seen from the US perspective. On the other hand, the ASC was starting from scratch and had to build up a set of basic standards. The FASB, unlike the ASC, has had to deal with quite detailed requirements because the FASB places a higher priority on comparability. The ASC, on the other hand, has stayed with the broad issues.

It is also interesting to note the small influence from EEC law to date. Perhaps this reflects the lead time in the standard-setting process rather than the eventual impact of the EEC on United Kingdom accounting practice. More impact may come through the implementation of the Seventh and other Directives.

The conclusion must be that, to date, the United Kingdom has responded mainly to internal pressures for change. International pressures have yet to cause a major reaction. The work completed by the IASC is considered by the ASC but the priorities reflect internal pressures.

The structure and due process of the ASC mean that its members look first to current internal problems and have no reason to take a broader view, unless the external pressures are also being felt internally. The same is true of other national standard setting bodies. The United Kingdom has often looked at and adapted accepted overseas solutions. But often the underlying circumstances have led to innovations which in turn have influenced overseas practice.

The United Kingdom response to international pressure for accounting change has been minimal, whereas United Kingdom involvements in international developments have been significant.

Appendix

The Appendix lists the IASC's Standards and current projects for which there is no United Kingdom Standard and offers a brief explanation or comment in each case.

Standards

IAS5   Information to be disclosed in financial statements. This is covered by the Companies Act.

IAS13   Presentation of current assets and current liabilities. This is covered by the Companies Act.

IAS14   Reporting financial information by segment. Although there is no United Kingdom standard, some information is required by the Stock Exchange and the Companies Act.

IAS16   Property, plant and equipment. ASC has a current project on assets and revaluations.

IAS18   Revenue recognition. Most United Kingdom companies comply with the provisions of IAS18 automatically. No standard is planned at this time.

IAS19   Accounting for retirement benefits in the financial statements of employers. An exposure draft (ED39) is being considered and a standard is expected in the new year. The approach is likely to be far less prescriptive than that proposed by the FASB.

         (Editor's note: The standard was issued in May 1988 as SSAP24 - Accounting for Pension Costs.)

IAS23   Capitalisation of borrowing costs. There is no specific United Kingdom standard on this matter.

IAS24   Related party disclosures. There is no United Kingdom standard, although work is progressing towards a standard.

IAS25   Accounting for investments. SSAP19 deals with part of the standard and the remainder is consistent with United Kingdom practice.

Other IASC projects

Accounting in highly inflationary economies.

         Hopefully the United Kingdom will not have to implement this standard.

Objectives of a general purpose financial statement, owners equity, liabilities and deferred credits.

         These are building block statements. Apart from *The Corporate Report* (1975), the ASC has not promoted conceptual studies. Perhaps, with the completion of the FASB's conceptual framework project for the time being, the ASC might support a United Kingdom study to see if any lessons can be learned from the US experience.

Disclosures in Financial Statements of banks.

         An EEC Banks Directive is currently being negotiated. It will eventually lead to United Kingdom legislation. Hence, the ASC does not see a need for work on this project ahead of the completion of the Directive. It is interesting to note that IASC has come out strongly against hidden reserves. The United Kingdom is a major player both in the development of the Directive and the IASC standard. There is a high probability that there will be another important success in international harmonisation with this topic.

**Table 8.1 Influences leading to the
development of a standard**

	Internal	United Kingdom law	External
SSAP 1	X		
2	X		
3	X		
4		Industry Act 1972	
5		Finance Acts	
6	X		
8		Finance Acts	
9	X		
10	X		
12	X		IASC
13	X		
14	X		IASC
15	X		
16	X		
17	X		
18	X		
19	X		
20			FASB and IASC
21	X		
22		Companies Act 1981	Fourth Directive
23		Companies Act 1981	Fourth Directive
SORP1		Social Security Act 1985	

**Table 8.2 Major influences on the method proposed
by each standard**

	Current United Kingdom practice	United Kingdom developed practice	Foreign standard
SSAP 1	X		APB18
2	X		APB22
3		X	
4		X	
5		X	
6		X	APB30
8		X	
9		X	APB43
10		X	
12		X	IAS4
13		X	
14		X	IAS3
15		X	
16		X	
17		X	FAS8 IAS10
18		X	FAS8 IAS10
19		X	
20		X	FAS52 IAS21
21		X	FAS13 IAS17
22		X	
23		X	
SORP1		X	

9

Accounting Standardisation in France and International Accounting Exchanges

Jean-Claude Scheid[1]/Peter Standish[2]

The theme of international pressures for accounting change directs attention to the interest groups or nations demanding change and to the groups or nations expected to change. It therefore directs attention to the economic consequences of this process and its resulting gains and losses. In other words, it expresses an essentially competitive process rather than, for example, international collaboration in research, unconcerned with resulting economic advantage.

This is an appropriately realistic view of the world of accounting and financial information, in which there are large prizes to be won in terms of international accounting practice, access to international clients and the commercialisation of computer software and financial information products (e.g. financial analysis services). Although this is the reality of international pressures for accounting change, a bystander might be forgiven for failing to understand what is involved. These pressures are frequently expressed in a coded language, which refers to harmonisation with its soothing overtones of reasoning together so that each will forgo personal or national advantage for the greater good of mankind.

Even to sound this note of Realpolitik in an analysis emanating from France may serve to confirm endemic Anglophone views that the French wish to be different in all things from the English-speaking world.

Let us first acknowledge the realities. If international accounting is viewed in terms of what is done, rather than what at times is said, it is

[1]Since March 1985, Director of Technical and Research Studies at the French Institute, the Ordre des Experts Comptables et des Comptables Agréés. His views are personal ones, expressed as an academic and not in his capacity as Technical Director of the OECCA.

[2]Spent seven months during 1986 in France expressly for the purpose of studying French accounting and in particular the Plan Comptable Général. The generous assistance of the OECCA in making facilities available and in assisting with access to its library and arrangement of interviews is gratefully acknowledged.

hard not to conclude that harmonisation occurs as and when non-English-speaking countries give up whatever indigenous accounting practices they may have developed in favour of Anglo-American accounting standards. In other words, harmonisation over the last few decades may be likened to early conversions of the heathen to Christianity or of the infidel to Islam.

Consider the evidence. Although the English-speaking world constitutes only a small proportion of the free world in population terms, there are no in-depth studies published in English of the accounting practices of foreign-language countries. Indeed, without the occasional surveys of international accounting practices by major public accounting firms, the English-speaking world might not even be aware that different practices exist in other places. The reasons for this indifference are not hard to find. In addition to the factors that have lead to the evolution of English as the commercial lingua franca, Anglo-American influence weighs heavily on international accounting practice and on the establishment and operation of the International Accounting Standards Committee. For the English-speaking world, disinterest in the accounting practices of non-English-speaking countries could easily commute into a self-serving belief that different accounting traditions are not intrinsically interesting and that they are in any case bound to fade away.

In short, are harmonisation and international pressures for change simply steps toward a sunny upland where eight happy clubs forever compete for the world accounting championship, played according to Anglo-American rules? Before concluding as spectators that the game is over, other realities need to be considered. Accounting practices, especially in the developed countries, are deeply rooted in commercial and fiscal laws as well as in a web of social conventions of behaviour. For this reason, it should not be lightly assumed that resulting national differences in accounting practices are bound to disappear, any more than it would be realistic to assume that differences between national languages will disappear. This is nowhere more true than in France, where a national structure for the specification and control of accounting practices, radically different from those in the Anglophone countries, has existed for nearly forty years.

Given these introductory remarks, the objective of this chapter is to explain the ways in which accounting concepts and practices have been or might be exported. In the first part, attention is drawn to the impact of Anglo-American accounting, partly as a result of Anglo-American investment in France. As could be expected, the indigenous French accounting profession would like to retain a role for itself, and some of its reactions to Anglo-American competition are noted. As regards financial reporting, the Fourth and Seventh Directives have stimulated major changes which are also considered.

The second part of the chapter explains the distinctive features of

French accounting, notably the Plan Comptable Général and its institutional framework. The core of the Plan is a standardised national accounting code which has no counterpart in the countries of the English-speaking world. An assessment is offered of the economic and social consequences of the Plan as it operates in France. A further issue is whether the French approach to standardisation of accounts and financial reporting offers solutions to some of the persistent problems concerning uniformity of accounting standards and practice in countries without a national accounting code.

Importation of accounting into France

In accounting, as in many other fields, it is difficult to establish the merit of what has been achieved by any one person or nation. Changes often have an obscure birth and their subsequent maturation depends on social context. Upon reflection, the evolution of French accounting can best be explained by means of an historical survey which, in this case, will show the effects of growing foreign influence. However, despite these effects, French accounting has retained distinctive features, which are discussed in the second part of the chapter.

As a general observation, there are few major contemporary differences between French annual accounts and those of the other principal western countries. Furthermore, regulation of accounting in France is as extensive as elsewhere in Europe, even if more limited than in the United States. Moreover, it may be noted that:

1. Audit guidelines of the French institute of registered auditors, the Compagnie Nationale des Commissaires aux Comptes (CNCC), are numerous and cover all major activities and aspects of the audit.
2. Although the major Anglo-American accounting firms (often referred to as the Big Eight), are amongst the larger firms practising in France, there are even larger indigenous French firms which have grown in recent times through mergers.

French accounting practices operate within a wider framework of international accounting co-operation, with France a member of the UEC, Groupe d'Etudes, IASC, IFAC–IAPC, and the OECD working group on accounting standards. As a result, most French professionals are acquainted with international accounting approaches and solutions, and apply many of them. Indeed, it is often hard to identify what stems from foreign influences and what derives from French views and opinions.

It is dangerous to split history into definite periods because many phenomena evolve rather than change abruptly. Nevertheless, the period discussed here, 1946-86, is divided into three sub-periods, as follows:

1. 1946-66: Accounting standardisation on a national scale, with insignificant foreign influence.
2. 1966-78: The beginning of significant international influence, both direct and indirect, mainly upon the French accounting profession rather than on French enterprises.
3. 1978 onwards: More evident international influence on the accounting practices of French firms and a measure of official recognition of that influence.

1946-66: The establishment of a national accounting code

In 1946, the Commission de Normalisation des Comptabilités was created to assist national economic planning through the development of a well-defined terminology for the titles of accounts to be used by enterprises. The Commission quickly produced the first national accounting code, the Plan Comptable Général, adopted in 1947. The Commission itself was transformed into the Conseil Supérieur de Comptabilité whose task was to adapt the Plan as required for each industry. The 1947 Plan was mandatory for nationalised enterprises but not for the private sector. Its distinctive features were:

1. Use of an all-numeric coding for accounts, organised in a structure of ten classes.
2. Recording of expenses according to their nature, not their functional purpose, and allowing for a subset of cost or management accounts separately from the financial accounts.

The Plan did not refer to accounting principles and only a few broad measurement conventions were indicated. At that time, French law was silent on the presentation of financial statements, though listed companies were required to appoint an auditor subject to approval by the court. Accounting was considered a technical matter, to be dealt with on the basis of professional accounting knowledge rather than by regulation. For these reasons, it took time for the 1947 Plan to become known and observed by enterprises.

After limited revision, the original Plan was replaced by the 1957 Plan. At the same time the Conseil Supérieur de Comptabilité was restructured as the present National Accounting Council, the Conseil National de la Comptabilité (CNC). A 1959 décret required that the Plan Comptable Général be adapted by the CNC for each recognised industry through the development of industry accounting codes (as had been earlier envisaged for the 1947 Plan). In the fifteen years from 1963 onwards, eighty-five adaptations were approved though some were never issued.

In 1965, two significant events occurred to change the process of accounting standardisation in France. The first related to the issue of information notes by the CNC on matters not dealt with by the Plan but of wide general interest. In acting this way, the CNC recognised the possibility of adapting the Plan on a partial but ongoing basis.

The second event related to a step taken by the French institute of registered public accountants, the Ordre des Experts Comptables et des Comptables Agréés (OECCA), to establish a standing committee to answer questions from members on issues not covered by the Plan. The committee decided at the outset that it would develop general statements of position on issues rather than deal with individual questions. In doing so, the OECCA was deliberately imitating the approach of the Anglo-American professional institutions toward accounting standard setting. It can be said that this was the first time that international accounting affected the evolution of French accounting.

In conclusion, the standardisation of this period was original from all points of view. There was little foreign influence, even as a result of the foundation of the Union Européenne des Comptables (UEC) whose aim was to promote an exchange of information within Europe on accounting matters. The important effects of the UEC were to come later.

1966-78: The beginning of international accounting co-operation

As far as France is concerned, this significant period can best be divided into two sub-periods, namely an initial period of indirect foreign influences (1966-73), followed by one of more direct influence.

1966-73: Indirect foreign influences

As noted above, the CNC began issuing statements on accounting outside the Plan. This occurred for several reasons. First, the development of industry accounting codes was very much in progress and it was thought wiser to address those needs by issuing limited statements rather than by undertaking a general revision of the Plan. Secondly, a 1965 décret matched the balance sheet and profit and loss account formats required for tax returns to those of the Plan Comptable Général. This décret was important in making the Plan more familiar to small and medium enterprises. Previously, requirements for tax returns and annual accounts were largely unrelated, except for some particular issues such as the revaluation of fixed assets for tax purposes. With the intrusion of taxation requirements into financial accounting, the CNC had to deal with the effects of tax accounting without waiting for an overall review of the Plan. Finally, as from 1967, the Commission of the EEC began to consider the harmonisation of differences between the various national requirements relating to company annual accounts. As the CNC was only at an early stage of considering a major revision of the Plan and as it was evident that the work of the EEC Commission would take a considerable time to carry out, the effect of this international influence in the short term was to delay change in France rather than to expedite it.

For all these reasons, the CNC worked on a case-by-case basis as, for different reasons, was the practice of the accounting standard-setting bodies in the Anglophone countries. In the period 1965-74 the CNC issued thirty-nine statements, in the following categories:

1. information notes (twenty-seven) on general accounting issues.
2. recommendations (two) on questions posed by the Government.
3. opinions (ten) relating to special activities or industries.

A growing concern by the government with investor protection was the next factor to bring French accounting closer to international practices. Of most direct importance was the new 1966 company law which, though having little to say on accounting and financial reporting, required as from 1968 that the auditor certify the sincerity and regularity of the annual accounts. This requirement had not previously existed and it was not clear what assurance had been imparted by auditors to company accounts. Thus the 1966 law marked a substantial forward step in the legal responsibility of the auditor. Given the lack of professional or official standards on the work of the auditor, however, there were no effective benchmarks by which to assess the sincerity and regularity of accounts and consequently the burdens placed on the auditor were not greatly altered.

At this same time, the Ministry of Justice pressed for the establishment of a separate statutory body for registered company auditors and in 1969, as a result, the Compagnie Nationale des Commissaires aux Comptes (referred to earlier) was formed and placed under its jurisdiction. Thus emerged the present distinctive organisation of the French accounting profession with:

1. Two institutions having near identical membership, one for registered public accountants (expert comptable) (OECCA) and the other for registered auditors (CNCC).
2. Separation of functions, whereby in respect of any given client, a person or firm is not permitted to act simultaneously as expert comptable and auditor.

The other important development reflecting concern with investor protection during this period was the creation in 1967 of the Commission des Opérations de Bourse, modelled to a considerable extent on the United States Securities and Exchange Commission, though without the power to demand separate accounting information from listed companies.

1973-8: Direct foreign influences
In 1971, the CNC began the task of revising the 1957 Plan whilst at the same time participating in the development of the EEC Fourth Directive. This latter involvement influenced the thinking of the CNC, especially

after the accession of Britain to the EEC in 1973, resulting in the incorporation into the 1979 revised Plan Comptable Général of the following three important concepts:

1. A true and fair view (image fidèle) as a criterion for the annual accounts.
2. Extension of the annual accounts to include explanatory notes (the annexe).
3. Specification of the basis of valuation and measurement underlying the annual accounts.

Reference has already been made to the Groupe d'Etudes which throughout this period was not only significant as the vehicle for presenting the viewpoints of the various European professional bodies to the EEC Commission but which had considerable influence on French accounting concepts.

A new accounting arena emerged at this time with the establishment in 1973 of the International Accounting Standards Committee (IASC), of which the French accounting profession was one of the founding members. Since the OECCA had already begun to formulate accounting issues in what could be regarded as an Anglo-American style with the establishment of its standing committee in 1965, the method of operation of the IASC was not novel to the OECCA. Nevertheless, OECCA participation has been a fertile channel for the introduction of foreign accounting ideas into France. Up to 1978 most of the subjects addressed by the IASC were already treated in the same way in France, but important contributions came from the following:

1. IAS1 – The standard strengthened the idea of supplementary disclosure by way of notes.
2. IAS3 – The standard added weight to the use of the equity method of consolidation (the threshold being lowered from 33 per cent to 20 per cent).
3. IAS5 – The distinction relating to intra-group receivables and payables found expression in the revised Plan Comptable Général.

A further direct foreign influence on French accounting was the operation in France of the principal Anglo-American accounting firms. Although present prior to 1973, it was in the ensuing period to 1978 that they became increasingly evident. Their contribution was manifold but primarily in audit methods, with the introduction by the Big Eight of techniques not well known at that time in France. It should be recorded, however, that several French audit firms were well aware of foreign developments, as illustrated by the foundation of ATH (Technical Association for Harmonisation) in 1968 by two large French firms to match the Big Eight in matters of audit and organisation. Moreover, keeping the American example in sight, the CNCC had from its inception in 1969 begun developing a complete set of audit guidelines for the statutory audit, beginning with the initial engagement. By the end of 1978, the major part of this task had been realised and was well in line with best practice in other countries, e.g. Britain.

To summarise this period, foreign influence introduced to France some important new concepts both in accounting and auditing. The effects were mainly evident in the proceedings of the major accounting institutions, viz the CNC, OECCA and CNCC, rather than at the level of individual business enterprises. Nevertheless, these influences were effective and crucial since the leading figures of the profession were persuaded by the need for French accounting to move toward accepted international standards.

1979-86: Influence of international accounting harmonisation

Since 1979, three important developments may be noted. First, bodies already established, such as IASC, the Groupe d'Etudes and the International Audit Practices Committee (IAPC), were a source for the persistent diffusion of new accounting concepts. Second, an accounting law was enacted to give effect to the EEC Fourth Directive and to embrace the financial statements set out in the Plan Comptable Général. Third, the EEC Seventh Directive, although not incorporated in the Plan Comptable Général, was introduced into France by a special law permitting more accounting alternatives for consolidated accounts than are available under the Plan for the accounts of individual enterprises.

Diffusion of international accounting concepts

The 1979 revised Plan Comptable Général, adopted in 1982, came into effect as from 1984. For French accountants and auditors this has been a change of the greatest importance since they have had to learn to interpret its three new concepts relating to a true and fair view, notes to the accounts and the explanation of accounting policies. For instance:

1. The extensive requirements for disclosure of notes initially resulted in an excessive volume of information without sufficient regard to materiality.
2. The concept of true and fair, intended to permit accounts to be drawn up on the basis of economic substance rather than legal form, introduced a validity criterion alien to French jurisprudence.

The diffusion of international concepts also increased as a result of French participation in international accounting standard-setting. For example:

1. Deferred taxation: some major French companies now follow interna-

tional standards on this issue although the CNC and the Plan continue to adhere to the recognition of tax liabilities as assessed by the tax authorities.

2. Lease capitalisation: although the law does not yet permit lease capitalisation on the balance sheet, the profession is aware of Anglo-American standards and the subject is one of active debate.

3. Retirement obligations: the legal authorities have resisted the idea of full recognition of liabilities, fearing a significant impact of periodic charges against earnings and taxable income.

As evidence of the increasing influence of international standards, the CNC has since 1981 adopted the practice of systematically examining standards issued by IASC for their conformity with French accounting rules, with the object of identifying and reducing areas of difference. Indeed, foreign accounting standards, especially those of the United Kingdom Accounting Standards Committee (ASC) and the US Financial Accounting Standards Board (FASB), are now more widely known and studied in France, though their individual significance depends on French accounting and tax law. For example, standards on extraordinary items have been of direct importance, whereas the immense effort expended by the British and American profession on inflation accounting has had little echo in France. One probable explanation is that, although inflation was also a major problem in France, the Anglo-American debates were taking place at the same time as the French profession was preoccupied with switching from the 1957 to the 1982 Plan. The FASB conceptual framework project has likewise no French equivalent.

The seventh directive

As has been much remarked in the English-speaking world, there has been rather halting progress in non-English speaking countries toward the general adoption of consolidation accounting as the means for portraying the financial performance of corporate groups. In this regard, France had not been notably different from other EEC countries, the Netherlands excepted, prior to the Seventh Directive. Following its adoption, the French government had several alternatives available for its implementation. One obvious route was to revise the Plan Comptable Général so as to create a national accounting code applicable to individual enterprises as well as to consolidated groups. This, however, would have encountered two major difficulties:

1. Annual accounts in France have statutory significance only at the level of the individual enterprise. By contrast, consolidated accounts are not adopted at the shareholders' annual general meeting and do not enter into the determination of distributable profit. In other words, they are

essentially for the information of investors. Since the Plan Comptable Général and its related accounting law apply solely to the individual enterprise, it would have been a complicated exercise from a juridical viewpoint to rework the Plan so as to include consolidation concepts, definitions and annual account formats. ⊀

2. Any major revision of the Plan would be no simple task. In this case it would only have been directed to holding companies which constitute a relatively small proportion of the total number of enterprises (unincorporated and incorporated) subject to the Plan.

Instead, the government took a more rapid route by enacting a law solely for the purpose of implementing the Directive. Because this law, passed in 1985, is outside the scope of the Plan Comptable Général, companies have considerable freedom to determine their choice of accounting policies when drawing up consolidation accounts. Moreover, the associated *décret* of February 1986 effectively permitted French multinationals to draw up consolidated accounts on either a US GAAP basis or some other modified Anglo-American basis, as might best suit their needs when raising funds on the international capital markets. For example, it is possible in the consolidated accounts for French groups to adopt LIFO, to take potential exchange gains and losses to the profit and loss account, to capitalise leases in the balance sheet, and even to move from an historical cost basis for the accounts, whereas none of these possibilities is available for individual enterprise accounts under the Plan Comptable Général.

The emergence of accounting legislation

Prior to the adoption of the Fourth and Seventh Directives by the EEC, there was no accounting law as such in France. The statutory position may now be summarised as follows:

1. The law of 30 April 1983 (Fourth Directive)
   This law applies to companies as well as to unincorporated enterprises and non-profit organisations. There is an associated *décret* for more detailed aspects of its application and the Plan Comptable Général itself has the status of an *arrêté* (i.e. a ministerial order).
2. The law of 3 January 1985 (Seventh Directive)
   The associated *décret* of February 1986, permitting wider freedom for the presentation of consolidated accounts, is referred to above.

In summarising events since 1979, it can be seen that international influences of two distinctly different kinds have affected French accounting, namely foreign accounting standards with their underlying concepts, and the introduction of accounting legislation resulting from agreement between the EEC member states. These influences have had profound effects at the level of individual enterprises, and especially French multinationals. The present operation of these influences and approaches is summarised diagrammatically in Figure 9.1.

Exportation of accounting from France

Any foreigner who takes time to examine accounting in France is likely to be astonished at the extent to which the culture of French accounting practice is unknown in the English-speaking world, even on the other side of the English Channel. Once more we see a language barrier having the twofold effect frequently observed in human affairs:

1. Impeding the spread of awareness and ideas from one society to another and enabling a society to live more comfortably with the assumption that what is not known of foreign customs is probably not worth knowing.
2. Facilitating the development of an indigenous culture that might not otherwise occur if, for any reason, it were easier to import practices and standards from elsewhere.

In this case, lack of awareness of the distinctive features of accounting in France cannot be explained either by a lack of documentary sources or by the claim that it has no more than national significance. Even if unavailable in English, there is voluminous literature on French accounting; its core, the Plan Comptable Général, has inspired or influenced the development of national accounting codes in other countries (notably, Belgium, Spain and various French-speaking African countries); and the concept of standardised formats for the annual accounts, introduced into Britain by the Fourth Directive, owed much to French ideas and experience. Without probing further the issue of why it might be that the English-speaking world has remained indifferent to these developments, the aim of this section of the chapter is to draw attention to those aspects of French accounting which have already contributed to international accounting or which appear likely to do so in the future.

A national accounting code

Accounting is often said to be the language of business. In related vein, it would be widely accepted that financial accounting and reporting is intended to communicate information from source to destination without significant changes in meaning. To be taken seriously as a language, albeit of a technical kind, accounting must exhibit the general characteristics required of any language. These are a shared vocabulary, essential for identification of time, place, objects and qualities, and a syntax, essential for articulating connections and expressing ideas. As

Figure 9.1
Accounting Regulation for Enterprises
France 1986

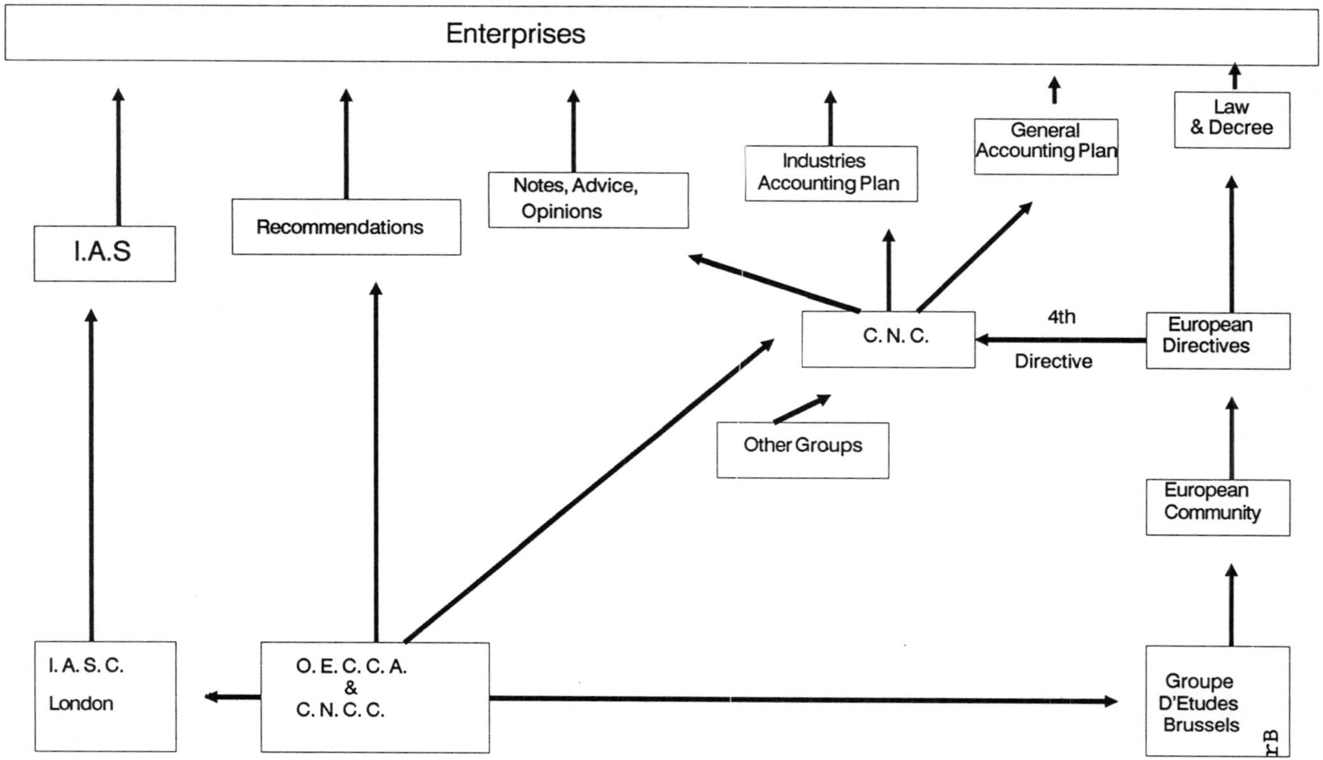

Enterprises

Law & Decree

European Directives

European Community

Groupe D'Etudes Brussels

F.B

General Accounting Plan

4th Directive

C. N. C.

Industries Accounting Plan

Other Groups

Notes, Advice, Opinions

Recommendations

O. E. C. C. A. & C. N. C. C.

I.A.S

I. A. S. C. London

regards the relative significance of languages, distinctions are often drawn between a national language and a dialect, according to how widely the language is understood across regions or economic classes. For the purpose of relating these ideas to accounting and its social context, the existence of different industries and types of commercial activity can be regarded as equivalent to economic regions, while the various groups with an interest in accounting represent the relevant economic classes.

As will be further explained, the requisite conditions exist in France for accounting to be understood across industries and economic interest groups, and for standardisation of its expression in formal communication. In other words, the formalised codification of accounting has effectively created a national accounting language. Can accounting in the Anglo-American countries be regarded as achieving a comparable effect, whether in the form of an accounting language in each country or as a supra-national language used throughout the English-speaking world?

To answer this question, we need to remind ourselves of the circumstances in which Anglo-American accounting evolved. Our present emphasis on accounting as an instrument of communication between parties at arms-length is of fairly recent origin. In the nineteenth century, at the time of establishing the institutions of the profession, the practice of accounting was largely directed to producing private information, and it took a long roll call of famous accounting scandals (Royal Mail, McKesson Robbins, Equity Funding, etc.) to bring about even modest changes in the attitudes of the profession. With the advent of the United Kingdom ASC and US FASB, associated in each context with varying degrees of statutory recognition for standards, it might be thought that the necessary conditions now exist for creating and maintaining the vocabulary and syntax of a national accounting language.

When regard is paid, however, to the attributes of accounting practice and financial communication in the English-speaking world, it becomes clear that what we are observing is not so much a language, as a set of co-existing dialects. This becomes more readily apparent when we consider the following:

1. At a primordial level, accounting is a procedure for classifying transactions on the basis of a code of accounts. For want of a national accounting code, each enterprise in the Anglophone countries is obliged to design its own code. This is an environment conducive to the creation of accounting dialects, in which enterprise codes lack generality and support data bases not readily understandable by outsiders. At a national level, accounting standards and statutory financial disclosure requirements contain terms intended to impose standardised classifications on annual accounts, but these terms are nowhere defined by reference to account codes.

The consequences are well illustrated by the painful affair of CCA. At the time of its introduction to Britain, CCA concepts were not widely known or understood within the profession. Without careful specification of what was to be done, there would inevitably have been widely varying interpretations of the proposals. Nevertheless, each successive exposure draft or recommended standard concentrated on financial reporting on a CCA basis but ignored the codification of the underlying accounting procedures. The outcome was that published CCA accounts incorporated a great deal of subjectivity and lacked clear meaning.

2. The uniqueness of accounting system design at the level of the individual enterprise forces the auditor to expend valuable time and effort in specifying and comprehending the client accounting system. As an outsider, the auditor cannot be sure from one year or client to another whether changes to a client system or differences between systems merely reflect idiosyncratic views about accounting objectives or whether they are driven by a fraudulent wish to extract advantage from behind the cloak of confusion. As is well known, there is a terrible price to be paid, in terms of damages for professional negligence, when wrong guesses are made.

3. The same underlying factors create endemic problems for financial statement interpretation. This is exemplified in graduate business schools, where it is normal to find courses designed to sensitise students to the tricks and traps of analysing accounts; in bank training programs for loan officers; and in typical financial analysis case books with their rogues gallery of misleading accounts. All this flows from the difficulty of assessing the particular nuances attached by the enterprise to the terminology in its accounts and the principles on which they are based.

The same set of conditions does not exist to this extent in France, due to the evolution of its national accounting code. Although the Plan Comptable Général originated in the conditions of World War Two, it was seen by early post-war governments and relevant senior officials as offering important advantages for national economic planning, for the development of reliable economic statistics and for more efficient tax administration. With the passage of years, goals and priorities have changed so that formalised national economic planning is now out of favour, while governments more recently have been giving attention to stimulating private enterprise and removing some of the politically induced rigidities in the French economy. Despite these changes, there is widespread consensus that the concept of the Plan Comptable Général has stood the test of time and that there is no case for abandoning it.

The 1982 Plan is organised as follows:

1.   A defined terminology for the titles of account classes, sub-classes

and individual accounts.

2.   Grouping of account classes into two principal divisions:

(a) Financial accounting

   Balance sheet accounts:
   (i)   Capital
   (ii)   Long-term assets
   (iii)   Inventory
   (iv)   Accounts receivable and payable
   (v)   Financial

   Income statement accounts:
   (vi)   Expenses
   (vii)   Revenues

   Special:
   (viii) Optionally available

(b) Management accounts:
   (ix)   Optionally available.

3.   An all-numeric coding, with account classes shown at the two-digit level and finer sub-divisions indicated by the addition of further digits for sub-classes or individual accounts.

The Plan is organised so that it may be applied at any of the following levels:

1. Expanded: Recommended in particular for listed public companies.

2. Standard: Required of all enterprises above a defined size.

3. Abridged: Optionally available for enterprises below a defined size.

The official text of the Plan Comptable Général is set out in a publication of 374 pages, with the code itself taking thirty-two pages. In style, the text is explanatory rather than legalistic. The Plan does not reach into every corner of the French economy or of commercial affairs (e.g. for the present, banks are exempted), but it extensively covers business activity, whether in the private or public sectors, non-profit organisations and public administration. Moreover, its successive versions have been a basic element in the training of French accountants for almost forty years. For these reasons, France can be said to have created a national language of accounting, for which the syntax and vocabulary are provided in the text of the Plan Comptable Général (and in the many commentaries on it).

As a consequence, the grounding received by accountants in the Plan can readily move with the individual from one task or context to another, whether it be the installation of a new accounting system, the design of an audit programme, dealing with financial failure and insolvency, or analysing annual accounts.

A national accounting council

In view of the early establishment of the institutions of the accounting profession in the Anglophone countries, it is not surprising that they were the first bodies to develop recommendations on accounting principles and statements of standards. However, without detracting from the expertise of the profession in financial measurement and the presentation of accounts, non-accountants are also widely involved in financial communication as recorders of initial data and final users of accounting reports. Accountants are no different from any other priestly caste in their tendency to mystify matters to a level well beyond the grasp of a reasonably intelligent person not having the same extended training. An even more fundamental point is that the measurement and valuation concepts employed by accountants are significant for issues of income and wealth distribution, which lie ultimately in the political domain where the voice of the accountant is only one of many with a legitimate claim to be heard.

In general, the profession in the Anglophone countries has tried to monopolise or dominate the standard-setting process. Along the way, it has had some sobering experiences of how politically sensitive accounting information can be. In some countries (e.g. Australia), it has had to cede authority in standard-setting to government. In France, however, the institutions of the profession were of too recent foundation and without either resources or authority to undertake standard-setting at the time when the profession was grappling with these issues in the English-speaking world. Moreover, France had already chosen a different path in creating a national accounting code, which does not necessarily obviate the need for statements of standards but does affect their subject matter and relative priorities.

From the outset, the task of developing a national code was assigned to a broadly constituted authority. The present national accounting council, the Conseil National de la Comptabilité (CNC), established in 1957, is the consultative organisation responsible for the standardisation of accounting in France, both in the public and private sectors. It has the following responsibilities:

1. Elaboration and diffusion of the Plan Comptable Général.
2. Publication of guidelines on accounting matters relating to the Plan.
3. Consideration and approval of adaptations of the Plan, in the form of

industry accounting codes.
4. Advice on accounting codes for use in public administration and by
   public authorities.

The CNC presently comprises 105 members, of whom approximately
two-thirds are drawn from the private sector and one-third from the
public sector. Its formal composition is as follows:

One	President.
Five	Vice-Presidents.
One	Secretary-General.
Thirty-five	Representatives of designated ministries and public authorities.
Nineteen	Representatives of organisations and commissions. specialising in accounting matters (e.g. financial analysts).
Twenty-seven	Professionally qualified accountants,
	Eight In public practice,
	Nine Registered auditors,
	Ten Chief accountants in enterprises.
Ten	Representatives of the national employers' federation, the chambers of commerce and industry etc.
Five	Representatives of trade unions.
Five	Public servants appointed for their standing.
Ten	Other persons appointed for their standing in the fields of accounting, law, economic affairs and finance.

The CNC is attached to the Ministry for Economic Affairs but operates
as an autonomous organisation. Its members are either *ex officio* or
appointed for renewable terms of three years. Collectively they constitute
the full assembly of the CNC which has the final power to make recommendations concerning the Plan and its application. In practice the full
assembly rarely meets, being perhaps somewhat unwieldy in size, and
recommendations are ordinarily made by a smaller group of thirty-five
members constituted as the Collège, or in rare circumstances by the
Bureau, comprising the President and Vice-Presidents.

The work of the CNC is organised through Sections, each directed by
a Vice-President as follows:

1st General principles.
2nd Financial accounting.
3rd Management accounting.
4th Industry accounting codes.
5th Public sector accounting.

Particular issues are dealt with, according to their importance, by
Commissions (e.g. consolidated accounts, computer based accounting) or
Working Groups (e.g. notes to the accounts, investment funds) to which

outside persons are frequently coopted. The CNC has a permanent secretariat (with a staff of about thirty-five), including nine Rapporteurs who are professionally qualified and provide technical support. Membership of the CNC includes many of the leading persons in French accounting and financial affairs, and its structure and operation clearly bring a wide range of talents and viewpoints to bear on accounting matters. For example, the Presidents of the OECCA and the CNCC are *ex officio* members of the CNC, the former also being a Vice-President and responsible for the First Section of the CNC.

Though the CNC only has authority to make recommendations, these have been consistently supported by successive governments. With a wide-ranging participation by senior public servants, the CNC no doubt has a realistic awareness of what will be acceptable to its political masters. The degree to which the CNC is an arm of government is quite difficult for any outsider (whether French or otherwise) to interpret, but as a matter of record it has been able to retain the long involvement of various members from the private sector known for their forthright views on aspects of the Plan and its underlying accounting principles. Moreover, there have been instances in which the need to arrive at workable compromises has produced concessions by particular government ministries or agencies as well as by private sector interests.

A significant role for the CNC, referred to previously, is to consider proposals for adaptation of the Plan Comptable Général to meet the needs of specific industries. To May 1986, forty-four industry accounting codes have been approved as adaptations of the Plan, and in a further fifteen instances the recognised industry federation has requested that the Plan Comptable Général be applied to that industry without modification. The net effect of these procedures is that each enterprise must keep its accounts in accordance with the Plan Comptable Général or, if it belongs to an industry for which there is an approved variant code, then in accordance with that code. The most common approved modifications to the 1982 Plan are for terminology that relates to the specific industry (e.g. the hotel industry code), though some industry codes deal with exceptional measurement and valuation issues (e.g. profit recognition on incomplete contracts, in the building and construction industry code). In comparison with the 1957 Plan, however, there has been notably less demand for variations to the 1982 Plan, perhaps reflecting the degree of development of computer-based accounting which in principle makes it easier to add optional features to the enterprise accounting system and to retrieve information in the form required by the Plan.

Standardised financial analysis

In the English-speaking world, the game of analysing annual accounts could be likened to the Olympic pentathlon. The task for the analyst is to comprehend accounts lacking standardised:

1. Terminology.
2. Formats for the income statement and balance sheet (Britain and Australia excepted) or the statement of source and application of funds.
3. Bases of measurement and valuation.
4. Scope and presentation of notes to the accounts.
5. Codification of the data base underlying the accounts.

Ironically, annual accounts must first be reprocessed into a standardised format before any serious cross-sectional analysis of company financial performance can take place. This can only be done, however, by accepting an unknown degree of processing error since the outsider has no reliable way of knowing what particular construction to put on the many singular items or explanations that appear in published accounts. With standardised codification and formatting of annual accounts, it is simpler in principle to construct data bases and to derive statistical conclusions of greater validity. To illustrate the point, there are in France two major data bases of corporate financial performance:

1. Centrale de Bilans de la Banque de France

   As a service to the business sector, the Central Bank, the Banque de France, has maintained since 1968 a data base on enterprise financial performance. This service is maintained by its department, the Centrale de Bilans, through extensive sampling (in 1982 covering 28,600 enterprises) across eleven broad categories of industry and commerce. Participation by enterprises is optional, with raw data furnished to the Bank on forms designed to match the requirements of the Plan Comptable Général and the enterprise income tax return (itself closely based on the Plan), so as to minimise the effort of compliance.

   The principal annual information produced by the Centrale is of two types. Firstly, each participating enterprise receives a report showing its financial performance in terms of key indicators and ratios, as well as average values for enterprises classified in the same industry. Secondly, for each industry category with sufficient participating enterprises to permit valid statistical inference, the Centrale reports a wide range of aggregate values, averages, ratios and frequency distributions.

The Centrale has also drawn on its data base to study the risk of business financial failure, using as a departure point the Z-score concepts and models developed by Altman. The objective has been to estimate the likelihood of failure by means of discriminatory analysis, using several different estimation models. Results have shown a strong ability to place enterprises in categories of probable failure or significant vulnerability.

2. DAFSA

This company is part of the DAFSA KOMPASS group, a quoted company largely owned by a consortium of French banks. DAFSA produces financial information services based on analysis of published company accounts, available to the subscriber in the form of annual reports for either individual companies or sectors. In this it can be likened to Extel Services in the United Kingdom and to Standard and Poors in the United States. It currently covers some 420 quoted French companies and in 1986 extended its service to companies listed on the Second Market. The emphasis is on presentation and analysis of serial fund flows, subdivided into operating and financing flows.

Both services produce information showing the classic range of indicators used in the English-speaking world, though in both the Plan Comptable Général and the work of the Centrale de Bilans and DAFSA there is a notable emphasis on identification of value added by the firm. In the case of DAFSA, this is then deflated by the general rate of price increase to show the real rate of growth for the enterprise. In the present context, however, what is chiefly significant is not so much the types of information provided by these services but the relative ease with which necessary data can be extracted from annual accounts and the higher degree of homogeneity in the resulting data base.

Audit risk and programme design

Professional negligence suits have arrived in the Anglophone countries somewhat like the Black Death. Auditors are horrified at the result but seem more concerned with seeking safe houses, such as limitation of personal liability, rather than dealing with root causes. Some of these have nothing to do with accounting as such (e.g. the class action system in the United States). However, one explanatory variable which does relate to accounting is the presence or absence of standardised codification in accounting system design because this directly affects the task of risk assessment by the auditor.

The existence of a national accounting code creates opportunities for specifying more precisely the operational tasks of the auditor and for reducing the time and effort required to comprehend client systems or significant changes therein. The effects of this on French accounting are apparent in two important areas:

1. The CNCC members' handbook includes an extensive audit manual (over 200 pages), structured to correspond to the Plan Comptable Général, with detailed audit guidelines for the various ledger accounts and cross-references to statutory requirements. In the absence of a national accounting code, it is not feasible for the professional bodies to offer the same extent of guidance.

2. Again taking advantage of the standardised accounting code, some of the principal French audit firms have developed a variety of software programmes offering, for example, the production of lead schedules for the audit working papers, ready interrogation of individual accounts and comparison with budget or prior period. Programmes of this type can be employed from one client to another, with the double effect of reducing the cost of audit programme design and maintenance, and the level of probable error in hypothesis formulation and inference for verification purposes.

It seems reasonable to infer that these factors explain in part the markedly lower extent of negligence actions against French auditors. As regards damages, the largest verdict to date is approximately 6 million French francs.

Computer-based keeping of accounts and production of annual accounts

Accounting software in the English-speaking world generally contains a set of operational controls (e.g. to prevent unbalanced entries), but otherwise presents the user with an open universe onto which must be mapped the individual accounting systems of the enterprise, both as regards the chart of accounts and the specification and formatting of the annual accounts. With a national accounting code, software can readily be developed with an inbuilt chart of accounts, either in standardised form or, depending on the complexity of the software, with possibilities for it to be subdivided according to various options.

To exploit these possibilities, a number of specialised enterprises have developed in France, the two largest being the listed public companies, CCMC and Sligos. Both companies are of comparable size (1985 turnover of approximately 900 million French francs), and offer a wide range of software for account keeping, preparation of annual accounts and the tax return, budgeting and financial planning, and audit. Their software available for sale or leasing is in all cases based on the standard version of the Plan Comptable Général, with various constrained possibilities for adaptation to the needs of the individual user. In addition, CCMC specialises in processing transaction data and producing periodic accounts for enterprises at several large-scale centres. In France,

OECCA members have a statutory monopoly on keeping accounts and producing annual accounts for those enterprises which do not choose to carry out these tasks internally. For this reason, it is the expert comptable who engages CCMC to provide services, not the end client.

Although the various commercial services in France for processing encoded data for enterprises are used by some large corporate clients, the major client base comprises small and medium enterprises. This may be compared with the classic phenomenon in the Anglophone countries of the shoebox filled with disorganised and often fragmentary records, reluctantly taken once a year to the accountant for purposes of the tax return. In contrast, the Plan Comptable Général has apparently been the basis for a significant improvement in the delivery of prompt and cost-effective accounting services to the business community, especially that part which is not able to afford its own internal accounting expertise.

Conclusion

During the period under consideration, France has progressed successively from relative unawareness of foreign accounting policies and methods, to active participation in the work of international accounting organisations, and finally to statutory adoption of foreign accounting practices. The present pattern of French accounting is therefore one in which distinctive indigenous practices and long-standing juridical approaches interact with more recent international imports. This mixture, though apparently operating without major practical problems, is bound to change in directions that at present are not readily predictable.

Two broad directions of change have emerged with significance for the future. The first concerns standard-setting. Under external influence, French standard-setting is now addressing a wider range of issues and operating in a more continuous manner. At the same time, the process used since 1946, namely, relatively infrequent revision of the national accounting code, has not been abandoned. As noted, there is no counterpart to this arrangement in the English-speaking world.

How the process of adapting the Plan will evolve is unclear. For example, given the pace of international change in demands for financial information, will it be possible for the Plan Comptable Général to retain sufficient general features to justify the claim that it is truly a national accounting code? Will the Plan be confined to accounting terminology and codification, or will it evolve as a more flexible instrument providing statements of standard and systematic information on approved departures from its overall structure?

In trying to forecast the answers, it is important to remember that the financial data base for almost the entire working for the French economy is based on the Plan Comptable Général, whether it be for financial management, audit, financial reporting, financial analysis, public

administration, national economic statistics, or ultimately the derivation
of the national accounts. A country that has created and learned successfully to operate this system is unlikely to allow it to crumble away.
On the other hand, French accountants are eager to learn about and
⋋ derive benefit from foreign or international accounting ideas and experiences. They are aware as their English-speaking counterparts that the
practice of accounting is a competitive game with much at stake.

The second change concerns perceptions of what accounting is and
what it is intended to serve. Foreign influences have induced profound
cultural change in French accounting, from a stage when it may have
been little more than a glorified form of arithmetic to a vehicle for
providing information of economic significance. The same may be said of
many other countries. In France this shift in emphasis has gone a long
way, as may be seen in the extensive statutory requirements for notes to
be attached to the annual accounts. In related vein, the test of 'true and
fair' is driving French accountants in the direction of a more judgemental
approach.

Whatever the future may hold for French accounting in terms of
absorbing foreign influences, it is clear that accounting in the English-
speaking world could in turn usefully absorb some of the qualities of
French accounting. Its distinctive features are those that have evolved to
deal with the very issues that have proven so elusive in the Anglophone
countries, where the concept and consequences of a national codification
of accounts have never been seriously considered.

References

Banque de France, 'Les ratios de la Centrale de Bilans de la Banque de
    France', *Note d'information No.43* (1980).
Banque de France, 'La détection précoce des difficultés d'entreprises par
    la méthode des scores', *Note d'information No.65* (1985).
Benedetti, A. and Malinvaud, E., 'Le dialogue entre comptables et éco-
    nomètres', *Economie et statistique*, (March 1977).
CCMC, *Manuel d'utilisation: Maxi 10, Traitement de comptabilité*, (1985).
CCMC, *Maxi 5*, Version 1.0, (1986).
CCMC, *Tenue 8*, Version 1.0, (1986).
Centre de Productivité des Transports, *Guide comptable professionnel des
    transports*, Vols. 1 and 2, Paris, Editions Celse, (1983).
Comité de Normalisation Comptable de l'Industrie Hôtelière, *Plan comp-
    table professionnel de l'industrie hôtelière*, (1983).
Compagnie Nationale des Commissaires aux Comptes, *Encyclopédie des
    contrôles comptables, Guide des Commissaires aux Comptes*.
Compagnie Nationale des Commissaires aux Comptes, *Recommandations
    relatives à l'exercice des missions, Guide des Commissaires aux Comptes*.

Conseil National de la Comptabilité, *Plan comptable général*, (1983).

Conseil National de la Comptabilité, 'Forum de l'OCDE: Harmonisation des normes comptables', *Bulletin trimestriel*, Supplement to No.63, (October 1985).

Culmann, H., *Le Plan Comptable révisé de 1979: comptabilité générale*, Paris, Presses Universitaires de France, (1980).

DAFSA, *Fiche DAFSA d'analyse financière: Manuel de l'utilisateur*, (1985).

Fédération des Industries électriques et électroniques, *Guide comptable des industries françaises de la construction électrique et électronique et informatique*, Société Auxiliaire de la Construction Electrique, Paris, (1983).

Fédération Nationale des Entreprises à Commerces Multiples, *Guide comptable des entreprises à commerces multiples*, Vols. 1 and 2, (1983).

Gélard, G. and Pham, D., *Comprendre le nouveau plan comptable*, Paris, Montchrestien, (1984).

Groupement des Industries Françaises Aéronautiques et Spatiales, *Guide comptable des industries aéronautiques et spatiales*, (1985).

Hannoset, R. and Mériaux, J., Plan comptable révisé et analyse financière, *Analyse Financière*, (1er trimestre 1981).

Kerviler, I. de, *Droit comptable (L'entreprise)*, Paris, Economica, (1986).

Lagarrigue, J.-P., *Le Droit comptable (Les Sources)*, Paris, Editions S.A., (1984).

Maeder, R. (Colloquium, 21 and 22 May 1979, organised by), *Plan comptable révisé*, Paris, Masson, (1980).

Ordre des Experts Comptables et des Comptables Agréés, Principes comptables, Nos. 1-17, *Encyclopédie permanente à l'usage des membres de l'Ordre*, Vol. 2, Series 1.

Ordre des Experts Comptables et des Comptables Agréés, *Les Principes comptables fondamentaux*, (1981).

Ordre des Experts Comptables et des Comptables Agréés, *Les rapports annuels des sociétés françaises (année 1984), Tome I: Les comptes annuels, (1986), Tome II: Les comptes consolidéa*, (1986).

Pérochon, C., *Présentation du Plan Comptable Français*, Paris, Foucher, (1983).

Pontavice, E. du, *et al.*, Le Droit Comptable Français en 1984: *Réflexions sur une réforme majeure*, *Revue Française de Comptabilité*, (October 1984).

Raffegeau, J., Dufils, P. and Corre, J., *L'Annexe des comptes annuels: Guide pratique*, Paris, Editions Francis Lefebvre, (1985, with supplementary update, March 1986).

Raffegeau, J., Dufils, P. and Corre, J., *Memento pratique Francis Lefebvre: Comptable 1986*, Paris, Editions Francis Lefebvre, (1985).

Sligos, *ECX MS/DOPS SPX*, Version 01.01, (1986).

Sligos, *ECX MS/DOS Comptelix 41*, Version 01.01, (1986).

Sligos, *ECX MS/DOS Syntix 41*, Version 01.01, (1986).

Syndicat National des Agents de Voyages, *Guide comptable professionnel des agences de voyages*, Paris, Editions Celse, (1984).

Valantin, J.-C., *Le tableau de financement: Pratique et interprétation*, Paris, Economica (1985).

Viandier, A., *Droit comptable*, Paris, Dalloz, (1984).

La Villeguérin (Collection), *Le code annoté de la comptabilité*, Paris, La Villeguérin Editions, (1986).

10
The Impact of International Pressures on Japanese Accounting: A Critical Perspective on the Emergent Issues

Sadao Takatera and Satoshi Daigo

It is now generally recognised that while new management methods and systems have been introduced into Japanese enterprises, the traditional management philosophy has been maintained unchanged as the core organisational culture. As part of this process, management systems have become subject to international influences and Japanese management has had to address the issue of how these systems can, and indeed must, be changed in response to the changing international business environment.

In a similar manner, the entry of large Japanese corporations into the international capital market has raised a number of fundamental issues relating to the need for, and the feasibility of, institutional change in Japanese accounting. Questions have been raised concerning the forms of change that are necessary for Japanese accounting and, not least in significance, the means by which any such changes might be realised given domestic resistance to them.

Any consideration of these questions must be based on a clear understanding of the institutional factors which have governed postwar Japanese accounting. Given this aim, the subsequent discussion is structured in the following manner. First, consideration is given to two distinctive features of Japanese accounting and their institutional determinants: (1) an institutional bias towards the lowering of accounting income and (2) some remaining possibilities for the enhancement of accounting income. Thereafter attention is given to some recent accounting changes in Japan which have been implemented in response to international pressures as well as domestic criticism. Finally a number of wider socio-economic influences are discussed in order to understand the sluggish manner in which Japanese accounting has responded not only to pressures to harmonise with international accounting standards but also to domestic concerns with improving the quality of financial reporting.

Institutional biases towards the lowering of accounting income

The most notable accounting phenomenon in postwar Japan has been the systematic under-reporting of accounting income as a result of both the inherent conservatism in business accounting and the unreasonable intervention of tax accounting in business accounting.

The inherent conservatism in business accounting

A number of institutional factors have resulted in an under-reporting of accounting income by the Japanese business community.

First, there has been a direct tendency to extend the conceptual definition of capital surplus. Immediately after World War Two, the American influence on Japanese accounting commenced with the Instruction for the Preparation of Financial Statements of Manufacturing and Trading Companies issued by the General Headquarters (GHQ) of the Allied Powers in 1947. These requirements were issued in a form that was consistent with prevailing American accounting usage and principles.[1] However the subsequent Business Accounting Principles (BAP) formulated in 1949 along the lines of the GHQ Instruction, and revised in later years, departed from the American principles by extending the conceptual definition of capital surplus so as to include the following two significant items:

1. Government grants and customers' contributions for construction, both being regarded as deferred revenue;
2. Positive differences (including debtors' gain) between the revalued or insured amount and the book value of related assets in inflationary context.

Although an extreme reliance on loan financing in an inflationary context has been a pervasive feature of post-war Japanese corporate finance, there has been no continuous accounting response to the impact of inflationary conditions on the financial positions of Japanese companies except for the upward revaluation of assets allowed by the Assets Revaluation Act of 1950. Under this Act, a positive difference on revaluation was deemed to be capital surplus. Furthermore, since the Act provided only an upper limit for the revaluation multiples for specific categories of assets, most corporations revalued their assets in accordance with their earning power. As a consequence, Davidson and Yasuba (1960) remarked that 'revaluation will confer more benefits on large businesses than small'. Evidence on the impact of these tendencies is shown in Table 10.1 which is based on the research of Nakai (1983). In the Table it can be seen that the debtors' gain in large Japanese corporations was the highest, compared with that for large corporations in Germany, the United

**Table 10.1 Rate of debtor's gain and adjusted income
to accounting income for large corporations of the world**

	1951-5	1956-60	1961-5	1966-70	1971-5	1976-80	1951-80
Japan	36	46	58	59	181	77	88
	101	108	114	117	193	76	123
USA	0	0	0	7	9	5	4
	72	84	88	91	78	70	79
UK	0	1	5	14	58	57	21
	86	86	96	99	125	90	99
Germany	23	16	22	14	68	44	33
	79	92	98	88	102	82	91

upper row: debtor's gain   lower row: adjusted income
        accounting income   accounting income

Kingdom and the United States. Moreover, except for the five year period 1976-80, accounting income in Japan was always lower than an adjusted measure of income (reported income + revenue shortage – expense shortage + liability holding gain – monetary asset holding loss) – a finding in sharp contrast to the situation prevailing in large American, British and German corporations.

The implications of tax accounting for business accounting

As foreign researchers have correctly recognised (Arpan and Al Hashim, 1983, page 29; Evans *et al.*, 1985, page 43), corporation tax law and regulations have had a great influence upon business accounting in Japan. This is because the 'business accounting based tax accounting' principle requires that financial statements and tax returns must conform in all respects.

When the principle was initially transferred from the German income tax system[2] to the Japanese Income Tax Law of 1899, it contributed to the diffusion of sound business accounting. If a corporation claimed certain expenses as allowable deductions for income tax purposes, it had to treat all those items as expenses in its business accounts. Hence, for example, in order to realise income tax savings through the full use of ordinary tax depreciation, it became necessary to write off fixed assets in the business accounts.

However, in the postwar period the 'business accounting based tax accounting' principle extended its application to special tax allowances, including the special tax depreciation which was introduced to encourage investment through tax deferment.[3] As a result, the principle necessarily resulted in the lowering of reported accounting income, because it is a prerequisite for income tax deferment to treat the full amount of such special tax allowances as expenses in the business accounts, even though they are not legitimate expenses from a normal business point of view. Moreover, the 'business accounting based tax accounting' principle also contributed to a concentration of the tax advantage among the relatively few profitable corporations that could absorb such extra depreciation charges.[4]

Such consequences of the tax accounting systems have been officially sanctioned. The Notification of the Ordinance on Audit Certification of Financial Statements, released by the Ministry of Finance (as administrator of the Securities Exchange Act of 1948) in 1957, unreasonably announced that the 'expensing' treatment of the special tax allowances should be regarded as 'fair and proper'. In addition, the 1962 revision of the Commercial Code (article 287b) legally sanctioned the expensing of specific provisions for uncertain future expenditures or losses which are generally unattributable to current operations. As a consequence, it was interpreted unjustifiably that the reserves for special tax allowances, being properly regarded as retained earnings as distinguished from liability provisions, could also be treated as specific provisions in business accounting.

Some possibilities for income enlargement

However, as has been noticed by some foreign observers, such 'conservative approach[es] to financial reporting [in Japan] are countered to some extent by accounting practices that may appear relatively unconservative' (Campbell, 1985, page 169). A number of such counter tendencies are discussed below.

The optional adoption of the 'lower of cost or market' method

While in the United States, United Kingdom and West Germany, a departure from the cost basis of inventory valuation is required when the utility of the goods is no longer as great as their cost, Japanese BAP leaves the adoption of the lower of cost or market method to management discretion. Thus, of the 300 leading Japanese corporations (excluding banking and finance corporations), only forty fully and forty-three partially adopted this method in 1984 (*Accounting Techniques and Reporting*, 1985, page 178). As Campbell (1985, page 162) has noted: 'from a United Kingdom or United States perspective, inventories may appear to be overstated in [most] Japanese balance sheets'. In other words, most

Japanese corporations are prepared to overstate their reported income in so far as they can avoid recording the loss which would result from the write-off of inventory.

A moderate provision for employees' retirement payments

In many advanced countries funded pension plans commonly have been adopted and pension liabilities equivalent to the actuarial present value of accumulated plan benefits have been reported through charges to current revenue. In Japan, however, a considerable number of corporations still adopt, either fully or partially, an employees' retirement payment plan rather than a pension plan. Moreover, the present Corporation Tax Law in Japan permits as an allowable deduction only 40 per cent of the possible total payment for all employees at the end of each fiscal year.

As a result of these conditions, of the 300 aforementioned corporations, 119 report an amount for the provision for employees' retirement payments that exactly equals the allowable deduction for tax purposes (*Accounting Techniques and Reporting*, 1985, pages 257-8). So there is no doubt that such an accounting policy results in considerable income enlargement, at least in the context of cross-national comparisons. However in the light of past records of the actual use of the provision, it should be borne in mind that even the 40 per cent basis may be considered generous.

A restrictive interpretation of provisions for loss contingencies

According to the FASB Statement No.5 or IAS No.10, reserves for loss contingencies must be created when the probability and amount of the future loss can be estimated. In contrast, Japanese BAP, before being amended in 1981, had been interpreted as disallowing in principle any provision for loss contingencies, other than for doubtful debts and product warranties, by reason of a guard against over conservatism. Only the supplementary disclosure of contingent liabilities, such as the fulfilment of liability guarantees or compensation for damages, had been required in corporate reports for the purposes of security regulation.

The unconditional admission of the pooling of interest method for corporate mergers

Japanese BAP permit the pooling of interest method of accounting for business combinations without any restrictive conditions, whereas most other countries have shown a marked tendency to place severe limitations on the adoption of this method. Moreover, any positive difference between the market value and the book value of transferred assets in mergers which would result from the application of the purchase method of accounting would be taxable in accordance with the Corporation Tax Law.

A research report of a study group on accounting for business combinations and separations established by the Japanese Accounting Association in 1984-5 found that of the 127 largest merger cases, 80 per cent (101) recorded the transferred assets at their book value. Market values were used in those cases where there were accumulated losses on the part of the merged companies. Lands were often recorded at their market values because they would not result in any depreciation charge on the post-merger income. Typically such write-ups tended to be undertaken to the extent necessary to eliminate the accumulated loss. As a result, merging corporations tended to enlarge their post-merger reported income whilst avoiding the higher depreciation charges or amortization of goodwill which would result from the adoption of the purchase method.

Recent accounting changes in response to international pressure

Although Japanese corporate accounting during the post-war era has exhibited tendencies towards both income lowering and income enlargement, these biases have been gradually amended in response to both international pressures and domestic reconsiderations.

Gradual relaxing of the 'business accounting based tax accounting' principles

First of all it needs to be recognised that the 'business accounting based tax accounting' principle which had been the fundamental cause of institutional income biasing has been relaxed in the period since 1967.

Several accounting scholars had persistently raised objections to the business accounting implications of the special tax allowances on the ground that they resulted in a distortion of income measurement. Moreover, in 1966 the Business Accounting Deliberation Council (BADC), the Japanese accounting standard setting body organised within the Ministry of Finance, issued an opinion that required the tax authorities to have a regard for sound business accounting.

As a result of these pressures, the tax regulations were amended in 1967 so as to permit the deduction of special tax depreciation even if it had been treated as an 'income appropriation reserve' in business accounting. Such treatment was then applied to other non-taxable reserves, e.g. inventory valuation reserves.

Exclusion of specific provisions in the commercial code article 287b

Despite the amendment of the bases for tax accounting, the expensing method for specific provisions for uncertain future expenditures or losses remained as an alternative method for income management. In fact until 1981 most profitable corporations had generally continued to adopt this method with the aim of understating income.

In the meantime, however, Japanese multinational corporations which were preparing consolidated financial statements to satisfy the listing requirements of the United States Securities and Exchange Commission had been compelled to reclassify the specific provisions pursuant to article 287b of the Commercial Code into earned surplus reserves. This in itself suggested that the expensing treatment of the special provisions allowed by the Code was not in accordance with sound accounting practice. Recognising this, bitter complaints were levelled against the relevant sections of the Code not only by critical accounting scholars but also by a few members of the Diet. As a result, in the 1981 revisions of the Commercial Code its specific provisions were abandoned so that now almost all non-taxable reserves (and including special tax depreciation provisions) have to be exclusively established through income appropriations.

Narrowing the interpretation of capital surplus

The conceptual extension of capital surplus, which had been another mechanism for the under-reporting of income in post-war Japanese accounting, was also forced to be amended as a result of both international pressure and domestic criticism. In 1974 BAP were revised such that government grants or customers' contributions for construction had to be directly or indirectly applied to the reduction of the cost of the related fixed assets, or would otherwise have to be credited to earned surplus.

However the revision was primarily a compromise between the provisions of the Commercial Code and the Corporation Tax Law in which these non-shareholders' contributions were ultimately treated as distributable or taxable income. The majority of the academic accounting community persisted in their broader interpretation of the capital surplus concept, with the consequence that Japanese public enterprises, such as municipal undertakings or government-owned public corporations, to which the Commercial Code and Corporation Tax Law did not apply, unfortunately continued with a wider definition of capital surplus.

Change was imminent, however. Some of these public enterprises, especially Japanese National Railways (JNR), had accumulated large losses and they were forced to change their accounting policies from ones of income lowering to those of income enlargement (or more precisely loss reduction). In addition, with the more general recognition of overseas accounting standards under which government grants or customers' contributions for construction are treated as deferred revenue or applied to the reduction of the cost of the related assets, and not least the issue of IAS Exposure Draft No.21 in 1981, the deferred revenue approach, which had been maintained by members of the critical school of accounting in Japan, has gradually superseded the capital approach in practice as well as in theory. For example, in the fiscal year 1977 JNR changed its accounting policy for government subsidies to the deferred revenue approach under which subsidies are allocated to revenue over the average useful life of the related assets (thirty years).[5]

Allowance of the provision for probable loss contingencies

Prior to the 1981 revision, Japanese BAP had been interpreted as being generally against provisions for loss contingencies, except for doubtful debts and product warranties (which were and are permitted as a valuation provision against accounts receivable or a provision for future liabilities rather than as a provision for loss contingencies *per se*). The business world had been dissatisfied with the restrictive treatment, however. Accordingly accounting policy makers were urged to amend their views on loss contingencies in order to enable Japanese corporations to provide for the possibility of compensation for damages or country risks, as commonly permitted in European countries and in the United States. Moreover, in practice a few corporations had even reported provisions for such contingencies, such as a compensation liability for medical ill-effects (Takeda Chemical Industries Co. Ltd.) or an investment loss from a joint venture in Iran (Mitsui & Co. Ltd.).

Given such circumstances, the wording of the section of the BAP relating to loss contingencies was amended in 1981 so that contingencies for losses could be created by charges to current revenue.

Some socio-economic determinants of sluggish accounting change

Although corporate accounting in postwar Japan has experienced some notable changes, progress has been slow and, as Campbell (1985, page 170) comments, the overall quality of financial reporting is still lower than in the United Kingdom, United States and many other industrial countries.

It is our view that a number of factors are implicated in this state of affairs, important amongst which are the inherent ambiguity of income measurement rules in Japan and the weak relationship between accountors and accountees.

Ambiguous income measurement rules

Looking over the Japanese BAP one repeatedly notices the words 'may be' rather than 'should be'. Such ambiguity itself has an ambiguous effect on accounting change, however. Not only can it evoke a sluggishness of response, enabling convention to confront the dictates of change, but it can also provide the basis for a flexibility of response that can sometimes cope with environmental changes without substantial revisions of the BAP.

According to the Japanese BAP and the Commercial Code, research and development costs, for example, can be treated as deferred assets with not less than one fifth of the total amount being written off annually within a five year period. A reporting entity therefore has within its discretion the possibility of allocating such costs to expense over five years, or less, or indeed to write them off as incurred. For this reason there is no need for the Japanese standard on research and development costs to be revised in response to recent international trends towards the immediate expensing of such costs. The ambiguity inherent in the present wording enables a requisite degree of responsiveness.

Weak arms-length relationship between accountors and accountees

In western societies sound arms-length relationships between accountors (reporting corporations) and accountees (shareholders, creditors, labour unions, consumers, etc.) have generally been maintained as a result of counter pressures against the accountors. Third party litigation against unfaithful management or negligent auditors, the accountees' claims of a 'right to know', and regulatory activity to promote the balancing of power through the disclosure of management perquisites or illegal payments have all served this role. In written contract based western societies, moreover, accounting numbers have been used as a basis for the arbitration of conflicting interests over management compensation or bond covenants. As a result, accounting measurement rules have received serious consideration from all related parties.

In Japan, in contrast, the relationships between accountors and accountees have been at less than arms-length and, as a result, Japanese financial reporting has not had to face continuous review and pressures for improvement.

The lack of such arms-length relationships in the Japanese corporate system stems from a number of socio-economic factors. First, the number of individual stockholders in Japan fell sharply from 68.5 per cent in 1950 to 28.4 per cent in 1983, while the holdings of institutional stockholders having interests in common with the invested corporations (such as affiliated banks or associated companies) rose rapidly. As a result of such developments the counter pressures of external investors and the stewardship consciousness of management weakened. Second, the dependence of labour's (or labour unions') moral consciousness, as well as their economic interest, on their employing corporations has also contributed to a weak arms-length relationship between the employer as accountor and the employee as accountee. The Japanese style of co-operation between labour and management partly stems from the organisation of labour unions by enterprise rather than by industry and partly from the life employment relationship that is more prevalent in Japan. For both reasons labour unions usually lack the counter power to question management's overly conservative accounting policies, not least in relation to their implications for wage restraint.

A third factor which promotes an asymmetry in accounting power in Japan is the lack of third-party participation in the accounting standard-setting process. The BADC is not an independent standard-setting authority but rather a mere buffer between the corporations and the state bureaucracy (Harrison and McKinnon, 1986, page 250). Informal negotiations between only the BADC (or the bureaucracy) and management representatives (Keidanren) virtually dominate the standard-setting process.

Finally, Japan is an ambiguous, verbal and promise-based society. People do not like and have not become accustomed to defining their claims and obligations on the basis of rigid numbers. In such a cultural context it should not be surprising that accounting information does not receive much consideration.

Concluding remarks

Notably, accounting phenomena in Japan, especially the institutional basis for the under-reporting of income, have been subject to amendment and no longer have such a substantial influence on income determination. As a result, Japanese corporate accounting is gradually conforming more to internationally accepted accounting principles. The changes in the accounting treatment of government grants and the acceptance of provisions for future contingencies are typical instances of cases where international pressures have hastened accounting changes in Japan. Indeed about one third of Japanese multinational corporations currently prepare consolidated financial statements in conformity with SEC standards.[6]

In the light of such developments, how should the impact of international pressures on accounting change in Japan be evaluated, not least from the perspective of the advancement of Japanese accounting? On the one hand, such pressures undoubtedly have contributed to the sound development of Japanese accounting. A wider questioning of the institutional biases underlying the under-reporting of income supported the challenges made by domestic critics who had hitherto been a reasonable but powerless minority.

Being realistic, however, the truth of the matter is that Japanese accounting policy makers, who were and still are honest spokesmen for powerful large corporations, accepted international pressures only when they resulted in insignificant adverse effects on those corporations (such as with the case of the deferred revenue treatment of government grants) or when they might even produce favourable effects (such as with the provisions for loss contingencies). As a result of such powerful inner pressures to protect the vested interests of the large corporations, the adoption of inflation accounting, through which the enormous debtor's gain unfairly obtained by a few highly geared large corporations would be disclosed, has been continually neglected. All too apparently there was little enthusiasm for responding to the international diffusion of inflation accounting initiatives since this would have provided useful information to public policy makers interested in the realisation of distributive justice in an inflationary context.

Moreover, so long as the effects of the 'business accounting based tax accounting' principle still persist, only some profitable corporations earning more income than the amount of 'necessary dividends plus special tax allowances' can fully enjoy the tax benefits. Needless to say, such concentration of tax advantages among large corporations results in tax inequalities in society. Whilst admitting that the specific tax allowances cannot be entirely eliminated from the income tax system, the prerequisites for such tax allowances could and should be only that the corporation fulfils the real conditions (such as investment in the fixed assets eligible for the special tax depreciation) rather than the present fulfilment of certain accounting conditions (whether it is using the expensing method or not).[7] Such a change would not only increase the equality of the distribution of tax advantages among corporations but it also would illuminate some of the ways in which accounting is implicated in wider aspects of socio-economic functioning.

Analysing the situation in such terms demonstrates that accounting change, particularly change orientated towards the correction of major biases, requires not only a reconsideration of existing measurement rules but also the promotion of symmetrical accounting power which will make more feasible the achievement of reasonable measurement rules.

Notes

1. The receptivity of Japanese accounting to external influences is an outgrowth of an institutional openness. To understand such receptivity it is necessary to understand the origins of Japanese accounting. See Takatera (1962, 1975).

2. Schmidt (1979) found that accounting policy decisions in German corporations had a tendency to lower accounting income in comparison with that of American corporations. Also see Coenenberg, Moeller and Schmidt (1984). Such an accounting phenomenon is also attributable, in our view, to the anachronistic maintenance of the 'business accounting based tax accounting' principle in the German income tax system.

3. Special tax depreciation was initially adopted in 1938, abandoned in 1946, and restored in 1951. Further, its use was extended after its restoration, in contrast to the use of accelerated amortisation in the United States which tended to be appealed to in emergency circumstances.

4. Butters and Niland (1949, page 61) observed that there is 'the systematic and pronounced tendency for the use of LIFO to be concentrated among [American] large corporations'. In our view, this is also attributable to the use of the 'business accounting based tax accounting' principle when accounting for the use of LIFO in the American income tax system.

5. The Nippon Telegraph and Telephone Public Corporation (the old NTT) was denationalised in April 1985 and its ownership is to be gradually transferred to the public. At the time of its privatisation, the old NTT's balance of the customers' contribution for construction amounted to about 2.6 billion yen, which was equal to 23 per cent of its total assets, and it had adopted an accounting policy under which customers' contributions were credited to the capital surplus. However, as mentioned above, the 1974 revision of the Japanese BAP, to which the new NTT was compelled to adhere, stipulated that those non-shareholders' contributions be credited to earned surplus or be applied to the reduction of the cost of the related assets. The new NTT then changed its accounting policy for the contributions from the capital approach to the BAP's second alternative method; that is, while contributions of this kind that are accepted hereafter are to be credited to the cost reduction account of the related assets, the balance of the contribution account at the time of the reorganisation is to be carried forward as it is.

   Such an inconsistent change of accounting policy in the new NTT presumably has a drastic impact on social welfare in two directions. Firstly, it would be expected to result in an extreme increase in the rate base upon which the new NTT is permitted to earn a fair return as compared with the consistent adoption of the cost reduction method. Secondly, as a result of such a non-retrospective accounting change, the balance of the consumers' contribution which would otherwise be attributed to the consumers through the reduction of charges, may fall into the hands of the government as the sole owner of the old NTT.

6. A recent survey of annual reports (written in English) published for

foreign investors in 1981, suggested that 53 of 147 corporations prepared consolidated financial statements in accordance with American standards and 77 corporations prepared them in accordance with Japanese standards. For details of the survey see International Committee of Kinki Chapter of JICPA (1983, pages 8ff). It was not until Sasebo Heavy Industries Co. published its annual report in 1985 (in English) that a Japanese corporation prepared its consolidated financial statements in accordance with International Accounting Standards.

7. Along this line, instead of the legal requirement for the 'expensing' or the 'income appropriation' treatment of the special tax allowances, the inter–period allocation of income tax deferments should be introduced into the unconsolidated financial statements as well as the consolidated financial statements.

References

Accounting Techniques and Reporting (in Japanese) (Eiwa Auditing Company, 1985).

Arpan, J.S. and Al Hashim, D. D., *International Dimensions of Accounting* (Kent Publishing, 1983).

Butters, J.K. and Niland, P., *Inventory Accounting and Policies* (Division of Research, Harvard Business School, 1949).

Campbell, L., Financial Reporting in Japan, in C. Nobes and R Parker, eds, *Comparative International Accounting* (2nd ed., Philip Allan, 1985).

Coenenberg, A., Moeller, P. and Schmidt, F., Empirical Research in Financial Accounting in Germany, Austria and Switzerland: A Review, in A.G. Hopwood and H. Schreuder, eds, *European Contributions to Accounting Research: The Achievements of the last Decade* (Free University Press, 1984).

Davidson, S. and Yasuba, Y., Assets Revaluation and Income Taxation in Japan, *National Tax Journal* (March 1960).

Evans, T.G., Taylor, M.E. and Holzman, O., *International Accounting and Reporting* (Macmillan, 1985).

Harrison, G.L. and McKinnon, J.L., Culture and Accounting Change: A New Perspective on Corporate Reporting Regulation and Accounting Policy Formulation, *Accounting, Organisations and Society* (May, 1986).

International Committee of the Kinki Chapter of JICPA, ed., *Annual Reports of Japanese Corporations: Cases and their Analysis* (in Japanese) (Seibunsha, 1983).

Nakai, B., Price-Level Adjustments Data of the Financial Statements of Japanese, American, British, and German Large Corporations (in Japanese), *Accounting (Kaikei)* (June, 1983).

Schmidt, F., *Bilanzpolitik deutscher Aktiengesellchaften, Empirische Analysen des Gewinnglaettungserhaltens* (Gabler, 1979).

Takatera, S., Early Experiment of Depreciation Accounting in 'National Bank' 1875-1879, *Kyoto University Economic Review* (April, 1962).

Takatera, S., Introduction and Diffusion of Depreciation Accounting in Japan, 1875-1903, *Kyoto University Economic Review* (April–October, 1975).

11
An International Focus on Accounting and Reporting Policies and Practices[1]

Mohamed Adel Elsafty

In the last few decades, it has become increasingly profitable for business enterprises to cross national boundaries searching for new opportunities. They operate and invest in countries as diverse as Brazil, Egypt, India, Japan, the United Kingdom and the United States of America.

Concurrent with the geographic growth of business operations, accounting and reporting[1] has assumed an international dimension. International accounting and reporting issues are increasingly becoming matters of concern to developing and developed countries and should be subject to multilateral consultations. Given the scope and complexity of the consequences of accounting these consultations should involve many interested parties, *inter alia*, representatives of Governments, inter-governmental groups and non-governmental bodies.[2]

The increasing role of transnational corporations and the new environment of encouraging their operations[3] has led many developing countries to be concerned about how they would account for their business transactions which have implications for gross national production, the balance of payments, tax revenues and the efficient allocation of resources, not to mention corrupt practices. This concern has underscored the need to regulate and monitor the accounting and reporting practices of transnational corporations. Accordingly, developing countries have continued to focus on four related issues:

1. Information disclosure.
2. Harmonisation of divergent accounting practices.
3. Standard-setting.

[1] Special thanks have to be given to Mr E.H. Wong of the United Nations Centre on Transnational Corporations for his help in providing material for this paper. Also thanks and gratitude to my son, Hecham, who while taking his G.C.E. and American University in Cairo entry examinations could find time for typing the chapter. His comments helped in clarifying many points.

4. Accounting education, training and research.

In the present era of an information revolution which does not take national borders or boundaries as barriers, most information comes from readily available public sources. Thus an important source of information concerning the global operations of transnational corporations is and should be their accounting records. How much of the information generated by the transnational corporations should be disclosed is an issue of continuing concern (and debate) to both home and host countries.[4]   In this regard it is pertinent to stress that information disclosure should aim at furthering understanding of the nature and economic and social effects of the activities of transnational corporations in home and host countries, and in international relations, particularly between developing and developed countries.[5]

Users of information need corporate reports which are comparable regardless of national origin and which disclose in usable form the economic and social information required for effective evaluation and decision-making. An important user group is governments, which need information for monitoring the implementation of various laws and regulations. Furthermore, comparable information is required for statistical surveys, production censuses, compilation of national income data, balance of payments, employment statistics, analysis of economic and financial indicators, setting monetary policies, etc. Regulatory agencies dealing with corporate affairs, national and transnational, need information for monitoring the activities of business enterprises. In this regard, all governments are equal in their needs for information, whether their countries are following free market economies, centrally planned (socialist) economies or any compromise between the two types. It could be said that the needs of free market economy countries are greater, that the availability and quality of information in those countries is better and that the information itself is more reliable.

Current accounting practices indicate that harmonisation appears to be necessary in many areas. For example, business combinations are accounted for using the purchase method, the pooling of interest method, or the new entity method. In accounting for investment in foreign operations, some business enterprises use the consolidation method while others use the equity method or the cost method. In addition, various valuation bases are used to determine the carrying amount of property, plant and equipment. Depreciation is based on more than one method. Several formulae are used in costing inventories. The costing of materials used in production is also subject to several methods. Furthermore there are several ways for translating foreign currency financial statements. Some countries require complete justification for new investments and there are several methods for this justification.[6]

Questions have been raised about the comparability of information disclosed by transnational corporations whose accounting and reporting policies and practices continue to differ from country to country. Users of information have experienced difficulties in comparing reports issued by transnational corporations for a variety of reasons, such as:

1. Certain items of information are disclosed in some reports but not in others.
2. Divergent accounting policies are applied and are not always disclosed.
3. Various accounting methods are used.
4. Different valuation bases are adopted.
5. Aggregate data are segmented by some entities but not by others.

Such a situation has given rise to the need to promulgate some international guidelines for harmonising the divergent accounting and reporting policies and practices of transnational corporations. An essential step in the harmonisation and standardisation process is to define the scope of information to be disclosed by transnational corporations. Currently, negotiations are taking place in the United Nations on a proposed formulation intended to promote greater corporate transparency. The appendix shows some points of agreement reached in this regard. However further efforts are still needed to refine these points further. Also the decision has not been reached yet on whether these points of agreement should be expressed in the form of a code of conduct or an international convention or just a resolution from the Economic and Social Council or the General Assembly. Several views have been expressed, and it is fair to conclude that several rounds of negotiations are still needed to further international understanding on both the substance and the form at issue. The difficulty that accounting and reporting are dynamic processes that need to evolve continuously to face new issues, situations and problems that emerge as business (and accounting) progresses must be taken into account.

It could be argued that efforts aimed at harmonising accounting practices and promoting information disclosure have been made by a number of international and regional organisations. For example the Council of the European Communities has promulgated accounting directives applicable to twelve European developed countries. Efforts under the auspices of the Organisation of African Unity have been made by the African Accounting Council but they are still in their infancy and the Council is facing financial problems. The guidelines issued by the Organisation for Economic Co-operation and Development (OECD) are recommended for adoption by several entities in its member states of developed countries, on several continents. Also some other efforts in several regional organisations in Latin America and Asia have reached different stages. It is also presumed that similar efforts must have been made in the socialist countries of Eastern Europe. At the same time, non-governmental efforts at harmonisation are being made, with a good degree of achievement, by the International Federation of Accountants Committee (IFAC).

However, while forty-three developing countries are members of the IASC and IFAC, more than eighty developing countries are not members of either.[7] It should also be mentioned that the majority of the members of the IASC board and the IFAC council are from developed countries. Furthermore, voting procedures in both bodies give developed countries the right and ability to block any decision, no matter how many members from developing countries support it. The practice used in the IASC for preparing accounting standards gives developed countries an edge.

The above mentioned efforts made by some regional entities are to be commended and in many cases they are of a highly professional nature, but those entities are, by definition, regional and not international. The United Nations is still the only available international organisation with the maximum universal representation. It also represents a very good and unbiased forum to deal with the technical issues (at least) of accounting regulation.

The United Nations Intergovernmental Working Group of Experts on International Standards of Accounting and Reporting differs from the aforementioned organisations in many important aspects. It provides for governmental participation and input from a greater number of countries, especially the developing countries. Its composition of thirty-four members, from as many countries, is based on the principle of equitable geographical representation. All Member States of the United Nations (159, as of July 1986) and observers are eligible for election to the Group on a rotational basis. There is also active participation (as observers) by representatives of intergovernmental organisations, standard-setting bodies, the accounting profession, trade unions and the business community.

The Group, meeting once a year under the auspices of the United Nations, serves as an international forum for multilateral consultations on international accounting and reporting issues.[8] Participants in the deliberations of the Group, working under the broad guideline of reaching agreements on issues to consensus rather than by voting, have achieved some useful results. Although its work is limited in scope to those issues of accounting and reporting falling within the scope of the work of the United Nations Commission on Transnational Corporations, and although the Group chose to postpone, for the time being, dealing with accounting and reporting issues related to banks and insurance companies, its work could be expanded to deal with all accounting and reporting issues and it could have more frequent meetings than once a year. But bearing in mind the present financial situation of the United Nations and the views of some important members of that organisation,[9] one cannot avoid the feeling that this is a distant goal to achieve.

Throughout the short time in which accounting and reporting have been dealt with by the United Nations, tangible results have been achieved.[10] The purpose of standard-setting has been agreed upon. The group also agreed on several criteria to be used in defining the applicability of accounting and reporting standards; that the selection and application of accounting policies should be governed by the concepts of user needs, materiality, substance over form, consistency, comparability and prudence. Furthermore, the discussions have dealt with several important areas of accounting and reporting by transnational corporations, such as foreign direct investments, property, plant and equipment, related party transactions, research and development, technology transfers, and foreign currency transactions. As in any sphere of life, agreement was reached in several fields, while in others it was not possible. But it is not an overstatement to say that the discussions helped all involved to understand the other point of view, and on many occasions helped in reaching common ground based on compromises. It is also true that the consensus in this field in the United Nations could serve as a catalyst in the harmonisation process and induce greater efforts to improve information disclosure by transnational corporations on the one hand and encourage governments to adopt the same criteria, standards and views as the United Nations, on the other.

In this regard there is now a general recognition that the work of the United Nations in the field of accounting and reporting could facilitate the efforts of many developing countries in setting accounting and reporting standards. It should be pointed out that many developing countries have not established standard-setting bodies or joined existing ones, while others have done so with limited resources and results. Something has to be done to facilitate that process in an economical way and in a manner and form that is universally acceptable, not only to the accounting profession but also to the world at large. One way of doing this would be for the representatives of countries to consult multilaterally in a truly universal manner on issues of universal concern. Another way would be to provide each and every developing country with comprehensive advisory services and a technical co-operation programme on standard-setting. In my opinion the first of these possibilities is the best and least expensive way of achieving tangible results. The best and true universal forum is, beyond any doubt, the United Nations.

One could argue that the United Nations is an intergovernmental forum, which should leave issues like accounting and reporting to the professions involved. Arguments could also be pursued about the results achieved in many countries, like the United Kingdom and others, which have left standard-setting to the independent accountancy profession. It is true that in many countries the accountancy profession, with little or no government interference and regulation has done a good job. But it took decades to reach the present stage of efficiency and one cannot ask developing countries to wait for the same period or even, drawing from experience gained by others, wait less time to reach the same stage that developed countries have reached today. Furthermore, developing countries need to promulgate accounting standards so as to:

1. Harmonise divergent accounting and reporting practices.
2. Promote adequate disclosure of comparable information, including non-financial information, giving a true and fair view of the financial position and results of operations.
3. Regulate the accounting and reporting activities of business enterprises.
4. Provide definitive criteria for the guidance of accountants.

The current regulatory and economic practices in many developing countries suggest that governments have leading roles to play in standard-setting and in enforcing compliance of standards by business enterprises. Standard-setting, if left to individual countries in all its aspects, including research work, drafting formulations and, above all, identifying and defining issues, could be a very costly exercise which would result in a duplication of effort and very divergent standards set by each country.

It could be argued that governments should leave standard-setting to the accounting profession, but in developing countries this is a luxury they could not afford. The profession in many countries is still in its early stages. It lacks the established tradition and the capacity to absorb new situations and adapt itself to meeting them. It also could be argued that standard-setting is a costly exercise that developing countries should best leave alone and direct their available resources to other fields that need those resources. I really do not see any merit in this argument. It even makes one suspicious that something lies behind such a forceful attempt to prevent developing countries from participating, on an equal footing, in standard-setting. Developing countries could not leave their interests to be taken care of by the goodwill of the standard-setting bodies. A positive case for change can be made on the basis of the fact that about twenty developed countries are represented by ten members on the board of one of the best known and supposedly unbiased standard-setting bodies located in one of the oldest democratic countries of the world, while at the same time 127 developing countries are represented by four members on the same board. How would any rational viewer look to this situation without suspicion? But the aforementioned board finds the situation normal, and it even speaks about 'the improvement' in the representation, because developing countries were represented by three members in the board until recently!

Implementation of accounting standards would be a difficult endeavour if the development of the accounting profession were lacking. In this context, it is now perceived that there is a need to promote the growth of the accounting profession both qualitatively and quantitatively in the developing countries. There is a growing demand for the services of accountants in most developing countries, but efforts to increase their number are being restrained by limited resources and inadequate education programmes, training schemes and research facilities. Opportunities for continuing professional education are also facing great problems of the same nature. It is evident that greater attention must be given to institution building, teacher training, curriculum development and continuous updating, the organisation of seminars, supplies of teaching material, research facilities, scholarship awards and the provision of internal and external (overseas) training assignments. All these need some sort of international supervision so as to pool and direct available resources to achieve the best possible results.

In conclusion, the needs are great in many areas; efforts to meet the needs are being made but they are insufficient and need harmonisation. I believe that the best body to meet this challenge is the United Nations. The United Nations work in this field is encouraging but needs enhancement. To build on what has been done in the United Nations is, maybe, the best course of action.

This could be done in stages: the first one would be strengthening the United Nations forum which deals with accounting and reporting, expand its mandate and have it meet more regularly. This forum could have, in the second stage, the task of reviewing standards set by standard-setting bodies and establish a more active dialogue with these bodies. In the third stage the United Nations forum could have the role of recommending acceptance of standards set by standard-setting bodies. And lastly, and according to the achievements of the first three stages, the United Nations could participate in the standard-setting process and in finding a way for its member states to implement the agreed standards. The time that should be allocated to each stage should be flexible so that achievements will be under continuous review, with necessary corrections being adopted.

Notes

1. Reporting was added here and will appear in many places in this paper as it is the basic need, without which accounting would become a theoretical science not related to the needs of end users.
2. It could be argued that representatives of the business community should also be included in the consultations. While they have legitimate rights to be raised in matters that affect them, we prefer that they should not be included in the first stages of consultations for two main reasons :
   (a) There are some contradictions between the needs of most end users for 'disclosure' and the natural desire of the business community, rightly or wrongly, not to disclose.

(b) The difficulty of devising an international forum that would include representatives of governments and private business enterprises. Although there is an example of this arrangement in the International Labour Organisation, its shortcomings do not encourage repeating the example. Furthermore, it would not be prudent, at least for some years to come, to suggest establishing a new international organisation for accounting and reporting.

However, one could envisage many ways that could be used to enable the views of the business community to have an impact on the consultations. As a matter of fact, the consultations conducted under the auspices of the United Nations include some representation of the business community.

3. Encouraging transnational corporations to operate in the developing countries can best be achieved by laws passed by legislative authorities in individual countries to encourage and guarantee the foreign investment and the transfer of its profits. Many international organisations, including the World Bank, have stepped up their promotion of foreign direct investment in developing countries by both governments and the private sector. The Bank also has promoted the expansion of the operations of the International Finance Corporation and its proposals regarding the conversion of existing external debt into foreign equity. Efforts are being made to establish a Multilateral Investment Guarantee Agency and an Emerging Markets Growth Fund to accelerate capital investment in developing countries.

4. Of particular importance is information concerning *inter alia* capital flows, technology transfers, management policies, corporate relationships, marketing strategies, personnel policies and development, environmental effects and corrupt practices.

5. The effects of transnational corporations in international relations are subject to divergent views. One example of the differences concerns the effects of transnational corporations on the views of some developed countries relating to South Africa, which may have affected these countries' relationships with developing countries.

6. In Japan the method used is called 'break and build', in the United States it is called 'Zero base value' and in Egypt it is '100 per cent justification.' Admittedly there are similarities between the three methods, but there are also points of difference which need certain accounting modifications depending on the method used.

7. At the last count (1984/1985) there were 127 developing country members of the Group of 77.

8. The mandate of the Working Group is set forth by the Economic and Social Council resolution no. 1982/67 (renewed in 1985). It stipulates *inter alia* that the Group 'should serve as an international body for the consideration of issues of accounting and reporting falling within the scope of the work of the Commission on Transnational Corporations,

in order to improve the ability and comparability of information disclosed by transnational corporations; should review developments in this field, including the work of the standard-setting bodies...'.

9. In a letter to the Secretary General of the United Nations dated February 26, 1986, the Permanent Representative of the United States of America to the United Nations stated that 'The Working Group performed some useful activities over the years. However the current work of the Working Group is of little usefulness to either the United States Government or to the business community. Discussion of accounting and reporting practices and standards is covered adequately by international professional groups such as the International Accounting and Standards Committee (IASC).' He concluded that his government 'has determined that it will not send delegates to the upcoming (1986) meeting of the Working Group,' and recommended further 'that the appropriate authority of the Economic and Social Council undertake to review the usefulness of the continuation of the working group in light of current severe budgetary restrictions.' However, these views are not shared by most members if by any at all.

10. See for example United Nations publication sales no. E.85.II.A.12-ST/CTC 152; sales no. E.85.II.A.13ST/CTC/85 and document no. E/C.10/1986/14.

Appendix: Disclosure of information[1]

Transnational corporations should disclose to the public in the countries in which they operate, by appropriate means of communications, clear, full and comprehensible information on the structure, policies, activities and operations of the transnational corporation as a whole. The information should include financial as well as non financial items and should be made available on a regular annual basis, normally within six months and in any case not later than twelve months from the end of the financial year of the corporation. In addition, during the financial year transnational corporations should whenever appropriate make available a semi-annual summary of financial information.

The financial information to be disclosed annually should be provided where appropriate on a consolidated basis together with suitable explanatory notes and should include, *inter alia*, the following:

1. A balance sheet.
2. An income statement, including operating results and sales.

---

[1]Official Record, 1983, Economic and Social Council, United Nations, (E/1983/17/Rev.1, pages 20-2).

3. A statement of allocation of net profits or net income.
4. A statement of the sources and uses of funds.
5. Significant new long-term capital investment.
6. Research and development expenditure.

The non-financial information referred to in the first subparagraph should include *inter alia*:

1. The structure of the transnational corporation, showing the name and location of the parent company, its main entities, its percentage ownership, direct and indirect, in these entities, including shareholdings between them.
2. The main activity of its entities.
3. Employment information including average number of employees.
4. Accounting policies used in compiling and consolidating the information published.
5. Policies applied in respect of transfer pricing.

The information provided for the transnational corporation as a whole should as far as practicable be broken down:

1. By geographic area or country, as appropriate, with regard to the activities of its main entities, sales, operating results, significant new investment and number of employees.
2. By major line of business as regards sales and significant new investments.

The method of breakdown as well as details of information provided should/shall be determined by the nature, scale and interrelationships of the transnational corporation's operations, with due regard to their significance for the areas or countries concerned.

The extent, detail and frequency of the information provided should take into account the nature and size of the transnational corporation as a whole, the requirements of confidentiality and effects on the transnational corporation's competitive position as well as the cost involved in producing the information.

The information herein required should, as necessary, be in addition to information required by national laws, regulations and administrative practices of the countries in which transnational corporations operate.

Transnational corporations should/shall supply to the competent authorities in each of the countries in which they operate, upon request or on a regular basis as specified by those authorities, and in accordance with national legislation, all information required for legislative and administrative purposes relevant to the activities and policies of their entities in the country concerned.

Transnational corporations should/shall, to the extent permitted by the provisions of the relevant national laws, regulations, administrative practices and policies of the countries concerned, supply to the competent authorities in the countries in which they operate information held in other countries needed to enable them to obtain a true and fair view of the operations of the transnational corporation concerned as a whole in so far as the information requested relates to the activities of the entities in the countries seeking such information.

Information furnished by transnational corporations to the authorities in each of the countries in which they operate containing [legitimate business secrets] [confidential business information] should be accorded reasonable safeguards normally applicable in the area in which the information is provided, particularly to protect its confidentiality.

With due regard to relevant provisions of the ILO Tripartite Declaration of Principles concerning Multinational Enterprises and Social Policy and in accordance with national laws, regulations and practices in the field of labour relations, transnational corporations should/shall provide to trade unions or other representatives of employees in their entities in each of the countries in which they operate, by appropriate means of communications, the necessary information on the activities dealt with in this code to enable them to obtain a true and fair view of the performance of the local entity and, where appropriate, the corporation as a whole. Such information should/shall include, where provided for by national laws and practices, *inter alia*, prospects or plans for future developments having major economic and social effects on the employees concerned.

Procedures for consultations on matters of mutual concern should/shall be worked out by mutual agreement between entities of transnational corporations and trade unions or other representatives of employees in accordance with national law and practice.

Information made available pursuant to the provisions of this paragraph should be subject to appropriate safeguards for confidentiality so that no damage is caused to the parties concerned.

Commentaries

12
Future Prospects for Research

Kenneth V. Peasnell

The papers presented at the Symposium and the resultant discussions dealt with a great variety of issues and aspects of the international forces affecting the work and organisation of accountants. My task is to identify what seem to me to be the issues which are both crying out for research and capable of being researched. My task has been made easier than I expected because of the frankness of the practitioner participants of the Symposium. Nevertheless, it should be recognised that my views are necessarily strongly influenced by my own research interests; another person might view the proceedings very differently. Comparative advantage suggests that I limit myself to trying to identify a few major areas suitable for research by the academic community, and this I have done.

Research can be valuable in at least two ways. Research can throw light on what is happening and why. Universities offer the intellectual atmosphere and combination of knowhow and talents where this kind of research can thrive, and it is in this direction which much academic research in accounting is now directed. To the extent that researchers are able to solve some of the accounting problems plaguing accountants, investors, businessmen and regulators, then their efforts are undoubtedly of value – but this is a much more difficult task. Whilst acknowledging the importance of problem-solving efforts, I will concentrate below on the first of these two areas for research.

Viewing the papers and discussions as a whole, two themes stand out. The first theme concerns the ways in which accounting practices, concepts and institutions have been and continue to be imported and exported; more generally, it deals with the economic, political and social forces at work in changing the practice of accounting in different countries and the central role played by the modern international audit firms in bringing about many of these changes. The second theme, clearly linked to the first, focusses on the pressures for and against the harmonisation of corporate reporting practices and standards.

The internationalisation of accounting is a widely noted phenomenon; not surprisingly, comparative accounting has proved to be a growth area for scholarly research, with at least one academic journal devoted to the dissemination of research findings in the area. Curiously enough, though, the large international accounting firms, which are playing such an important part in the internationalisation of accounting, are receiving very little serious attention from scholars. This neglect is due in large measure, no doubt, to the fact that accounting firms are not (yet) limited liability companies with shares listed on the stock exchanges; they are under no legal obligation and have little economic reason to publish details of their financial affairs and business operations. The numerous mergers between accounting firms are, almost by definition, friendly and private occasions conducted largely behind closed doors. The resultant lack of data means the researcher faces a daunting task. Yet the absence of serious study means that all we are left with is anecdote and light-weight journalistic pieces. Given that so little of substance is known about firms which are virtually household names, it is perhaps not surprising that doubts should be raised in Congressional circles about the beneficial nature of their operations. Much criticism has been expressed, in and out of the courts, of the quality of audit services and how these might be being corrupted by the other services offered.

What is needed is a serious study of the forces which have led to the remarkable growth of the international accounting firms. Don Hanson modestly assures us that the growth of Arthur Andersen is due in large measures to the growth of its clients; they were lucky, so to speak, in their audit assignments. This begs the question, though, as to why their clients should turn to their auditors for management services. What is it about the audit function which encourages the growth of the consultancy side of the business? Is it the advantage also possessed by banks, namely, knowledge of need and opportunity? Transaction cost theories developed by Oliver Williamson and others and applied with much success in the study of the development and growth of industrial companies might help us to understand the 'accounting industry' to a far greater and more rounded degree.

The papers by Paul Rutteman and Allan Cook provide fascinating examples of divergent accounting practices and cogent cases for international harmonisation. Tentative evidence of the diversity of types and methods of transnational reporting adopted by European multinational companies is provided by Archer and McLeay. Irritating and inconvenient as this disharmony might be for international investors, multinationals and governments alike, these papers leave us in no doubt as to formidable problems which have to be overcome before matters can be much improved. The resources devoted by IASC and others to international harmonisation are at present very small, judged both in absolute terms and in comparison with the national (particularly US) standardisation programmes.

The key policy issue concerns the likely gains from committing more money and manpower to harmonisation efforts. In this regard, it would be helpful to have more research on the uses made by investors of foreign companies' financial statements. After all, it is perfectly possible that United Kingdom investors, say, make little or no use of financial statements when buying and selling Japanese, German or even American equities, viewing the accounts as monitoring and bonding devices rather than as direct decision aids for investors. To the extent that overseas investors act as price takers, concern over lack of international harmony might be misplaced.

Following this line of thought further, we might gain greater understanding if more attention were paid to inter-country differences in the functions served by corporate financial statements. After all, financial statements are not the only sources of information about companies, nor are they the only means of motivating and monitoring management; harmonisation efforts should take account of the possibility that variations in financing patterns, bases for compensating executives, taxation and pricing controls might be the cause of international differences in corporate reporting practices, rather than differences in competence, skills and 'standards'. At the moment we simply do not know the answer.

Scheid and Standish provide a very good example of a different corporate reporting environment in their account of the French Plan Comptable Général – a centralised and rigorously standardised structure for the specification and control of accounting practices which has been in operation since just after World War Two and which is completely at variance with the British-American system. They exhort us to consider whether this might not be a good model for Britain and America to follow, and clearly estimation of the likely costs and benefits is called for. The scope such a codified system of accounts offers for cost savings in financial statement analysis would appear to be considerable. In this context, it would be very helpful to have some information about whether or not the Plan really results in greater comparability than in Britain and the United States, in the sense of resulting in less variations in choices of reporting techniques, or whether it is merely largely cosmetic in character.

Elsafty argues for more attention to be paid to the wishes and interests of the developing countries and for a greater say in the international standard-setting programme. He looks to the United Nations to get more involved than hitherto. Study of the needs of the developing countries is overdue. Little is currently known about the uses government officials and others in these countries are making (or hope to make) of the financial statements of transnationals.

I will conclude by pointing out an area where research has been carried out that is of relevance to the concerns of practitioners. Much academic effort, especially in the United States, has been put into trying to ascertain whether or not share prices 'reflect' what is known and publicly available about companies; in particular, whether the market is 'fooled' by straightforward, transparent manipulations of reported profits. The evidence strongly supports the view that the market is 'efficient' in this respect. It is therefore interesting to note Geoff Mitchell's remark that it is believed in some quarters that the City marks down the shares of companies which are big spenders on research and development, implying either that investors are irrational or that research spending is largely money down the drain. Prior research would tend to make one sceptical of the irrationality argument, but this is an area undoubtedly warranting further research and one where the techniques for doing the research are well developed.

13
Future Perspectives for Practice and Research

Jack Shaw

My contribution to the review of the earlier chapters and the discussion they stimulated during the Symposium comes from the perspective of practice. Because this attempt to provide a summary reflects impressions gained from all the chapters and discussions, and because what struck me as the most important or most pervasive points emerged in the context of more than one analysis, I hope I may be forgiven for not referring to individual authors. The reader will have already identified the provenance of much of this commentary.

Whether in practice, teaching, or professional administration, British accountants have, I fear, demonstrated remarkably little knowledge of accountancy and reporting practices elsewhere. We seem remarkably little concerned with the way our discipline is developing elsewhere. This isolation from other international trends has its domestic parallel in what seems to be the institutional isolation of accountancy bodies in the United Kingdom from developments in either the academic world or the 'real world' of business and finance.

British introspection is demonstrated, for example, in chapters betraying a lack of knowledge about what is going on even among our near neighbours in Europe. As well as being our geographical neighbours, they are, under the expanding European Community, our economic trading partners and our political associates. It is therefore not surprising to find so little British response to international developments either of accountancy techniques or of financial reporting. We notice instead an apparent determination to defend particular British interests including what appear to be narrow and sectional concerns.

The detachment of our professional societies is demonstrated by the network of institutions and agencies which appear to exist in their own remote world unpopulated by those directly concerned with the creation of wealth. There are largely international political organisations such as the UN Group of Experts and various agencies of the European Commission. There are largely economic organisations such as the OECD. There are various 'professional' organisations including, of course, IFAC and IASC (as well as FEE now uniting UEC and the Groupe d'Etudes). Senior and experienced people within these organisations sometimes seem unimpeded by any concern for the practical implementation of their proposals; at other times they appear to be only too conscious of some narrow, sectional interest to which they feel they have to pay attention.

Within the United Kingdom, our own Accounting Standards Committee has behaved in a similarly disengaged fashion. It is still wrestling with some fundamental issues like accounting for changes in price levels, and for the consequences of corporate reconstructions. Perhaps accountants have become too much concerned with the political processes of negotiating consensus instead of providing the theoretical framework and practical experience to guide policy makers. We have not found the right mechanism for ensuring that the politicians who legislate understand our technical and professional concerns.

One lesson for the British in this review of international experiences is that the commitment of resources to the attainment of clearly defined strategic objectives is frequently rewarded by success. The French experience, among others, demonstrates this. We in Britain therefore have to give high priority to the definition of strategic objectives for our discipline and profession. We also have to make a major commitment to their attainment – submerging minor differences to achieve a major advance. Perhaps we are not good enough at either definition or commitment!

But this focus on perceived weaknesses of the United Kingdom only serves to emphasise the intensity of our national introspection. This was a symposium dedicated to international horizons. The place which British accountancy bodies have and expect in the world today is largely a consequence of our history. In times past Britain was a major force in the world economy in terms both of wealth creation and as a source of capital investment. It is not surprising, therefore, that British perceptions and practices were so widely exported. But our international position in the creation and investment of wealth is now relatively weaker (except, perhaps, in the provision of an international market for capital movements and in international expertise in the management of investments).

Since the 1940s it is the United States which has been the economic engine of the capitalist world. It was therefore to be expected that American practices and preoccupations would become a dominant force in the accounting and reporting developments. That is as true in the field of management accountancy as in financial accounting and the evolution of capital market theory. In the chapters in this volume the pervasive nature of the influence of the United States was acknowledged explicitly in reference to the structure of practice firms, the organisation and objectives of the FASB and the role of the IASC as a means of seeking acceptance of primarily American concepts and practices.

A number of obvious questions follow from these observations – some of which have been considered in the various analyses presented earlier.

What is the role of the non-capitalist countries in the development of accounting thought? Can we expect in the long run to preserve two international languages of economic performance and measurement? As the United States yields its dominant position of economic leadership to Japan can we not expect the next tide of leadership in accounting developments also to come from there? (Despite the post-1945 'Americanisation' of the Japanese economy it seems likely that Japanese attitudes to materialism and the different political and financial structure of the Japanese economy will produce something quite different from 'American practice with a Japanese accent'!) If Europe as a whole succeeds in creating an effective counterweight to Japanese economic power, will European accounting influences again become important? And if so, from which part of Europe?

But probably the most important long-term consequence of the Americanisation of accountancy is the challenge it has brought to traditional perceptions of professionalism. The professional ethos developed largely in Britain during the second half of the nineteenth century was exported with those who were the agents of its economic and political power. The perceptions of professional responsibilities both influenced the formation of the accountancy institutes and were reinforced by them. These perceptions were quite different from those developed in the dramatically different economic and social conditions of the United States in the mid to late twentieth century. The difference can be seen clearly in the more recent struggles to strike an appropriate balance between classic professional objectives and pressing commercial concerns; between the traditional awareness of wider social responsibilities and obligations and the now starker desire for satisfaction of personal aims and objectives.

For the individual such a balancing involves the reconciliation of personal responsibility with personal satisfaction; for the institutions it involves balancing public demands of social duty with the claims of members for support, and sometimes protection, in meeting the individual demands and pressures on them. The emergence of transnational firms of practising accountants attempting to apply common standards and common practices in many different economies and cultures raises a number of issues of concern to these firms and to the accountancy institutions.

One of the major implications for the accountancy institutions seems to be that the transnational firms themselves behave progressively like self-contained institutions. The firm specifies for itself standards of qualification for entry and the means of maintaining competence; it provides its own programmes of education and training, creates its own technical development and research activities; it codifies (or standardises) techniques and practices to be applied and creates its own internal procedures to monitor and secure compliance; it provides a very effective means of peer-group support for any member who meets its norms of behaviour and is attacked from outside – and equally effective discipline on those who do not conform!

The transnational firm thus becomes the most effective conduit for securing the international harmonisation of accounting standards and practices. The individual members of such a firm have to respond to different local cultural influences, but the resources of their firm help them not only to respond but enable them to modify and, in part, overcome the consequences of local differences. The firm's management structures and their operational practices all tend towards transnational harmonisation. Perhaps, most importantly, their major patrons (clients) – the multinational and transnational corporations – have a direct interest in achieving the international harmonisation of accounting measurement and reporting.

Interestingly, in the course of the discussions stimulated by the chapters collected in this volume, the suggestion emerged that commitment of a professional firm to achieving leadership of development in the discipline of accounting should be acknowledged institutionally by seeking to secure universal acceptance of that firm's practices and procedures.

The 'classic' perception of the badge of 'professionalism' was inescapable personal responsibility in the exercise of individual judgement. But obviously, the greater the extent of specification of procedures and practices and the more effective the mechanisms of surveillance and compliance, the less scope there is for the exercise of individual personal judgement. There is no question but that 'the rules' have to be obeyed: the issue is, how is 'the rule' specified? A requirement not to exceed thirty miles per hour requires no judgement (but does need accurate measurement) whereas the need to drive with due care and attention demands skilled judgement. The more precise the specification, the less scope for judgement: the wider the definition of objective, instead of the precise means of achieving it, the more the need to exercise judgement.

The analyses in the earlier chapters prompt the thought time and again that a key issue for accountants worldwide – in practice and in research – is the resolution of this conflict between a 'legalistic' approach and a 'judgemental' approach. It is another balance which has to be struck – between the precise specification of detailed procedures which will usually (but not always!) achieve a desirable objective and the definition of broad objectives which impose a duty on individuals to identify and use appropriate procedures.

The process of finding that balance takes us back to further consideration of an earlier comment in this review. I suggest that the resolution of conflicting responsibilities to exercise independent judgement and to conform to norms of conduct will only emerge through political processes. The professional institutions themselves, although subject, of course, to their own internal political pressures and processes, are not now seen as having sufficient authority to resolve matters of public interest. Questions of accounting measurement and reporting touch the public interest very deeply – at national and international levels.

The extent of this public interest probably means that politically negotiated solutions are inevitable. The forum must be one in which *all* interests can feel they have an opportunity for representation. Thus the need for participation takes the issue out of the hands of the professional societies. A need for transparency – of debate, of objective, and of means of achieving the objective – reinforces that pressure. And finally the perceived need for mechanisms of effective enforcement weakens the traditional authority of the 'self-regulating' professional bodies.

In the United Kingdom we have seen the impact on accountancy practice of political pressure from the European Commission through our own Parliament. Our Accounting Standards Committee has not found the way to achieve an equivalent effect. Given the apparent difficulty of accountants to influence legislators and the lack of an effective supra-national legislative forum it is little wonder that the IASC sometimes expresses its disappointment at the slow progress towards the international harmonisation of accounting.

It is because I believe that it is inevitable that a politically-negotiated resolution of those accountancy issues which affect that public interest will emerge that I urge on all concerned with research and practice the need to inform politicians of the issues and implications. (To the extent to which we, as accountants, are concerning ourselves with matters which do not touch the public interest, we may be enjoying ourselves but we are also behaving irresponsibly!)

There is one particular aspect in all this which interests me as an auditor – or as a former auditor! The present basis of the United Kingdom accountancy profession's claim to exercise self-regulation and to control the specification of accounting standards rests, in part, on the United Kingdom model of corporate reporting. If you regulate the auditor, the argument goes, you effectively regulate his or her client, so you achieve universal acceptance of professional prescription. But that depends on the authority of the auditor and the extent to which failure by the client to accept the auditor's view is condemned (formally or informally) by the community at large. It also depends – as will the perceived authority of the auditor – on the ability of the auditor to exercise and to demonstrate his or her independence from the client. Thus we return again to the earlier questions of defining professional authority and responsibility and balancing them against commercial pressures.

To conclude, let me pose some questions to which accounting practitioners have got to find answers. Answers are needed not just to define the place of accountants and of accountancy in society but to help in specifying priorities for the research efforts of accountants during the latter years of this century.

When are you going to start paying attention to what is going on elsewhere in Europe, in the Pacific and in centrally-managed economies?

Does standardisation or even harmonisation really matter either to developing countries or to local indigenous businesses operating in any one country?

What is going to be done about standard-setting in the United Kingdom? Should those who seek to set standards simultaneously be designing ways of circumventing compliance? Should they be seen to behave as the agents of those whose 'flexibility' in practice they claim to be seeking to restrict? Should standards be subjected to close textual analysis to establish support for unlikely meanings of the words, or even the punctuation?

Is statutory regulation of accountancy practice inevitable? (Look at the experience in United States; look at the Financial Services Legislation in the United Kingdom.)

Finally, let me express a personal hope that the answers to these and many other questions will not be inconsistent with the acceptance by accountants of individual responsibility for their judgement and for the views they express on the basis of that judgement. That is true for practitioners and for teachers and for researchers. Acceptance of the priority of our responsibility to others will achieve more relevant standards of conduct and practice than by trying to tackle our problems the other way round. When we abandon personal responsibility for professional judgement we will surrender control over the development of our discipline and over the definition of standards by which our professional performance will be judged by the community.

Index